# GOD'S STORY

## ANNE GRAHAM LOTZ

THOMAS NELSON
Since 1798

NASHVILLE   DALLAS   MEXICO CITY   RIO DE JANEIRO   BEIJING

Published in Nashville, Tennessee, by Thomas Nelson. Thomas Nelson is a registered trademark of Thomas Nelson, Inc.

Thomas Nelson, Inc. books may be purchased in bulk for educational, business, fund-raising, or sales promotional use. For information, please e-mail SpecialMarkets@ThomasNelson.com.

Unless otherwise indicated, Scripture quotations used in this book are from the Holy Bible, New International Version (NIV). © 1973, 1978, 1984 by International Bible Society. Used by permission of Zondervan Publishing House. All rights reserved.

Scripture references indicated KJV are from the King James Version of the Bible.

ISBN: 978-0-8499-2092-9

**The Library of Congress has cataloged the earlier edition as follows:**
Lotz, Anne Graham, 1948–
    God's story : finding meaning for your life through knowing God / Anne Graham Lotz.
    p. cm.
    ISBN: 978-0-8499-1531-4
    1. Bible. O.T. Genesis I–XI—Meditations. 2. Christian life—Meditations. I. Title.
BS1235.4.L67        1997        222'.1106—dc21
97-28113    CIP

*Printed in the United States of America*
09 10 11 12 13  RRD  7 6 5 4 3 2 1

# CONTENTS

*Dedicated*

*to*

# YOU,

*especially when life doesn't make sense*

# MY GRATITUDE FOR THE WOMEN . . .

God has used several men and women to encourage, guide, and help me in creating this book; I am grateful to each one. But as I prayerfully consider those who have had the greatest influence, I am especially struck by the number of women who have come into my life at one time or another without whom this book would not have been written.

Virginia Leftwich Bell, my grandmother, now living in heaven, who taught me to read and whose love for me made God's unconditional love easy to understand . . . .

Ruth Bell Graham, my mother, who is also in heaven, who made God's Word "more to be desired than gold" by her own example and whose loving encouragement, sensitive insights, and unwavering support kept me going during dark moments of weary discouragement in this project . . .

Morrow and Rachel-Ruth, my beloved daughters, who are living evidence of the fullness of God's blessing in my life and who have greatly expanded the dimension of my joy, and whose pride in this project has been a delight.

A. Wetherell Johnson, whose thoughtful and powerful exposition of Genesis 1–11 first opened up for me the wonder of God's timeless truth in personal, practical application . . .

Brenda Bateman and the AnGeL Ministries staff, Helen George, my personal assistant, and Marjorie Green and the AnGeL Ministries prayer team, all of whom have given consistent and loyal service as a constant reminder to me of God's sufficiency to supply all my needs—especially when I am overextended.

Laura Kendall and the staff members at Thomas Nelson who have maintained not only their patience but also their enthusiasm for this project from the beginning, exemplifying God's faithfulness to complete that which He has begun . . . .

Sue Ann Jones, whose professional skill has nudged my writing upward toward excellence, that God's glory in the earliest days of His story might be revealed to you and reflected in your life . . . .

## . . . AND FOR THE WIND

As I began writing this book, the work was laborious and slow. Each sentence was written, rewritten, then written again. I felt like a person who was straining at the oars of a boat with no wind to fill the sails and propel it across the water.

Then, early one morning, my Bible reading led me to 2 Samuel 5:17–24, where David was planning his advance against the Philistines. God instructed him, "As soon as you hear the sound of marching in the tops of the balsam trees, move quickly, because that will mean the Lord has gone out in front of you."

Who would be marching in the tops of trees except angels . . . or the wind of the Holy Spirit?

I immediately prayed that passage of Scripture for myself. I earnestly asked God to send the wind so that I could advance in my writing.

Later that day, still straining at my computer, I called my mother to ask her to join with me in praying for the wind. She made a few comments that immediately quickened my spirit as well as my mind. Then she described sailing on a large boat, with the tranquillity of total quietness broken only by the loud *snap!* as the wind filled the sails and the boat shot across the surface of the sea. She prayed that God's peace and quietness would descend upon my heart, broken only by the loud *snap!* of the wind as the Holy Spirit Himself filled my mind, carrying me swiftly through this project.

As I hung up the phone, the wind began to blow! Words and thoughts came readily to mind. Within five weeks of that telephone conversation, the rough draft of this book was finished!

Thank you, dear Mother, for your prayer.

And thank You, dear God, for the Wind.

# Genesis: The Memoirs of an Eyewitness

What a difference an eyewitness can make! Especially when the truth is being sought and there are conflicting opinions about what has taken place. This difference was dramatized by the emotional and legal turmoil our nation experienced during the trial of O. J. Simpson, who was accused then acquitted of the slashing deaths of his former wife, Nicole Brown Simpson, and her friend Ron Goldman. Later we experienced this lack of an eyewitness during the trial of Timothy McVeigh, who was accused and convicted of the bombing of the Alfred P. Murrah Federal Building in Oklahoma City, and in the still-unresolved murder of the doll-sized beauty queen JonBenet Ramsey.

Our country might have been spared multiple millions of dollars, weeks and months of preoccupation, and the misery and agony of minutely detailed analyses as well as at least one verdict that incited hostile division in an already emotionally overwrought public if there had been just one credible eyewitness in each case. Such a witness is powerful because the testimony is irrefutable, clearly and simply setting forth what someone has actually seen with his own eyes, heard with his own ears, or touched with his own hands.

This holds true not only for criminal justice but for the origin of the universe, our planet, and the human race. If a credible eyewitness could be found for Creation itself, he or she would substantially reverse and alter our conclusions. One such conclusion about the origin of the universe is the theory of evolution, which has been widely accepted in our nation's schools as the scientific explanation for the existence of everything. But wherever it is taught, there is usually sharp disagreement and radically conflicting opinions. Some states have gone so far as to try to pass legislation making sure evolution is presented as a theory rather than fact and requiring creationism to be presented at the same time as an alternate possibility. While the debate rages, it is time to recognize that there was an eyewitness to Creation and the earliest years of human history. This eyewitness has gone on record, giving testimony to the truth about our origin, and that enormously impacts the meaning of our lives today. His testimony can be found in Genesis, the first book of the Bible.

On November 8, 1981, the *New York Times* reported results of a data analysis by a computer at the Technion, Israel's institute of technology in Haifa. Scholars fed the computer information related to the Pentateuch, the first five books of the Bible—Genesis, Exodus, Leviticus, Numbers, and Deuteronomy—including facts, style of writing, and vocabulary. After analyzing the data, the computer concluded that a single author wrote all five books.

According to Jewish tradition and biblical testimony, Moses was the single author of the first five books of the Bible, also known as the Law of Moses, written in approximately 1450 BC. Scholars believe he compiled historical family records into an accurate account of the years that preceded his time. The family records on which Genesis 1–11 are based are each indicated by the phrase "This is the account of . . ." (Gen. 2:4; 5:1; 6:9; 10:1; 11:10, 27). This means that Genesis is essentially an eyewitness account of man's earliest years!

Yet who was the eyewitness of Creation? Who saw and recorded the events of the first two chapters of the Bible before man even existed? The simple yet astounding answer is God Himself! Perhaps God revealed the events to Moses in a vision, much as He revealed the future to John in the book of Revelation. Perhaps He carved the words in stone, the same method He used to give the Law to Moses on Mount Sinai. However it was given, there is nothing in all of literature that can match the grandeur, the majesty, and the drama of the Creation account. It stands by itself as an unparalleled literary pinnacle that gives eloquent testimony to the glory of the almighty God of Creation.

Regardless of how God did it or who served as His instrument for human authorship, 2 Timothy 3:16 says it is not conjecture but fact that God Himself is the final Author. The first eleven chapters of Genesis are God's eyewitness memoirs of Creation.

In most courts of law, the credibility of an eyewitness is attacked because the opposing parties are afraid of the verdict to which such testimony could lead. For instance, although there was no actual eyewitness to Nicole Brown Simpson's murder, the character of any witness—police officer, chauffeur, houseguest, or friend—who might have pointed a finger at the defendant was fiercely attacked in order to destroy his or her credibility and thus weaken the testimony's impact on the jury.

God's eyewitness testimony of Creation is no exception. There is no portion of the entire Bible more attacked and maligned by those who are secular and religious than the first eleven chapters of Genesis. Why? Because of the enemy's fear of the verdict that would result from an eyewitness testimony of our beginning. And what would such a verdict be? The verdict is that God is our Creator, He has established basic directions for living the life He has given us, and we are accountable to Him—for everything!

What difference does this make to you and me? Perhaps the most notable difference is that it makes life make sense as it answers our basic questions: Does life have any real meaning? Where did I come from? Why am I here? Where am I going?

Without this awareness, feelings of meaninglessness, even worthlessness, can easily creep into our lives. Sometimes we look at modern celebrities and can't help but feel some envy for their wealth and influence. Yet one of the most famous (and sometimes infamous) celebrity icons, singer-actress Madonna, has been quoted as revealing, when asked if she was happy, that she is a tormented person. Comedian Eddie Murphy has wondered aloud, when he seems to have everything anyone could want, why something seems to be missing in his life. Actor Harrison Ford referred to his feeling of meaninglessness when he said he always wants what he doesn't have. Kurt Cobain, former lead singer for the rock group Nirvana, described a big empty hole inside himself. When he tried to fill it with drugs, money, fame, thrills, success, and sex, it just got bigger. Finally, the hole got so big he felt there was no escaping it, and he took his own life.

What really gives meaning to your life?

Is it the possession of more and more material things?

Is it the pursuit of a higher income, a higher degree, a higher office?

Is it the preoccupation with pleasure, sports, entertainment, physical fitness, sex?

Is it the pattern for living drawn by your peers? Your psychiatrist? Your parents? Your psychic?

Is it the priority of selfishness that insists on having everything you want, doing everything you can, saying anything you feel, seeing anything you like?

Is it the power of politics? Of popularity? Of position? Of prestige?

How many of the items on this list have you pursued only to come to the same empty conclusion King Solomon did when he moaned, "I have seen all the things that are done under the sun; all of them are meaningless, a chasing after the wind"?[1]

As we conclude the first decade of this millennium, I hope you'll join me in earnestly seeking and finding meaning for our lives, not in any of the above areas, but at the beginning of time at the beginning of the universe in God's eyewitness account of Creation on the first pages of Genesis.

What has been your attitude toward Genesis? Have you argued with its history? Have you scoffed at its science? Have you rejected its theology? Could it be you have missed one of the most obvious facets of this fascinating book, which is that it is God's eyewitness account of Creation? It is history from God's perspective, recorded in His own words. It is God's story.

The primary purpose of Genesis is to reveal God. Nowhere is God revealed as powerfully as He is in the first eleven chapters—unless it is in the Gospels through the person of Jesus of Nazareth. Yet Jesus did not "begin" in the Gospels at Bethlehem. He was already there in the beginning, before time and history began. Our minds explode and our hearts soar as we discover not only God the Father and God the Spirit but also God the Son in the very first verses of the Bible.[2]

The apostle John tells us, "This is the message we have heard from him and declare to you: God is light; in him is no darkness at all."[3] The primary characteristic of light is to reveal itself. John was giving us the astounding truth that God has revealed Himself to us through the "message" of the apostles and prophets that we refer to as our Bible. And this thrilling self-revelation begins in Genesis at the beginning of human history and the dawn of God's story.

While Genesis has been popularized for its practical application to everyday modern life by Bill Moyers's television series and by psychotherapist Naomi Rosenblatt's Bible studies, many people seem to be missing the point. For example, Rabbi Burton L. Visotzky, professor of interreligious studies at the Jewish Theological Seminary, calls Genesis "an ugly little soap opera about a dysfunctional family."[4]

At the other end of the opinion spectrum, Bishop Stephen Neill was a missionary bishop who helped form the Anglican Church in India, then went on to become the professor of missions at Hamburg University in Germany. In a lecture to his students, one of whom was my brother-in-law, he said, "More Hindus have come to faith in God through Genesis than any other book because Genesis clearly shows the world did not just happen but was created, not by 350 million gods and goddesses (as the Hindus believe), but by one God."

It makes no difference if the reader is Hindu, Muslim, Jewish, Catholic, or Protestant, the primary purpose of Genesis is to reveal the glory, the character, of God and what He has done. Unless it is read and studied with this purpose in mind, it will remain something of a controversial mystery. We study God's revelation of Himself not only to know the truth but in order to know Him more fully and intimately so that we might find our meaning and fulfillment and satisfaction and joy—our very life—in Him.

Several years ago when my family visited England, we did many of the things tourists generally do, including visiting Windsor Castle, where the queen goes from time to time for a long weekend. We were impressed by the castle's lavish decor, but I personally found it difficult to enjoy the guided tour of the rooms that were open to tourists because I was constantly wondering what was not in view. I found myself intrigued by the closed doors. The little doorknobs looked as though they might lead into secret compartments. I was dissatisfied with the superficial public tour because I wanted to see what was behind those closed doors.

In the same way, the book of Genesis is something of a closed door for many people. Although the stories of Creation, Adam and Eve, Noah and the Flood, and the Tower of Babel are fairly familiar, there seems to be a great lack of understanding about what meaning these stories have for our lives today. And as the average reader begins to search for the meaning, he or she is easily distracted by the debate among scholars as to the reliability and historical accuracy of Genesis, leaving the reader with even less confidence in the relevance of Genesis to modern life. While many may be intrigued by the stories, the average person cannot seem to penetrate the closed doors.

In the pages that follow, I hope you'll let me be your tour guide through not only the main events of God's story that are obvious to even the most casual reader but also into the "rooms behind the closed doors"—places inhabited by God Himself! And in finding God, in coming to know Him as He describes Himself in His own words, you will find more than a deity who created the universe. As you come to know Him, you will inevitably come to know His ways, His love, His power. As you come "face-to-face" with the Creator of the universe, you will find the meaning of life for which you have been searching.

Our "tour" winds through the first eleven chapters of the book of Genesis, beginning in the dark void of eternity filled only with God and moving quickly into the glorious dawn of His story . . .

# The God You Can Know

GENESIS 1:1–3

When our youngest daughter was small, we sent her off to a summer camp on Cape Cod. Following her arrival, the counselor gathered all the other girls together who would be living in the same cabin with our daughter and inquired, "Do you know who Rachel-Ruth's grandfather is?"

A little chorus went up from the circle of campers, "Noooo, who is Rachel-Ruth's grandfather?"

The counselor replied in a very dramatic tone of voice, "Rachel-Ruth's grandfather is the world-famous Billy Graham!"

As the counselor paused for effect, one little camper spoke up and said in an awed voice, "You mean Billy Graham the wrestler?" to which another, much more worldly-wise young lady said as she elbowed the first one in the ribs, "No, stupid, Billy Graham the singer!"

While the youngsters recognized my father's name and knew he was important and famous, none of those little campers really knew who Rachel-Ruth's grandfather was!

I find that many people today have the same kind of knowledge of God. They know He is up there somewhere, they may even be familiar with His Name, and they know He is famous and important and powerful—but they haven't a clue as to who He really is!

An incredible diversity of people claim they know God:

President George W. Bush and President Barack Obama;

Mahmoud Ahmadinejad of Iran and Benjamin Netanyahu of Israel;

Pope Benedict XVI and the Dali Lama;

Reverend Jeremiah Wright and Reverend Billy Graham;
Secretary of State Hillary Clinton and Governor Sarah Palin.

All of these people say they know God! But can all these people, who live out such extremely different lives and beliefs, really know Him as He truly is? Or do some of them just know *about* Him?

That same question occurred to me several years ago when I was invited to address the national prayer breakfast of a large secular convention. In my talk, I challenged the thousands of people at the event to gain real happiness by developing a right relationship with God through faith in Jesus Christ. Then, as I took my seat at the head table following my address, the master of ceremonies walked to the podium, looked down at me very condescendingly, and said in a scathing tone of voice, "Mrs. Lotz, we think you need to understand that we all have our own gods. Some of us call our god Buddha; some call him Mohammed; some call him Gandhi or Confucius or the Force. Some of us call our god Messiah, and some may even call him Jesus."

I didn't say anything at the time because I had already delivered my message as clearly as I knew how. But I thought to myself, *I don't want to know God like that. I don't want to know the names other people call Him. I want to know the name He calls Himself. I don't want to know what someone says He may or may not be like. I want to know what God says about Himself. I want to know His thoughts and emotions and plans and personality and character traits. With all of my heart, mind, soul, and being, I want to know Him as He truly is!*

My experience at the prayer breakfast wasn't the first time I had felt confirmed in my desire to know God in truth. That desire became an earnest quest twenty-one years ago when I studied and taught the book of Genesis for the first time. One result of that study was an overwhelmingly strong desire to know God in as much reality as did the biblical characters I was studying.

I didn't want to know *about* Him. I didn't want to know Him as a casual acquaintance. I wanted to know Him as Adam knew Him—I wanted to walk with Him and talk with Him.

I wanted to know Him as Enoch knew Him—I wanted His presence to so fill my life that I would be enveloped in it, aware of nothing else except Him.

I wanted to know Him as Noah knew Him—I wanted to risk my reputation and everything I have and am to be obedient to His call in my life. I wanted to care more about what God thought than what the world around me thought.

And I wanted to know Him as Abraham knew Him. I wanted to trust God in every situation. I wanted to have Him as my friend and have Him count me as His friend.

So I made that kind of relationship my goal. I made the deliberate decision to seek to know God as He truly is, and my pilgrimage of faith through in-depth study and application of His Word and my obedience to it continues until this day. Although I do not know Him as well as I want to or as well as I should, I know Him more closely and personally than I would have believed possible twenty years ago. And I pray I will know Him better next year than I do today.

I invite you to join me in this rewarding search to know God so well through His story that His eternal person, His infinite power, His unlimited love, and His matchless glory give meaning to your life and joy to your heart and purpose to your step.

Who is this God of the universe who leaned out of nowhere to interrupt eternity with the glorious dawn of His story?

Who is this God of glory whose very Presence can give:

> fulfillment to the empty . . .
> healing to the broken . . .
> forgiveness to the sinful . . .
> freedom to the bitter . . .
> purpose to the meaningless . . .
> help to the helpless . . .
> courage to the fearful . . .
> strength to the weak . . .
> reality to the religious . . .
> hope to the hopeless . . .
> love to the loveless?

Who is God? Who is this One we can know?

The glorious dawn of God's story begins with the stunning yet profoundly simple statement that in the beginning He created everything (Gen. 1:1)—which means that in the beginning, He was already there. He is eternal.

## THE GLORIOUS ETERNITY OF GOD

It is impossible to comprehend eternity. It's been defined as three stages of time: everything before Creation, everything that has taken place or will take place from Creation until the end of the world, and everything that will take place after the end of the world. It stretches back farther than the human mind can reach—

    whether through anthropology,

        or geology,

            or archaeology,

                or astronomy,

                    or microscopes.

It stretches ahead farther than the human mind can imagine—

    whether through science fiction,

        or political projections,

            or scientific observation,

                or telescopes.

While the Bible gives no explanation or definition for God, the opening statement of Genesis makes it clear that God as Creator is eternal and therefore not bound by time.

## God Is Not Bound by Time

God created time—the time we know as sixty seconds in a minute, sixty minutes in an hour, twenty-four hours in a day, seven days in a week, fifty-two weeks in a year, and however many years there will be in your life . . . however many years there will be in human history.

God created time, but He doesn't live within it Himself. He's not bound by or limited to it. In fact, Peter states that "with the Lord a day is like a thousand years, and a thousand years are like a day."[1] Could it be that the billions of years attached to various aspects of our planet and solar system are in actuality part of the mystery of eternity where there is no time as we know it?

Perhaps this characteristic of God helps explain the "days" of Genesis 1. Since God is not bound by time, could the six days of Creation be twenty-four-hour days on our time clock while at the same time being thousands or even millions of years on God's time clock?[2]

Several years ago, a movie was released entitled *Back to the Future.* In the movie an old professor designed a car that could be set for a certain date. By driving at a certain speed, the professor could break the time barrier and arrive at that date. Although the driver of the car could be living in 1997, he could set the date for 1950 or 2020, drive the right speed, and arrive at that date. The idea was that 1950 or 2020 or 1997 or any date all occurred simultaneously if the time barrier were broken. But God has not just broken the time barrier; He lives without one because He is eternal.

The eternity of God can mean wonderful comfort in the face of something as final and frightening as death. If you have recently lost a loved one who had faith in God, perhaps you have wondered, "I've buried my loved one. Her body is in the ground, and I know she is with Jesus. But does she just sort of float around somewhere up there with Him until she gets her resurrected body? And will she wait for years and years, longing to be reunited with her loved ones?"

When someone dies who belongs to Christ, that person is ushered into the presence of Christ in eternity and enters a timeless state. Although on our time clock hundreds of years could elapse before the resurrection day, on eternal time it could be just a few moments. So your loved one may have no concept of waiting to be reunited with you, in terms of earthly time.

This concept may partially explain predestination. God says whoever believes may come to Him,[3] but when you come, you learn that you were chosen "in him before the creation of the world."[4] This seeming contradiction is possible because God transcends time. For Him, all history—past, present, and future—is now. He sees everything at once. He doesn't see you now then wait thirty years to see you then. He sees all of your life from the beginning to the end at one time. Therefore He can choose you, yet at the same time you can have free choice.

Perhaps one of the most profound, thought-provoking applications of this concept concerns Jesus Christ, who hung on a Roman cross for six hours of earthly time.[5] However, since Jesus Christ is Himself God, could it be that those six hours of earthly time were an eternity on His time clock?[6] Did Jesus Christ, as the Lamb of God sacrificed for the sin of the world,[7] actually suffer an eternity of God's wrath and punishment for your sins and mine while hanging on the cross?

Regardless of the answers to these provocative questions, we can find personal reassurance in the fact that God is not bound by time. He is not only with us now, in the present,[8] but He is also simultaneously in the future, preparing the way for us[9] and working to answer our prayers of faith.

What are you worried about in the future?

Are you worried that you will become a financial burden to your children?

Are you worried about pending surgery or ill health that may incapacitate you and leave you totally dependent on others?

Are you worried about the future of your children—their physical safety, financial security, and spiritual well-being?

Are you worried about your career and if it will take you where you want to go?

Are you worried that you may not be able to adapt to all the technological changes in our world today and thus be unable to cope in your business?

Perhaps you are like the little girl whose mother found her sobbing uncontrollably. When the mother asked her what was wrong, the little girl raised a tear-dampened hand, pointed to the wall, and said between her sniffles that she was afraid of the nail that was protruding there. The mother gazed at her in consternation and asked why on earth she would be afraid of the nail on the wall. The little girl burst into a fresh deluge as she sobbed, "I'm afraid that one day I will have a little girl, and she will grow up and bump her head on that nail!"

What nail on the wall are you afraid of? Whether they are real or imaginary, worries about our future can rob us of our peace and joy at present.

## God Is Not Bound by Space

You and I can only be in one place at any given time because we are bound by space. Right now I am at my desk in my home. As much as I might like to be with my dad four hours away or with my son in California or with my daughters in Texas, I can only be in one place, and for now it's right here, in my study, working at my computer. But God can be everywhere at once. God, in all of His fullness, is present

> with pastors in Bosnia trying to keep the unity of the Spirit in the midst of generations of division,
>
> with Christians in Sudan seeking to glorify God in the midst of an earthly hell,
>
> with Christians in South Africa seeking to love one another equally,
>
> with the underground "house" church in mainland China praying for those in authority,
>
> with the missionaries in the jungles of Colombia seeking to present the gospel despite the threat of the drug lords,
>
> with the single mothers working in the inner cities of America, seeking to raise children who are honest, God fearing, drug free, hardworking, contributing members of society,

with the government politician who seeks to do what is right,

with me, as I write this book,

and with you as you read it!

On Christmas Eve, 1968, Frank Borman, James Lovell, and William Anders, while orbiting the moon in *Apollo 8*, were so aware of the presence of God in space that they publicly read the first ten verses of Genesis to the listening world thousands of miles away. When James B. Irwin, an astronaut with *Apollo 15*, actually walked on the surface of the moon, he said he looked out into the inky blackness, saw our planet looking like a blue marble suspended in space, and was overwhelmed with the conscious awareness that God was present on the surface of the moon! And God was! And God is! He is not bound by space.

Whom are you praying for who is separated from you? A child off at school? A spouse on a business trip? A family member who lives in another city or state or country? What comforting encouragement to know that God is not only fully present with you but also with those from whom you are separated, hearing and answering your prayers of faith for them.

Only once in eternity has God been bound by time and space. It was a time of His own choosing when, in the person of Jesus Christ, He "made himself nothing, taking the very nature of a servant, being made in human likeness. And being found in appearance as a man, he humbled himself and became obedient to death—even death on a cross!"[10] How awesome to consider that the Creator of the universe, unbound in time and space for all eternity, chose to be bound

by a woman's womb for nine months,[11]

by planet Earth,

by a manger bed,[12]

by an infant's body, crying helplessly for something to eat,

by the body of an adolescent that grew in wisdom and stature
    and favor with God and man,[13]

by the body of a man that knew weariness and hunger,[14]

by cords that took away His freedom to do what He wanted,[15]

by a Roman cross,[16] with His hands and feet pinned by spikes so that
    He could only move His head, by a borrowed tomb . . .[17]

Why? So that you and I might be set free from the problems that threaten to bind us and keep us from fulfilling God's intended purpose for our lives. Free from . . .

*Free From:* ↴

emptiness,

   brokenness,

      sinfulness,

         bitterness,

            wastedness,

               loneliness,

                  helplessness,

                     fearfulness,

                        weakness,

                           religiousness,

                             hopelessness . . .

free from any hindrances that would keep us from living our lives as He would have us live them—for Him! Praise God! We can be free, truly free at last, from all that binds us, because the One who is gloriously eternal, unbound by time and space, was willing to be bound!

## THE GLORIOUS DEITY OF GOD

The opening phrase of Genesis reveals the divine nature of God. It states, without giving room for even reasonable doubt as to His existence, that "in the beginning *God* . . ." (Gen. 1:1, italics added). In this statement two attributes of God's divine glory are revealed: He is greater than Creation, and He is separate from Creation.

### God Is Greater Than Creation

  Just as a potter is greater than the jar he forms,

    and an artist is greater than the canvas he paints,

      and an author is greater than the book she writes,

        and a programmer is greater than the computer he designs,

        and a musician is greater than the instrument she plays,

God is greater than that which He has created! And God has created everything![18]

He is not one of several gods. He is absolutely supreme over everything!

God is greater than Creation. This means there is nothing in my life—

    no circumstance or crisis,

      no organization or administration,

no individual or alliance,

no problem or pressure,

no habit or heartache,

no sickness or grief,

no king or criminal,

nothing visible or invisible—

*nothing that is greater than God!*

What are you facing that is greater than you are?

An emotion?

A habit?

A person?

A problem?

A responsibility?

A schedule?

A crisis?

An illness?

A committee?

Praise God for His deity! He is the Creator who is in authority over everything, fully able to control that which not only seems but is beyond our abilities to handle.

## God Is Separate from Creation

The New Age movement—and the Eastern religions such as Hinduism from which it comes—would have us believe that we are all gods with amnesia. The New Agers' philosophy, in essence, calls upon us to wake up the god within ourselves through a mystical experience that often involves an altered state of consciousness. But their philosophy is exposed as the deception that it is by the first phrase in the Bible, "In the beginning God . . ."

I was recently told by a university religion professor that her "inner reality" was God. Perhaps you have heard someone say, "There is a god within each of us." Or, "I see God in a sunset." Or, "I see God in an act of human compassion." Or, "I call it my inner reality; others call it Mother Earth or the Higher Power. You may call it God, but it's all the same thing."

No, it's not the same thing. God Himself is not in a sunset or in an act of human compassion any more than an artist is in his painting or a musician is in his music. You and I may see reflections of the artist's or musician's personality in his work, but the person himself is separate from it. Likewise, you may see the reflection of God's personality in a sunset or in an act of compassion, but He Himself is not in either one. He is separate from His Creation. What an important truth! This means:

When something is wrong, He can right it.

When something is broken, He can mend it.

When something is lost, He can find it.

When something doesn't work, He can fix it.

When something is hurt, He can heal it.

When someone is dead, He can raise him!

My failures, sins, mistakes, and shortcomings in no way dilute or deplete or weaken or harm God! If a man in India kills a cow, he has not killed God. If a giant redwood tree is cut down, nothing of God is cut down. If the entire planet and all that exists as we know it explodes in a nuclear holocaust, nothing of God is destroyed. God is a Person; therefore there is never even a slight possibility of pantheism.

Praise God for the glorious dawn of His story! He is separate from and greater than Creation, yet He chose to humble Himself and become part of it when He took on the form of a man. And as Man, the One who is greater than Creation submitted Himself to it—to the heat of the day, the cold of the night, the storms on the sea. On occasion, His deity was revealed when He calmed the sea or cleansed the leper or gave sight to the blind or raised the dead, but for the most part of thirty-three years, He lived in subjection to the very things He had created. Why? So that you and I might have the power, through faith in Him, to overcome the empty, broken, sinful, bitter, meaningless, lonely, helpless, fearful, weak, religious, and hopeless world of which we are a part.[19]

The eternity of God is revealed in the phrase "In the beginning . . ." The deity of God is revealed in the word ". . . God" (Gen. 1:1). And His activity is revealed in the last phrase of the first verse, ". . . created the heavens and the earth."

## THE GLORIOUS ACTIVITY OF GOD

All the way through the first chapter of Genesis, the phrases "God blessed," "God made," "God created," and "God said" stand out. The impression given is that God, as Creator, is busily active in several ways.

### *God Is Active in Big Ways*

There are 400 billion stars in the Milky Way galaxy.[20] Our sun is 150 trillion miles from the center of our galaxy. Our galaxy is just one of a cluster of thirty galaxies, and the closest galaxy to ours, the Large Magellanic Cloud, is 978 trillion miles away![21] Astronomers estimate there are more than 100 billion galaxies. And each galaxy has more than 100 billion stars![22] And each of those hundreds of billions of stars was personally hung in space by the Creator who has not only numbered them all but knows each of them by name![23] The very first words of Genesis tell us, "In the beginning, God created the heavens." I can't conceive of any activity much bigger than that!

What big things are you facing?

A big decision about a career change or a child's schooling or a marriage proposal?

A big commitment like accepting the marriage proposal or buying a new house or beginning a new job or becoming a new parent?

A big responsibility such as caring for elderly parents or supervising an office staff or rearing teenagers or being the sole provider for your family?

A big problem such as the disease that is claiming the life of your loved one or the broken relationship that is ruining your life or the debts that are greater than your income or the lawsuit pending against you?

The very first verse of the Bible tells us that God is active in big things! But God also "created the heavens and the earth." As Creator, He is active from the telescope to the microscope!

### *God Is Active in Small Ways*

The "earth" implies chemical elements and matter—molecules and atoms. It includes things that cannot be seen with the naked eye. In fact, a square foot of soil can contain over one billion organisms![24]

God created snowflakes, no two of which are alike. He created a spongelike pad between the head of a woodpecker and its bill to absorb the shock when the bird strikes a tree. He created small barbs along the feathers of each bird—as many as one million barbs per feather!—that act like zippers to lock the feathers together, not only waterproofing the bird but enabling it to catch air under its wings so that it can fly. He created seventy-five thousand miles of blood vessels in the human body that carry blood to over sixty trillion cells! More than one million of these cells are white antibodies, each one designed to fight just one kind of germ or virus. He created nerve cells that connect the human body to the brain like tiny telephone wires, with messages traveling along them up to three hundred miles per hour![25]

God is active in small ways in the universe, on our planet, in our bodies, and in our lives! What do you think is so small that it's too small for God to notice?

A small tear?

A small hurt feeling?

A small kindness?

A small insult?

A small sin?

A small lie?

A small need for love or encouragement?

A small article of clothing?

A small bite of food or a sip of water?

A small word of praise?

A small worry that is robbing you of your joy?

Nothing is too small for the Creator's attention and activity!

God as Creator is active in big and small ways. And God as man was also active in big things like raising Lazarus from the dead,[26] feeding five thousand people with five loaves of bread and two fish,[27] and calming a stormy sea.[28] And He was active in small ways like noticing a widow giving her mite at the temple[29] or taking a child on His knee[30] or touching a leper[31] or caring for Mary's feelings when she was criticized for pouring the contents of her alabaster box at His feet.[32]

Yet the One who is God-man, active in big and small ways, allowed Himself to be nailed to a Roman cross where He could not move His hands or feet. For the first time in all eternity, He ceased activity when He deliberately refused to take the next breath, and died. He lay cold, silent, and totally still for three days in a tomb. Why? So that you and I might have eternal life![33]

Praise God for the temporary inactivity of the One who is gloriously active in big ways and small ways and unseen ways!

### God Is Active in Unseen Ways

Although God was actively involved throughout the Creation process, in the beginning the "earth was formless and empty, darkness was over the surface of the deep"

(Gen. 1:2). If you and I had been present at that time to view the earth, we would have been able to see no outward, visible evidence of God's activity at all. In fact, we might have had the impression that because we could not see any evidence of His activity, He was not doing anything. Yet at that very time, "the Spirit of God was hovering over the waters" (Gen. 1:2). He was personally, invisibly, actively preparing planet Earth to receive His Word and be transformed into a place of beauty and purpose—a place that would reflect His image and bring Him pleasure.

Whom are you praying for whose life is "formless"—with no apparent purpose or meaning? Whom do you know whose life is "empty"—void of satisfaction and fulfillment? Is there someone you love who lives in the "darkness" of depression or ignorance or confusion? Are you concerned for a friend whose life is like "the surface of the deep"—undulating, unstable, always changing, and moody?

Even though you have prayed without ceasing, have you seen no evidence of God's activity in that person's life? Have you therefore concluded that God is not active? Or that He has not heard your prayers? Or that if He has heard you, He just doesn't care? Or if He cares, He simply is unable to do anything about it?

Place your faith in the God of Creation! He cannot be less than Himself. And He is active whether or not you and I can see evidence of His activity. In answer to your prayer of faith, the invisible, silent Spirit of God will move and hover over the heart and mind and will of your loved one, preparing him or her to receive His Word and thus be transformed.

The Word the Spirit uses in your loved one's life may be a verse or passage of Scripture that you share with him or her or something heard on radio or TV or in church. God is active, but He does not always act according to our timetable. He is very patient. But don't mistake His patience for inactivity; understand that very often His activity is unseen.

You and I must place our faith in the God of Creation, who is active in big ways, small ways, and unseen ways. Sometimes God tests and strengthens our faith by withholding evidence of His activity from us so that our faith is in Him alone. The men and women of God in the Old Testament were commended for faith that "is being sure of what we hope for and certain of what we do not see."[34]

Following the resurrection of Jesus Christ but before His ascension, He spent forty days and nights, coming and going among His disciples. At one point, two of His disciples were walking along the road to Emmaus when suddenly Jesus appeared, walking with them. Then, just as suddenly, when they broke bread together, He disappeared.[35] At another time that same day, His disciples were gathered together in the Upper Room in Jerusalem with the windows barred and the doors locked. Suddenly Jesus was in their midst; then just as suddenly He disappeared.[36] Jesus appeared again suddenly to His disciples on the shore of Galilee after they had been out all night fishing.[37]

During the forty days when Jesus suddenly appeared to His disciples, then just as suddenly disappeared, could it be He was teaching His disciples to live by faith? Whether or not they could see Him, He seemed to be teaching them to be confident He was actively present and involved in their lives.

His involvement is always at His own initiative. Because God is active in big ways and small ways and unseen ways and initial ways.

### God Is Active in Initial Ways

In the billions of years that stretch back into the mystery of eternity, God decided to create the universe as a home for planet Earth, which would be a home for man. Why? What prompted God to act? "Who has understood the mind of the LORD, or instructed him as his counselor?"[38] The answer that reverberates through the millenniums is . . . no one . . . no one . . . no one . . . no one . . . no one. God stands in the august solitude of Himself. When He acts, it is because He Himself has taken the initiative and made the decision to do so.

God took the initiative

to create the universe: "And God said . . . ,"
to create the earth: "The Lord God made the earth . . . ,"
to create man: "Let us make man in our image . . . ,"
to create the home: "The Lord God had planted a garden . . . ,"
to create woman: "I will make a helper. . . ."

And God took the initiative to send His own Son to earth to be our Savior: "For God so loved the world, that he gave his only begotten Son . . ."[39] He took the initiative to draw us to His Son that we might be saved.[40] He took the initiative when He raised Jesus Christ from the dead and placed the entire universe under His authority.[41] He took the initiative to send His Holy Spirit to live within us when we receive His Son by faith as our Savior and Lord.[42]

Your life and mine, both physical and spiritual, depend upon God's initiative. Praise God for the glory of His initial activity!

How unbelievably awesome is the One who created everything!
Our heads should bow,
our knees should bend,
our wills should yield,
our hands should serve,
our minds should worship,
our hearts should love

the One whose glory is revealed in the beginning through His eternity, deity, activity, and identity.

## THE GLORIOUS IDENTITY OF GOD

The Hebrew word for God in Genesis 1:1 is *Elohim*, and it occurs more than two thousand times in the Bible. *Elohim* is a plural noun, but in the Bible it is used with singular verbs. In other words, it implies by its definition and usage that God is one God—yet at the same time more than One. For example, "In the beginning God" reveals one person. Then, "the Spirit of God was hovering over the waters" reveals another person. "And God said, 'Let there be light'" reveals to us the third person as the living Word of God goes forth.[43]

A dramatic example of God's plurality is found in the first chapter of Genesis when God said, "Let us make man in our image, in our likeness...." Note the plural pronouns. But in the next verse the pronouns are singular: "So God created man in his own image, in the image of God he created him; male and female he created them" (Gen. 1:26–27). Again and again, God reveals His plural identity in the Bible.[44]

The mystery of His identity as three persons in One is hard to comprehend. One classic illustration is that of water, which retains its key elements and properties but can appear as liquid, steam, or ice. While God's Personhood and power do not change, He reveals Himself as Father, Son (living Word), and Spirit. Although no explanation is totally satisfying, we can worship the God who, if small enough for us to understand, would not be big enough to create us and be worthy of our worship.

*God the Father*

While God is the almighty Elohim, eternal, divine, and active, He is also very personal and loving.[45] It was God's idea to bring you and me into existence that we might know Him, because He loves us even though He knew we would sin and break the relationship with Him for which we were created.[46] It is God who demonstrated His love to us, not by making us healthy, wealthy, prosperous, and problem free, but by planning our redemption from sin, sending His own Son as a sacrifice through whom we might have forgiveness of sin and reconciliation with Himself.[47] God loves each and every person who has ever been born into the human race! God loves:

> the Eskimo living in an ice hut,
>
> the Chinese living in a bamboo lodge,
>
> the African living in a mud hut,
>
> the homeless living in a cardboard box,
>
> the Bedouin living in a tent,
>
> the Native American living in a teepee,
>
> the royals living in a palace,
>
> the slum dweller living in a housing project,
>
> the city dweller living in a high-rise penthouse,
>
> the president living in the White House,
>
> the peasant living in a farmhouse,
>
> the orphan living in a state house,
>
> the criminal living in a prison house,
>
> the soldier living in a guard house,
>
> the beggar with no housing at all . . .

God loves the whole world! God loves you! And God loves even me! And Jesus said we could call the God who is love our "Father."[48] In fact, the New Testament says when we come to Him in Christ, we can call Him "Abba, Father," which means "Daddy."[49]

A little girl was riding on a commuter train, flitting from passenger to passenger, totally uninhibited as she smiled, laughed, and talked with those making the routine journey from the center of the city to the outlying suburbs. Everyone wondered if her parents were on the train since she seemed equally comfortable with whomever she met. Suddenly the train was plunged into blackness as it entered a tunnel. The little girl gave a terrified squeal and flung herself into the arms of a gentleman sitting near the front of the car. And all the passengers knew who her father was. While she was friendly with everyone, only her father could give her the comfort and security that was based on her personal relationship and knowledge of him.

Nowhere in the Bible does it say that everyone on planet Earth is a child of God. But the Bible does say God loves everyone on planet Earth, and we can call God our Father when we come to Him in a personal relationship through faith in His Son.

*God the Son*

John's gospel begins with the astounding statement that "in the beginning was the Word." The Greek translation for "word" is *logos*, which means the outward expression of all that God is. Plato once said that he hoped one day there would come a "logos" from God that would make everything clear. John said He has come! "And the Word was with God . . ." as another separate, supreme Being. "And the Word was God." Although the Word is another separate Person from God the Father, He is no less in power, position, or personality. Because He is God the Creator! "Through him all things were made; without him nothing was made that has been made. . . . The Word became flesh and lived for a while among us. We have seen his glory, the glory of the One and Only Son who came from the Father, full of grace and truth."[50]

The "One and Only Son who came from the Father" is the logos of God through whom God created everything, and His name is JESUS! Jesus Christ is in the first chapter of Genesis as the living Word of God that goes forth every time we read the phrase "and God said." "He is the image of the invisible God. . . . For by him all things were created: things in heaven and on earth, visible and invisible, whether thrones or powers or rulers or authorities; all things were created by him and for him. He is before all things, and in him all things hold together."[51]

Have you ever wondered what God is like? While we glimpse the revelation of God's glory in Genesis, we see it fully in Jesus Christ.[52]

A little boy was pestering his father, who was trying desperately to get some paperwork done. So the father thought he would distract his small son. He handed him a piece of paper and a pencil and told him to draw a picture of a dog. Two minutes later the little boy proudly handed his busy father the picture. It was the stick figure of a dog. The father, making an extra effort to be patient, gave his little nuisance another piece of paper with the instructions to draw an elephant. Two minutes later, the paper was dutifully handed in with another stick figure drawn on it. The father gave the child one piece of paper after another, telling him to draw a lion, a frog, a dinosaur. Each time, the paper was handed back to him within a matter of minutes. Finally the father felt he had a stroke of genius. He knew something that should occupy his son for hours. He dramatically handed his son what he informed him would be the last piece of paper and told him to draw a picture of God. The father smiled smugly to himself, believing he had outwitted the youngster and would now have some uninterrupted work time. To his astonishment, the little boy began busily drawing and within the usual two minutes was prepared to hand his paper back in. The father exclaimed in exasperation, "No one knows what God looks like!" to which the little boy replied with the confidence of youth, "Well, they will now."

No one knew what God looked like until He revealed Himself through His Son.[53] But when Jesus Christ came to earth, everyone then knew what God looked like[54]—because God is exactly like Jesus!

The glory of God the Father is made visible and accessible to us through God the Son. And the glory of God the Son is made real and accessible to us through God the Spirit.

*God the Spirit*

The same Spirit that hovered over the surface of the deep in the second verse of the Bible is the same Spirit that fully indwelt Jesus Christ[55] and is the same Spirit who ever lives before the throne of God at the center of the universe.[56] In John 14 Jesus speaks of Him as the Spirit of truth,[57] because He always works through the truth, which is incarnate in Christ and written in the Scriptures.[58] He is also referred to as the Counselor because He gives wisdom, direction for living, and understanding of the truth.[59] And He is called the Holy Spirit because He is totally separate from sin.[60]

This wonderful Spirit of God is available to live within you when you repent of your sin and, by faith, invite Jesus Christ to come into your life as your Lord and Savior.[61] In fact, without the "seal" of His presence in your life, you have no eternal credibility with the Father.[62] But with the "seal" of His presence you have the guarantee of a heavenly home and all the blessings of God.

A few weeks before I began to write this book, both of our daughters became engaged to be married! As a pledge of their serious intent, the steady boyfriends gave their prospective brides beautiful diamond engagement rings. It was hard to know which sparkled more, the rings on the fingers of our daughters or the gleam in their eyes! Our daughters thought of 1,001 ways to use their left hands in order to flash their rings! And before leaving the house, each made sure she had carefully cleaned her ring! Although the rings were gorgeous, what really produced the light in our daughters' eyes and the blush on their cheeks was the knowledge that each ring brought with it the pledge of marriage within a few months.

The Spirit of God is our spiritual "engagement ring."[63] When we receive Christ by faith, He gives us His Spirit as His pledge guaranteeing we will receive all He has promised—acceptance by God, forgiveness of sin, and a heavenly home, to name just part of our inheritance![64]

When have you invited Jesus Christ in the person of His Spirit to live within you? It is possible to feel His love and presence, to know something of His grace and power, simply because you are near someone in whom He lives; yet you may not have Him living within you. In other words, if Jesus Christ lives in my husband and I am with my husband, in a sense I am "with" Jesus Christ, and it is possible to be aware of His presence even though that awareness is through my husband. One difficulty with this vicarious arrangement is that when I become separated from my husband, I also become separated from Christ. What a difference it makes when you invite Jesus Christ, who has been with you, to come live inside of you. He will never leave you or forsake you, nor can you ever be separated from Him.[65]

Jesus explained to His disciples that "the world cannot accept him [the Spirit], because it neither sees him nor knows him. But you know him, for he lives with you and will be in you."[66] The disciples knew the Spirit because the Spirit indwelt Jesus, and they were with Jesus. But when Jesus went back to heaven, God sent the Holy Spirit at Pentecost to live in the disciples.[67] It makes all the difference in this world and in the next to have the Spirit of God, who has been with you, come to live within you.

Because I stay so busy at home, when a friend comes to the door, I answer it but stand in the doorway with the person remaining on the porch with the screen door between us. We can talk about our children, discuss places to shop for good bargains, laugh at humorous anecdotes, and answer each other's questions. My friend can even look longingly over my shoulder at the inviting warmth of my kitchen, and I can be aware that she wants to come in, but I keep her standing on the porch until finally she says she has to go. I respond by thanking her for stopping by and saying it was good to see her. Even though I carried on a conversation with my friend and enjoyed her company, I never actually invited her to come inside from outside the house.

Do you have a screen-door relationship with the Holy Spirit? Do you know what it is to talk to Him in prayer, to listen to what He has to say by reading your Bible, and even to enjoy His company as you go to church and mingle with Christians? But have you kept Him standing outside your life because you have been unwilling to repent of your sin and have never invited Him to come inside? The Spirit of God is a gentleman. Although you can be aware that He looks long-ingly into your life, yearning to enter into all that you are, He will not force His way into your life. He waits to be invited. Haven't you kept Him waiting on the doorstep of your life long enough? Invite the triune God—the Father and the Son in the person of the Holy Spirit—to come in!

In the Old Testament, the glory of God appeared to the children of Israel as a pillar of cloud by day and a pillar of fire by night as they were led for forty years in the wilderness.[68] On occasion, the glory of God would envelop the tabernacle and later the temple with a golden glory cloud as a manifestation of God's presence.[69] When Moses pleaded with God to show him His glory, God instructed Moses to hide in the cleft of a rock and He would pass by, allowing Moses to only see His back.[70] And Moses, after ascending Mount Sinai to meet with God, descended with God's glory reflected visibly on his face.[71]

But the Bible says God's glory is no longer revealed in a cloudy, fiery pillar; it is no longer revealed in a golden, glowing cloud; it is no longer reflected from the backside or on someone's veiled face. The glory of God is within you and me through the Spirit of God, who indwells us when we receive Jesus Christ by faith as our personal Savior and Lord! You and I are the display cases for God's glory as His living temples.[72] "And we, who with unveiled faces all reflect the Lord's glory, are being transformed into his likeness with ever-increasing glory, which comes from the Lord, who is the Spirit."[73]

There is no experience more thrilling,
no adventure more exciting,
no relationship more satisfying,
no goal more rewarding,
no joy more lasting,
no meaning more fulfilling,
than personally glimpsing the revelation of God's glory in the dawn of His story and being the living revelation of His glory to the world!

IVAN ANGELOV was president of his church's denomination in Bulgaria when, in 1945, he was imprisoned by the Communists. In prison he was physically beaten again and again because of his faith in God. After one extremely severe beating, he crawled back into his cell and cried out in abject despair, "Oh, God, I cannot endure it any longer!"

Then, in the solitude of his desperation and confinement, Pastor Angelov suddenly heard a loud voice from an invisible Presence respond, "Fear not! I am with you!"

Ivan felt his entire being flooded with strength and energy as he stood up and walked around the cell into which he had crawled just moments before. Within minutes, the armed guard came and dragged him before the major to be interrogated again. The major asked with consternation, "What happened? I just had you beaten until you could only grovel on the ground! How is it that now you are walking?"

Pastor Angelov lifted his head, looked the major clearly in the eye, and answered in a ringing voice, "God spoke to me!"

The major put a gun to Ivan's head, threatening to pull the trigger. Without flinching, Ivan told the major to go ahead and shoot because, he said, he wasn't afraid. But instead of shooting him, the major had him returned to his cell, where he remained for eight long years. During his imprisonment, Pastor Ivan Angelov endured this type of brutality again and again.

Finally, the day came when he was released from prison. As he was passing the railroad station, he was confronted with a loitering, drunken bum. As he looked more closely, he recognized the bum as one of his cruelest prison guards who had personally beaten him time and time again. In fact, the guard had been so sadistic that the Communists had severed his party ties.

Suddenly Pastor Angelov was filled with the love of God for the wretched man. Without bitterness, he put his arm around his former tormentor and told the astounded man about the God of the universe, whose glory had invaded his prison cell.

The former guard's life was profoundly changed by the living revelation of God's glory in Ivan Angelov. Like Ivan Angelov, who glimpsed God's glory in his prison cell, or the guard, who glimpsed it in Ivan Angelov, my prayer is that each of us will glimpse God's glory as it is revealed in the dawn of His story.

# 1

## *I Fill Your Emptiness*

GENESIS 1

S ir Isaac Newton once had a miniature model of the solar system in his office. The sun was positioned in the center of the model with the various planets displayed in orbit around it. One day a fellow scientist walked into his study and when he saw it exclaimed, "My! What an exquisite thing this is! Who made it?"

Sir Isaac Newton replied, "Nobody." The scientist looked amazed as he said skeptically, "You must think I am a fool. Of course somebody made it, and he is a genius."

Sir Isaac Newton got up, walked around his desk, and put his hand on the shoulder of his friend as he said earnestly, "This thing is but a puny imitation of a much grander system whose laws you and I know. I am not able to convince you that this mere toy is without a designer and maker; yet you profess to believe that the great original from which the design is taken has come into being without either designer or maker. Now tell me, by what sort of reasoning do you reach such incongruous conclusions?"[1]

The same sort of reasoning that believes in the evolution of the universe from an amoeba in some prehistoric pool would lead to the conclusion that a bomb set off in a garbage dump could produce an intricate Rolex watch! All of creation makes a mockery of such reasoning!

When have you observed the blazing glory of a tropical sunset
> or an exquisite lady's slipper tucked into a rocky crevice in the forest,
>> or a baby's birth and first lusty cry,
>>> or a bird weaving her nest, hatching and feeding her young,
>>>> or the soft, silvery shimmer of moonlight on the ocean waves,

or a hummingbird suspended in air,
or a V-shaped flight of geese migrating north,
or the blinding flash of a jagged bolt of lightning
splitting the darkness . . .

when have you observed these things and wondered, as Sir Isaac Newton's friend did, *My! What an exquisite thing this is! Who made it?*

When we thoughtfully consider the world around us, we instinctively know our environment is not some haphazard cosmic accident but the handiwork of a Master Designer. The earth did not come about by the snap of some giant fingers but was deliberately planned and prepared in an orderly progression of events. Like planet Earth around us, our lives are not a haphazard cosmos, either. They were deliberately planned to be filled with the beauty of love and joy and peace and purpose—with God Himself. Such plans for our lives, as for planet Earth, need careful preparation.

## FINDING MEANING IN THE PREPARATION OF THE EARTH

In the beginning, there was nothing in the universe except a vast, endless emptiness. There was no time,
no history,
no life, no light,
no sound.

Just an immense black hole. Then, in all of that eternal empty nothingness, there was a misshapen blob that swirled in water, minute in size compared to the endless expanse surrounding it. It was enveloped in inky blackness, empty of everything and anything we might name, recognize, or find familiar.

One of the very first steps the Creator took to fill the emptiness with life and beauty and eternal purpose was to prepare it by His Spirit: "Now the earth was formless and empty, darkness was over the surface of the deep, and the Spirit of God was hovering over the waters" (Gen. 1:2).

### Prepared by the Spirit of God

The preparation by the Spirit of God may have taken days, weeks, months, years, or millenniums! The only information we are given is in the second verse of Genesis when we are told that "the Spirit of God was hovering over the waters."[2]

The invisible Spirit of the Creator enveloped and permeated the misshapen blob that was dangling in the midst of the vast black hole.

The description of planet Earth as it existed in the beginning is also an amazingly accurate description of the lives of many people today—lives that are formless, with no shape or discipline or character; lives that are void of meaning and joy and satisfaction—empty on the inside; lives that are in the darkness of ignorance, depression, despair, separated from God; and lives that are covered with water—the "deep"—having no stability or security.

How does a person whose life is empty experience changes that will result in a full, happy, meaningful life? The first necessary step is the preparation of the Spirit of God.

Penny and Johnny Sanders have been close friends for years. I first met Penny when she began attending the Bible study class I was teaching. Soon after she committed her life to Jesus Christ, she began praying for her husband, Johnny. Johnny never went to church, drank up to a fifth of alcohol and smoked three packs of cigarettes every day, and was dangerously overweight. Penny not only prayed for Johnny herself but enlisted the prayers of others for him.

Although Johnny was a successful businessman, he was not a reader. He never even read the daily newspaper. But several months after Penny began praying for him, they were both invited to a church Sunday school class social. At the social they heard several Sunday school class members discussing plans for a Bible study. To Penny's astonishment, Johnny indicated he was interested in joining it but expressed the opinion that he would get more out of it if he had his own Bible. Penny intensified her prayers! She knew Father's Day was approaching, and she used the opportunity to suggest to him that she and the children would like to give him a Bible.

Within a few days Johnny asked Penny to go to the local Christian bookstore and help him select his gift. He began his selection process by pulling from the shelves all the various Bible translations he could find. Then he sat down on the floor of the store, spread the Bibles out around him, and began to compare the various features and language. He finally decided on one, and Penny purchased it for him.

He began his search for God with a bottle of liquor in one hand and his new Bible in the other! Within a short period of time he was convinced through his reading that God loved him and had the power to transform his life. For the first time in his life, he got down on his knees in prayer, confessed his sin, asked for forgiveness, and invited Jesus Christ to come into his life and take control.

Within one week, Johnny quit drinking, smoking, and overeating as the joy and peace of God flooded his heart and mind. He enlisted in the weekly Bible study, which continued the wonderful transformation of his life. As of this writing, his children each know and serve the Lord, he himself is an elder in his church, he sponsors a Christian youth fellowship at a local university, leads a men's weekly breakfast Bible study, and bears radiant testimony to the power of God to transform an empty life into one filled with the blessing of God through the preparation of the Spirit and the power of the Word.

*Prepared by His Word*

God brought about change in planet Earth not only through the advanced preparation of the Spirit but through the daily proclamation of His Word. The phrase "and God said" occurs ten times in the first chapter.[3] Was His Word like a still, small voice whispering in the darkness?[4] Was His Word rumbling and loud like a peal of thunder?[5] Was His Word full, musical, reverberating like the sound of rushing waters?[6] Or was it an expression of what was on God's mind, communicated by an Agent, a Person who carried out exactly what God wanted?[7] Regardless of the form, we know that every day[8] of Creation, God's Word went forth, every day it was received, and every day some change took place in response, until progressively, day after day after day, the earth was transformed from emptiness to fullness of life and beauty.

Is your life empty? Do you want to experience real, lasting, God-pleasing change so that you are filled with satisfaction, peace, joy, love, purpose—abundant life? Then don't look to

a drug,

a bottle,

a pill,

a therapist,

a once-a-week trip to church, or even

a weekly Bible study.

Look to God's Word for yourself. Read your Bible every day in order to understand, apply, and obey it.[9]

As we long to grow not only in our faith but in our Christian character so that others can readily see Christ in us, we need to live in the power of the Holy Spirit

4

and in obedience to His Word. This transformation is a continual process that is brought about by daily saturating ourselves in the Scriptures, then living it out on the anvil of our experience.[10]

Do you know someone who is desperate for change? Someone who is:

controlled by alcohol?

dependent upon drugs?

embittered by injustice?

crippled by abuse?

bound by anger?

isolated by pride?

depressed by worry?

consumed by jealousy?

panicked by fear?

God's Word has not lost its power since the beginning of time! The same power that transformed planet Earth from that which was void, dark, without form, and in a fluid condition to that which was teeming with life, clothed in beauty, and reflective of the image of God is available today to change and fill empty lives. There is no life so shattered and devastated that it is beyond God's power to redeem and transform it. The process of transformation that invariably takes place through the preparation of the Spirit and the daily application of the Word is illustrated by what took place in the beginning of planet Earth.

## FINDING MEANING IN THE TRANSFORMATION OF THE EARTH

In the beginning, the earth was empty of any real, life-sustaining substance. It was suspended in blackness, swirling in water, with no discernible shape.[11] The first change necessary was to illuminate the darkness in which it existed.

*The Illumination*

In the beginning there was no dawn to end the night,

no sun to warm the day,

no moonlight reflected in the swirling water,

no silhouettes against the sky,

no sky,

no horizon,

just a never-ending night! "And God said, 'Let there be light,' and there was . . ."! (Gen. 1:3). What was that first light like? Was it a soft, gradual illumination of the darkness? Was it a shaft of brilliant glory? And how was it possible since the sun, moon, and stars were not brought into existence until the fourth day of Creation?[12]

Scientists tell us that there is light in the universe apart from the sun, such as phosphorescence or the light from radiation or the aurora borealis. And the Bible tells us physical light is associated with the very presence of God—so much so that in heaven there will be no need for a sun, moon, and stars, because the light of God's glory will illumine everything.[13]

Perhaps on the first day of Creation God lifted the veil that had hidden Him from earth, and in some way the glory of His presence was revealed! Perhaps it was an explosion of light energy similar to the "big bang" referred to today as a theory of Creation. Whatever the unknown technical explanation may be, we know the light came in response to God's Word.

God didn't leave our environment in a murky, dusky twilight. "God saw that the light was good, and he separated the light from the darkness. God called the light 'day,' and the darkness he called 'night.' And there was evening, and there was morning—the first day" (Gen. 1:4–5).[14]

While the light described was literal, it has wonderful analogy and personal meaning for you and me, because light in the spiritual sense represents the truth, clarity, spiritual understanding, and discernment we receive from God's written Word. The psalmist praised God because "the unfolding of your words gives light; it gives understanding to the simple."[15]

In what area of your life do you need illumination? Discouragement about the future and the direction we have chosen, depression over the lack of fulfillment in our lives, or disillusionment by our previous attempts to find meaning for life through organized religions can all plunge us into the darkness. Do you ever wonder,

"Why am I here?"

"What is the meaning to my life?"

"Why is genuine happiness so elusive?"

"Why am I lonely in a crowd?"

"Why am I so restless inside?"

"Why do I feel guilty?"

"Why do I feel afraid?"

"Is there a God?"

"What is God like?"

"How can I know God?"

"Is there life after death?"

"Where am I going?"

God's written Word and the answers we find there turn our darkness into light. God's Word "is a lamp to my feet and a light for my path."[16]

I wonder if the mind of Saul of Tarsus searched for truth through similar questions. He had filled his life with organized religion in order to find God and through Him, meaning for his life. He testified that he was "circumcised on the eighth day, of the people of Israel, of the tribe of Benjamin, a Hebrew of Hebrews; in regard to the law, a Pharisee; as for zeal, persecuting the church; as for legalistic righteousness, faultless."[17] Yet he lived in the darkness of ignorance, thinking he was serving God while all the while he was separated from Him. While he pursued with a vengeance what he perceived to be the truth, suddenly "a light [blazed] from heaven, brighter than the sun."[18] And Saul of Tarsus was confronted with the revelation of God's glory in the person of Jesus Christ! While the light temporarily physically blinded him, at the same time it opened his spiritual eyes to the truth. Later he exclaimed, "For God, who said, 'Let light shine out of darkness,' made his light shine in our hearts to give us the light of the knowledge of the glory of God in the face of Christ."[19] And the life of Saul of Tarsus was forever changed through his personal encounter with Jesus Christ from that of a blasphemer to a proclaimer of the truth—from one who left destruction in his path and was headed for eternal darkness to one who offered eternal life in Jesus' name[20] and ran his race of life for "the crown of righteousness, which the Lord, the righteous Judge, will award" on that day.[21]

Jesus Christ, the living Word of God, is the light of the world![22] The apostle John said that "in him was life, and that life was the light of men."[23] His life is our light—our meaning, our reason for living, our fulfillment and satisfaction and joy and peace!

Many people today are searching for the Light. I talked to the nephew of a dear friend who was looking for the Light in Buddhism. He shared with me that he felt he would find the Light when he could adequately describe the difference between the colors black and red!

I talked to another young man seated beside me on an airplane. He was going on a backpacking trip into the Adirondack Mountains because he believed the mountains he worshiped were the Light! On my trips to India, I have met various Westerners making the trek to a guru because they were seeking the Light through meditation and human homilies!

Where are you looking for the Light? Are you searching for the Light through
a career?
a family?
a reputation?
an education?
money?
travel?
entertainment?
pleasure?
sports?
sex?

John says the Light has come! He is the living Word who was in the beginning with God, who Himself was God, who became flesh! His name is Jesus![24]

Whom do you know who is living in darkness without a personal relationship with Jesus Christ and therefore is separated from God?[25] Surely, if God could lean down out of heaven and invade the life of Saul of Tarsus, shining His Light into Saul's life in such a way that his life was transformed, He is able to do the same for you and me and anyone we know!

Once the Light penetrates the darkness, our understanding and wisdom are enlarged. The dimension of our lives is increased.

## The Dimension

In the beginning, when the light appeared, it revealed a planet that was black and white and gray. There was no color. The planet was just a misshapen blob submerged in water. If we had been present, all we would have seen would have been some prehistoric, stagnant pond. To the untrained eye, it would have appeared to have no potential at all.

Do you know anyone like that? Sometimes, even with the Light on, only God can see the potential in a human life. The potential can be totally invisible to others, submerged in waste, in filth, in sin and rebellion and violence. How do you react to such a person? Sometimes, a person's life can be so hopelessly ugly I just want to turn the light off! But praise God! He turned the Light on and began to draw out the potential: "And God said, 'Let there be an expanse between the waters to separate water from water.' So God made the expanse and separated the water under the expanse from the water above it. And it was so. God called the expanse 'sky.' And there was evening, and there was morning—the second day" (Gen. 1:6–8).

When God separated the waters below from the waters above, forming an atmosphere in between, He increased the earth's diameter by approximately 120 miles.[26] Apparently this involved the formation of a type of vapor canopy over the earth. It may have appeared something like the ice rings around the planet Saturn or the cloud cover that shrouds Venus.[27]

The vapor canopy would have made the earth like a greenhouse. On the earth, under the canopy, there would have been

> no great air-mass movements,
> > no hurricanes,
> > > no tornadoes,
> > > > no monsoons,
> > > > > no typhoons,
> > > > > > no rain,
> > > > > > > no thunderstorms.

The canopy would have served as a giant terrarium, with the dew condensing and watering the earth, making rain unnecessary[28] while maintaining a uniform temperature.[29]

Scientists tell us that today the atmosphere weighs approximately 5.7 quadrillion tons![30] But the atmosphere held much more water than that in earth's first days. Think of the pressure on the earth when it was smothered and swirling in billions and billions of tons of water! Can you imagine the power of God's Word that lifted those billions of tons of water up from the earth into a vapor canopy? The earth was still "under" the pressure, but with the expanse and new dimension, it had breathing room!

Do you feel overwhelmed and smothered by pressure? Are you desperate for "breathing room"? Do you try to escape the stress through

> an extended vacation,
> > therapeutic counseling,
> > > alcohol,
> > > > drugs,
> > > > > entertainment, or
> > > > > > a romantic liaison . . .

only to find when you stop to assess your condition you are no better than you were before, because the pressure is from within?

Only God has the power to lift the pressure from within you. Your circumstances may remain the same, but He has the power to give you breathing room. He can give your spirit peace and rest,[31] even as He gives your life a new dimension.

When the Light enters your life in the person of Jesus Christ, He enables you to think new thoughts, feel new emotions, and make wise choices because He gives you His mind and heart and will.[32]

When my children were babies and toddlers, I remember feeling that the dimensions of my mind seemed so small. I thought in small thoughts, and I talked in small words. I longed for a larger "adult" dimension to my mind. I received it through the daily study of God's Word. I would slip into a quiet place before the children got up in the morning or when they took their naps in the afternoon or after they had been tucked into bed at night, and in that quiet place I would read my Bible, talking to God about His thoughts, which are bigger than anyone's,[33] and His Words, which are not just intellectually stimulating but comforting and challenging and life changing! Day by day He enlarged the dimension of my mind.

Not only our minds but our emotions can be given a new dimension through the power of God's Word. Following a message I had given in Pretoria, South Africa, a young man came up to speak with me. He told me he had been sexually and physically abused as a child, rendering him incapable of giving or receiving love as an adult. I prayed for him and noticed afterward that he faithfully came to every meeting and sat on the front row, taking in everything that was said with earnest, rapt attention. On the last day of the meetings, he came up to me, gave me a hug, and told me God was opening up his heart and life to other people. His emotions were taking on a new dimension as he received God's Word.

While God's Word is not like a magic wand, it does have the power, when applied by the Holy Spirit, to give a new dimension to your mind and emotions and also to your will. Have you lacked the willpower to stay on a diet, conquer a bad habit, or develop disciplines necessary for character? Until I began to receive God's Word daily, I never had the willpower to get up early in the morning for a time of prayer. I lacked what has been called "blanket victory"— victory over those blankets in the early-morning hours! But God has given my will an added dimension so that I am now able to do what I formerly could not.

Does your life feel confined? Do you sometimes have the uneasy feeling that something is missing, that there must be something more to life than what you are experiencing? That you are not fulfilling your potential? Open your heart and mind to God's Word. Use this book as an aid to reading your Bible on a daily basis, and increasingly, God will expand not only the dimension of your heart, mind, and will, but He will give you a foundation for your life.

*The Foundation*

God's Word went forth to a planet submerged in water and laid the foundations of the earth with the command, "Let the water under the sky be gathered to one place, and let dry ground appear. And it was so. God called the dry ground 'land,' and the gathered waters he called 'seas.' And God saw that it was good" (Gen. 1:9). The word *seas* is plural, meaning several seas or oceans, yet God gathered them all into one place, meaning they were all at sea level. The water of the oceans, to this day, does not rise above sea level except in a storm or during high tide, because God set the boundaries in the beginning. As God gathered the waters into one place He raised the land, formerly submerged in water, so that the earth had not only illumination and an enlarged dimension but a foundation as well.[34]

Several years ago the multitiered parking deck at our area's largest shopping mall suddenly collapsed without warning in the middle of the night. Coming right after the busy Christmas shopping season when the deck had been jammed with thousands of cars, everyone was enormously relieved that no one was injured and only one car was damaged. As the dust and debris settled, questions began to arise: "How could a deck newly built by a reputable contractor collapse? There had been no crush of cars to add weight, no storm or wind to add pressure, no recent accident to have caused damage. From all outward appearances, there had been no problems. Everything looked exactly as it was supposed to. What went wrong?"

When the investigation of the accident was completed, it was discovered that the steel beams used in the foundation of the parking deck were flawed and cracked. Although it had withstood days and weeks of heavy activity, underneath the surface it had been constantly weakening until it could no longer stand. One large area had given way to the weakness, dragging down an entire section. As a result, no part of the structure was safe. The entire multimillion-dollar deck had to be dismantled piece by piece, then rebuilt with a foundation that included beams strong enough to support the weight it was designed to hold.

Many people today are living lives that to all outward appearances seem to be working successfully. Then, with no prior warning, a wife of twenty-five years abandons her family—for another woman. Or a young couple making honor grades in an Ivy League school murders their newborn infant. Or a reputable attorney holding national responsibilities commits suicide. Or a well-known, well-liked athlete gives expression to his rage and beats his wife.

All around us we see lives collapsing with broken hearts and broken homes and broken hopes—with shattered minds and shattered emotions and shattered bodies. What has gone wrong? The foundation on which the majority of people are building their lives is cracked and flawed.

On what foundation are you building your life?

What feels right?

What works?

What everyone else is doing?

What research and opinion polls say is best?

How stable is your foundation? When an unexpected crisis comes, will your life remain firm and steadfast, or will it all collapse? Each one of the above "foundations" is makeshift. Like the undulating waters that covered planet Earth, these "foundations" change from day to day. What feels wrong today feels right tomorrow. What worked yesterday doesn't work today. Everyone else may be doing the same things, but those same things can be fads that in the long run prove to be unhealthy, unwise, unprofitable, unsuccessful, and unfulfilling. And research and opinion polls can be so manipulated as to be very unreliable.

Our nation today illustrates the danger and tragedy of living without a firm foundation. Our Pledge of Allegiance refers to the fact that America is "one nation under God" that offers religious and individual freedom. As she destroys the very foundation that has made her strong, refusing to allow public and private acknowledgment of God in her government and educational institutions for the sake of toleration and political correctness, she is growing morally and spiritually weak. Increasingly, America will be unable to adequately respond to national crises in

health,

education,

welfare,

immigration,

race,

crime,

Medicare,

social security,

government

corruption,

the deficit . . .

The list is like a time bomb waiting to go off and destroy all that she has been.

The Bible tells us there is only one foundation for individual or national life that will last, regardless of the crisis or pressure, and it is the foundation of Jesus Christ: "For no one can lay any foundation other than the one already laid, which is Jesus Christ."[35]

Jesus Christ never changes.[36]

He will never leave you nor forsake you.[37]

Nothing can ever separate you from His love.[38]

His grace is always sufficient, and His power is made perfect in weakness.[39]

His Word never fails,

His promises are true,

and everything He says comes to pass.[40]

The foundation of faith in Jesus Christ is one on which you and I can build our lives with confidence, knowing it will last, not only for our lifetimes but for all eternity as well.

As Jesus concluded His Sermon on the Mount, He said, "Everyone who hears these words of mine and puts them into practice is like a wise man who built his house on the rock. The rain came down, the streams rose, and the winds blew and beat against the house; yet it did not fall, because it had its foundation on the rock."[41]

The Creator wants us to have a strong foundation for life, and He wants the lives we build on that foundation to be filled with satisfaction, fulfillment, beauty, and fruitfulness. This is reflected in the third day of Creation, which not only involved laying a foundation but also bringing forth vegetation that made the earth fruitful and beautiful.

*The Beautification*

Up until this point, the cold, colorless earth was as bleak and barren as the lunar landscape looks today. It consisted only of water and dry ground. There was:

no grass,

no moss,

no flowers,

no ferns,

no bushes,

no shrubs,

no trees,

no cacti,

no fungi,

no lichens,

not even any weeds! "Then God said, 'Let the land produce vegetation: seed-bearing plants and trees on the land that bear fruit with seed in it, according to their various kinds.' And it was so. The land produced vegetation: plants bearing seed according to their kinds and trees bearing fruit with seed in it according to their kinds. And God saw that it was good. And there was evening, and there was morning—the third day" (Gen. 1:11–13).[42]

Through the power of His Word, God brought beauty to the barrenness and added color to the drabness. Notice this time God did not create anything new. He just called it forth from what was already present, because apparently that which was necessary for plant life was in the soil.

Several months ago, a friend delivered several loads of topsoil to our house, dumping it in the front yard. Within a week's time, the mound of black dirt was covered with a soft, green mantle of small plants. The weeds had sprung up because the elements necessary for plant life were already in the soil.[43]

I wonder what it would have been like to watch the bleak, barren, desolate planet suddenly softened with

spidery ferns,

exotic orchids,

waving palm trees,

velvety moss,

scarlet poppies,

majestic sequoias,

lush raspberries,

gnarled apple trees,

weeping willow trees,

carpeted fields of grass,

until it was breathtakingly beautiful! What does the land of your life look like? Is it drab and devoid of the real beauty of joy and happiness? Is it barren of any lasting meaning? Is it desolate from lack of love? Perhaps it is even ugly because of the scars of sin and suffering. If God, through the power of His Word, transformed planet Earth into something that was beautiful, He can do the same for you.

Years ago, in the highlands of Scotland, a group of fishermen stopped in the local pub for something to drink after having been out at sea all day. They ordered their drinks, then began to tell their "fish stories." As one fisherman described the fish that got away, he threw his arms out to demonstrate how large the fish had been. He didn't see the little barmaid who had come up beside him, and his gesture hit her tray, sending the drinks crashing against the newly whitewashed wall. The entire pub was silenced by the crashing glass as everyone watched the ugly brown stains from the drinks appear on the wall. Before anyone could react, a patron who had been sitting quietly in the corner jumped up, took a piece of charcoal from his pocket, went to the wall, and began to sketch around the stains. As he sketched, the ugly brown marks were transformed into a magnificent stag in full flight across a highland meadow. Then he signed the drawing. His name was Sir Lanseer, Great Britain's foremost wildlife artist. His masterful touch had transformed the ugly stains into a very lovely and valuable picture.

It doesn't matter if your life has always been dry, barren, bleak, desolate, and ugly, or if it has become that way because of some tragedy or crisis. If you submit your life to the skillful touch of the Creator, He has the power to transform you into someone who is beautiful—beautiful not because of a toned physique or flawless skin or a perfect figure or manageable hair but because the life of Christ radiates from within you: His joy sparkling from your eyes, His love lighting up your face, His peace softening your expression, His purpose lifting your chin, His presence causing you to walk with confidence.

Planet Earth became beautiful. It had a blue sky, a variegated green earth, turquoise seas, and multicolored flowers. But the Creator wasn't finished with the way it looked. He surrounded it with jewels as He studded the sky with stars, hung the moon in place, and took away the coldness by giving it the warmth of the sun. But earth was not just some celestial bauble beautified for the Creator's collection. It was also given purpose and direction.

## The Direction

At this point in time, planet Earth was spinning round and round rather aimlessly rotating on its axis[44] but seeming to go nowhere. On the fourth day of Creation, God, through the power of His Word, gave it direction when He said, "'Let there be lights in the expanse of the sky to separate the day from the night, and let them serve as signs to mark seasons and days and years, and let them be lights in the expanse of the sky to give light on the earth.' And it was so. God made two great lights—the greater light to govern the day and the lesser light to govern the night. He also made the stars. God set them in the expanse of the sky to give light on the earth, to govern the day and the night, and to separate light from darkness. And God saw that it was good. And there was evening, and there was morning—the fourth day" (Gen. 1:14–19).

The emphasis does not seem to be so much on the fact that the lights were made but that they were made for a reason: to give direction and purpose to the earth for days and years of time, for signs and seasons, for navigation and migration. Because life without direction is just existence.

In what direction are you headed? Has the direction of your life been controlled by the direction of others, like a leaf caught in the river current? Is your life spinning around aimlessly in a self-preoccupied existence with no real purpose or meaning or focus? How do you get your life focused? Do you long for a sense of purpose, a clear-cut direction, a goal to live for that makes living worthwhile? Then submit to the Creator's voice—His Word that reveals His specific and personal plan for your life.

When my children were small, I felt my life had no real direction. Although I knew I was to raise my children to be committed Christians as well as socially responsible and contributing members of their generation, I felt my life beyond my identity as a mother and wife was somewhat aimless and empty. I became deeply convinced there was more to life than I was experiencing.

I began studying and eventually teaching the Bible to other women like myself who were searching for meaning and direction in their lives. Through the daily study of His Word, God increasingly focused my life on Himself. Whether teaching my class of five hundred women or mopping up spilled juice or preparing and serving meals for my family or speaking to an audience of ten thousand evangelists, my whole life has become focused in worship of God as I desire to know Him through His Word, through life experiences, through relationships, through responsibilities and opportunities and difficulties. As a result, He has filled my life to overflowing!

*The Animation*

The earth at this stage was in living color, but it was like a still-life painting. There was no movement or activity or feeling. There were no

    singing birds

        or roaring lions

            or soaring eagles

                or barking dogs

                    or quacking ducks

                        or trumpeting elephants

                          or grunting pigs

                            or howling wolves

                              or leaping fish . . .

Nothing. There was no sound or movement of life at all. "And God said, 'Let the water teem with living creatures, and let birds fly above the earth across the expanse of the sky.' So God *created* the great creatures of the sea and every living and moving thing with which the water teems, according to their kinds, and every winged bird according to its kind. And God saw that it was good. God blessed them and said, 'Be fruitful and increase in number and fill the water in the seas, and let the birds increase on the earth.' And there was evening, and there was morning—the fifth day. And God said, 'Let the land produce living creatures according to their kinds: livestock, creatures that move along the ground, and wild animals, each according to its kind.' And it was so. God made the wild animals according to their kinds, the livestock according to their kinds, and all the creatures that move along the ground according to their kinds. And God saw that it was good" (Gen. 1:20–25, italics added).

God had called forth the plants and trees from the life in the soil. He had made the sun and moon and stars from the light. But to produce the fish, birds, livestock, and wild animals, He created something brand-new when His Word went forth on the fifth day of Creation.

The Hebrew word for "create" is *bara*. It literally means to bring forth something out of nothing. *Bara* occurs once in the first verse of Genesis when "God created the heavens and the earth," bringing them forth from nothing. It occurs again in verse 21 when God "created the great creatures of the sea and every living and moving thing with which the water teems," bringing forth animal, bird, and sea life from nothing. What was it that had not existed prior to this and was therefore called forth from nothing? If there was already life in plants, trees, and vegetation, what was so unique about the life brought forth on the fifth and sixth days that it had to be created?

The uniqueness of the life created on the fifth and sixth days was that it was life with conscious awareness and feeling. In contrast to everything that had come into existence previously—the sun, moon, stars, sky, seas, dry ground, and vegetation—the fish, birds, livestock, and other wild animals could think and feel. Where there had been no feelings or emotions or thoughts or awareness of life, now Planet Earth was teeming with these things.

In the same way, God's Word brings life to human existence today. Abundant life! Eternal life! Fullness of life! Do you feel dull?

Lethargic?

Apathetic?

Indifferent?

Depressed?

Despondent?

Dysfunctional?

Empty?

In Jesus Christ you can find the life you are missing and looking for in

accumulating material things,

increasing your income,

traveling to unseen places,

tasting exotic foods,

driving fast cars,

flying fast airplanes,

riding fast bikes,

promoting your reputation,

furthering your education,

partying with friends,

indulging your whims.[45]

Jesus said one of the reasons He came to earth was to give you and me fullness of life.[46] Why settle for less?

In the beginning, the Creator was not stingy with our environment. He filled it with life. Planet Earth was progressively transformed as every day God's Word went forth and every day God's Word was received. Each day's change prepared the environment for the next day's change until it was totally transformed. Yet it was as though it waited for something. In the same way a church sanctuary, all decorated, waits for the bride, and a nursery, all equipped, waits for the baby, planet Earth was prepared but waiting to be completed.

## FINDING MEANING IN THE COMPLETION OF THE EARTH

All of the daily changes seemed to be setting the stage for the climax on the sixth day. "Then God said, 'Let us make man in our image, in our likeness, and let them rule over the fish of the sea and the birds of the air, over the livestock, over all the earth, and over all the creatures that move along the ground.' So God created man in his own image, in the image of God he created him; male and female he created them" (Gen. 1:26–27).

Earth had been waiting for man![47] Man himself was the climactic jewel of Creation! Everything prior to his existence was created and made in preparation for him. Once again the Hebrew word *bara*, meaning to bring forth something out of nothing, is used, not just once, but three times in one verse, as though to emphasize and draw attention to the fact that nothing like man had ever existed in the universe prior to his creation. Through the power of God's Word, man was brought into existence from nothing.

What was—and is—so unique about man that he required a special act of Creation? There was already inanimate life in plants and trees. There was life with feeling and conscious awareness in the fish, birds, and animals. We know some animals are so similar to man that they can be used in medical research for human benefit. There have even been successful cases of animal tissue and organs being transplanted into the human body. What sets man so distinctly apart from the animals that he required a separate creative process of God? The distinct difference between man and all other animals and life forms is that man was created in the image of God.

By creating man in His own image, God fixed a gulf between animals and man that will never be bridged. Animals always have been and always will be animals. Man always has been and always will be man. The fossil evidence confirms this. No one has ever found the "missing link," and no one ever will, because it's missing! It doesn't exist! Since Creation, approximately ten billion human beings have been born, yet there is not a single recorded case of one ever being genetically less than a human being. Man was created in God's own image, completing the creation of the environment.

## Man Reflected God's Image

What is life in the image of God? It is life with a capacity to know the Creator in a personal relationship.[48] It is a soul that communes with God and has eternal value in His sight. Man was created

to walk and talk with God,
to love and obey God,
to listen to and learn from God,
to serve and please God,
to glorify and enjoy God forever!

Jesus defined our meaning for existence when He prayed, "Now this is eternal life: that they may know you, the only true God, and Jesus Christ, whom you have sent."[49] Knowing God in a personal, pure, passionate, and permanent relationship is the ultimate human experience. Knowing God is the meaning of human life. It is the reason for our existence. It was the completion of all the changes God made in the environment in the beginning. And it is the completion of all the changes God is making in your life at the present.

The changes brought about by God's Word in your life and mine are not primarily for the purpose of making us good or successful or happy or wealthy or prosperous or problem free. The primary purpose of these changes is that we might know God fully and intimately so we can reflect Him in all we are and say and do, bringing glory to the One Who created us.

Is your life complete? Do you feel you are waiting for something, but you don't know what? Do you have an aching loneliness, a hunger pain of the spirit, a yearning deep inside yourself for something? For Someone? Then get in touch with your Creator. You are hungry for God. You were created with a capacity to know Him in a personal, permanent, love relationship. That capacity is empty until you establish the relationship with Him for which you were created.

After God had prepared the environment through His Spirit and His Word, after He had transformed the environment by bringing in illumination, expanding the dimension, laying a foundation, clothing it in beautification, giving it direction, and filling it with animation, He completed the environment with the creation of man, who not only reflected His image but who, praise God! also received His blessing.

## Man Received God's Blessing

The blessings of God are His benefits. Recently my son took a new job. One of the questions he asked his new boss was what benefits he could expect as an employee of the company. He wanted to know if he would have moving expenses, housing allowance, health insurance, and transportation in his annual salary package. When considering a job, the benefits can induce us to make a long-term commitment while the lack of benefits can keep us from such a commitment.

Once man was created, he was committed for the long term. And the Creator, in His grace, showered the man with benefits that would make his commitment to life a joy and pleasure: "God blessed them" (Gen. 1:28). Every day the man would be excited to wake up, eager to go to work, rejoicing in who he was and the opportunities he had during the day, sleeping peacefully at night in harmony with the world around him because he was blessed by His Creator.

The blessings of God became even more precious to me on an early June day in 1983. It was the first day my children were out of school for the summer, and I took all three of them to celebrate at a special downtown restaurant in our city. Two hours later, in the middle of the day, we returned home to find the front door broken down and everything of value gone! I will never forget the sick feeling of walking through my house and seeing the empty places where antique furniture had been, the space where my grandmother's clock had been, the blank wall where the mirror had hung, the drawers of my silver chest partially open to reveal their emptiness. Cameras, jewelry, silverware, and even the little silver baby cups and spoons my children had used as infants that had been displayed on a cabinet—gone!

The police who came and dusted the house for fingerprints said there was nothing that could, or would, prevent thieves from entering when they set their minds to it. Apparently they had "staked out" our house for some time, and once the thieves had decided to rob our home, it was just a question of when.

That night I crawled into my bed—the same bed that the thieves had so neatly turned back so they could take the pillowcases off the pillows to use as sacks in which they carted off my things! As I lay there in the darkness, thinking of what the police had said, I felt myself growing icy cold with the realization that there was nothing I had that could not be taken from me:

21

My health could be robbed by illness.
My education could be outdated by more advanced knowledge.
My house could burn to the ground.
My children could leave home.
My husband could drop dead from a heart attack.
My youth could be robbed by old age.
My reputation could be robbed by gossip . . .

I could not think of one thing I had that was permanently secure! And then it was as though the light came on in my mind's eye. I knew I had "an inheritance that can never perish, spoil or fade—kept in heaven" for me.[50] I had the blessings of God that could never be robbed from me! As I lay in bed, surrounded by a home that had been violated, I began to count my blessings. I fell asleep counting my blessings, and when I awoke in the morning they were still on my mind. And my joy was back!

As I drifted off to sleep, I had thought of so many permanent blessings of God in my life that I listed them the next morning on paper in alphabetical order to remember and meditate on them. The list itself has become a blessing!

I am:

Accepted by God,
Beloved by God,
Chosen by God,
Delivered by God,
Enlightened by God,
Forgiven by God

I have:

God's grace
Hope
An Inheritance in heaven
Justification
Knowledge of God
God's love
God's mercy
God's nearness
Oneness with God
Peace
Quickening of the Spirit

I am:

Redeemed

Sealed with the Holy Spirit

Treasured by God

United with other believers

Validated as an authentic child of God

I have:

His Wisdom

And one day I will be **exalted** with Him to live in heavenly places![51] Praise God, from whom all blessings flow! If He doesn't bless you and me, we won't be blessed, because all real, permanent blessing comes from Him!

God is the Creator, whose purpose for you and me is the same as it was when He created our environment in the beginning. He wants us to reflect His image so that we might receive His blessing. "God saw all that he had made, and it was very good. And there was evening, and there was morning—the sixth day" (Gen. 1:31).

In the end, the Creator stood back. He surveyed the transformation of the environment that had followed His loving and careful preparation. Then He looked at the man and woman He had created in His own image, with a capacity to be His close, personal friends, and He was pleased.

✐♥

HIS NAME is Lon. He was a good Jewish kid from a good Jewish family. He went to the synagogue every Sabbath, read the Torah fluently in Hebrew, and was bar mitzvahed at age thirteen. He believed God existed, answered prayer, and one day would accept him into heaven, based on his heritage.

At the age of fifteen, he decided the synagogue was no longer relevant to his life, but drinking and girls were. So he gave his life over to having fun. He enrolled in the University of North Carolina at Chapel Hill as a chemistry major, joined a fraternity that was 50 percent Jewish, and plunged into the party scene with gusto. The summer of '69, between his sophomore and junior years, he worked as a waiter in the Catskill Mountains. Since he was always up for a good time and he was in the vicinity, he went to the concert at Woodstock. While there, he got heavily into drugs. His experience with LSD and other psychedelics convinced him he had found the real meaning to life. When he returned to school, he encouraged 60 percent of his fraternity brothers to turn to drugs. He became one of the leading drug pushers on campus, obtaining the illegal substance from Amsterdam, then selling it anywhere and everywhere on campus. Because he never showed up for class, he was the only student to ever flunk honors chemistry. In fact, he stopped going to all his classes because, while taking LSD three or four times every week, he was convinced he didn't need to. His senior year, he was pictured in the yearbook sitting in a tree with four of his friends, smoking dope.

One day he was sitting on a wall with a friend in downtown Chapel Hill, totally tripped out on LSD, when he made the observation that rather than his life getting better, it seemed to be getting worse. Instead of becoming more loving, kind, and gentle, he was getting more selfish, mean, and ugly. His friend listened to him, then turned to him and with glazed eyes replied, "Lon, maybe you're not getting worse. Maybe you're just getting honest with who you've been all the time." The casual, offhand remark rocked Lon's world. Because he knew it was true. The drugs were unlocking and exposing his inner self as being immoral, unethical, and selfish, and he didn't like what he saw. He suddenly knew he needed help. Drugs were not the meaning of life he thought they were. He quit taking drugs and began to look for meaning in religion.

Lon plunged into Taoism, Confucianism, and Buddhism, seeking help for his internal problems. But in the same way cancer seems to grow more rapidly when exposed to oxygen, he felt his friend had opened up his inner self, and the exposure caused the ugliness in his life to mushroom in size and scope. In desperation, he sought help from the local rabbi, but nothing in orthodox Judaism could help or change his hurting soul. At that point, he acknowledged he had nothing, no answers, no resources with which to live life, so he decided to kill himself. He reasoned, "What is the point of living a life that is totally meaningless when you just die in the end? Why not just kill yourself now and get it over with?" But he was lazy and a procrastinator, so he put off killing himself.

In the spring of '71, he was walking down the street with his dog. Right in front of a van covered with Scripture verses, mounted with loudspeakers that continually played hymns, and manned by a freak who preached to those passing by as he handed out tracts about Jesus, Lon's dog got into a fight. As he pulled his dog away, he looked up into the man's eyes; they exchanged greetings, and Lon walked away. Several blocks down the street, Lon was suddenly struck by the awareness that he had seen what he was searching for in the eyes of the fanatical preacher! He had thought there was no real meaning to life, but he was convinced that if there was, that man knew what it was.

The preacher-man appeared in town every Saturday. Every Saturday Lon observed passersby spit on the man, curse him, crumple up his tracts, and throw them back in his face. Out of sympathy and as an act of kindness, Lon took the tracts he was handed, but he never read them.

Six weeks later, Lon couldn't stand the misery anymore. He went to the man one Saturday and asked if he could talk to him sometime. The man readily agreed to talk to him that day. Lon, suddenly frightened, rejected the offer, saying they would have to meet the next week. As he walked away, the man cupped his hands around his mouth and screamed at Lon, "You may not be here next week."

Lon ran around the corner of the building, terrified and embarrassed to be yelled at on the street by the fanatical preacher. But like a knife to his spirit, he realized the preacher's words were true; he might not live to see the next week. In fear, he lived each day so carefully he took steps one at a time, didn't walk under ladders, and carefully looked both ways when he crossed a street.

Lon decided what he needed was a Bible. He had never before seen or read one, so he went to the local bookstore. He was astounded at how much they cost but finally found a small one for three dollars, which was half of all the money he owned. He bought it, but when his fraternity brother ridiculed him for doing such a stupid thing as to spend half of his money on a Bible, Lon took it back. But as he returned it, he told God that if He was real and if He was who He claimed to be, He would just have to give him a Bible to read.

The following Saturday, Lon was waiting when the strangely painted van pulled into town and the preacher began to set up for another day in Chapel Hill. Lon sauntered over to him and said he was ready to hear the full sales pitch. The man opened up his Bible and for two hours explained who Jesus is and what it meant to know God personally through faith in Him. Like a dry sponge soaking up water, Lon thirstily drank in every word. The man concluded by asking him if he wanted to invite Jesus into his life. Lon didn't have the faintest idea what that meant, but he was sure he didn't want to do whatever it was, so he said no.

The man responded, "Okay, but do you have a Bible to read?" When Lon shook his head, the man opened up the back of his van and pulled out a brand-new Bible and handed it to Lon. When Lon refused it because he couldn't pay for it, the man insisted it was a free gift. As Lon accepted the gift, he remembered what he had said to God and became even more afraid because he seemed to be into something that was really getting serious.

He took the Bible back to his room and began reading the gospel of Matthew. He pored over the Sermon on the Mount six times before he could go on. Jesus seemed to have more to say in one sentence than all of his professors had said in an entire semester at school. When he read Jesus' words of invitation, "Come to me, all you who are weary and burdened, and I will give you rest. Take my yoke upon you and learn from me, for I am gentle and humble in heart, and you will find rest for your souls,"[52] Lon knew he had found exactly what he had been searching for. All of his life he had been looking for peace for his soul.

Not knowing what to do, Lon got down on his knees and made a deal with God: "God, I don't know if You're real, and this Jesus character is confusing, but He said if I would come to Him, He would give me peace and rest. So I'll tell You what I'm going to do. I'm willing to try You for a month. If during that month You can prove to me You can give me peace and rest, I'll give You the rest of my life. But for the next month, I'll do whatever You say. I want to give You the same shot I gave those other religions. But God, I want more than a warm, fuzzy feeling. I want real proof. So I'm going to lay it on the line. My dog has mange. I've been rubbing medicine into him for weeks, and it hasn't helped. I'm going to quit giving him the medicine. If You heal my dog of the mange, I'll know You're real."

Within three days, Lon's dog was healed of the mange! And Lon knew somehow he had backed into the living God of the universe! One week later, he knew God had come into his life. He was filled with inner peace and joy coupled with deep contrition for sin. Three weeks later, he went back to the street preacher and told him what had happened. The man started to cry like a baby, then called for his wife to get out of the van; when he told her, she began to cry. They hugged Lon, then told him he needed to be baptized. Lon refused, explaining because he was a Jew, he couldn't go that far. But during the following week, he became convinced that if he had given his life to God, he had to go all the way in his commitment. So he went back to the preacher the next week and was baptized in a little pond outside of Chapel Hill.

The Creator must have stood back and surveyed the transformation of Lon's life from that of an empty, pleasure-seeking, drug-pushing, LSD-tripping college dropout to a man who went on to graduate from a theological seminary and is now a full-time preacher of the gospel, filled with peace and joy.

If God can fill the emptiness of planet Earth so that it reflects His glory . . .

If God can fill the emptiness of Lon's life so Lon reflects His glory . . .

He can fill the emptiness in your life so that you reflect His glory too!

# 2

I AM THE GOD OF CREATION

## I Mend Your Brokenness

GENESIS 2

When our children were small, invariably on Christmas Eve my husband and I would stay up late to put together some toy we had bought unassembled. We would nail, hammer, and saw with increasing determination as well as frustration when the last piece was out of the box and the last screw inserted, yet the toy didn't work. Finally, we would come up with a little piece of paper in the bottom of the box that said, "Read carefully. Manufacturer's directions for assembly."

We could have saved ourselves a lot of trouble if we had just followed the directions in the first place! We have ruined many Christmas toys with the attitude, "This thing is so simple, anyone can put it together. We don't need to read the directions."

I remember we had that attitude toward a little red tricycle we were going to give our daughter Morrow one year. My husband pulled the pieces of the tricycle out of the box and said, "Well, anybody can put the wheels on it." But when he finished putting the wheels on it, every wheel seemed to angle in a different direction! We never were able to get that little tricycle to run properly, simply because we had not bothered to read the manufacturer's directions for assembly.

Many people approach life the way my husband approached that little red tricycle. They treat life as though it's so simple they can live it their own way. They sort of guess their way along. It's not until their lives don't work that it occurs to them to look around for directions.

God as our Creator has specific directions for our lives. If we live according to His directions, our lives work—we are blessed, and we experience life the way it was meant to be lived. If we ignore or reject His directions, we do so to our own detriment and experience much less than He intended.

28

As we observe society today, particularly in America, we observe increasing chaos and confusion at every level because society is ignoring and rejecting the Manufacturer's directions for assembly. All around us are

broken lives,

broken dreams,

broken families,

broken homes,

broken people,

broken hearts,

broken hopes.

But God never intended us to be broken. He did not just create you and me, plop us down on planet Earth, and say, "Happy birthday! Now you can guess your way through life." Instead, He has given us directions, which form a pattern that will prevent breakage of our lives and will help to mend the brokenness already present if we follow it.

## Finding Meaning in a Pattern to Live By

Life on planet Earth is fast becoming a rat race, a dogfight, and a mad scramble to get ahead that is leaving brokenness everywhere. We desperately need a pattern to live by that will enable us to live our lives successfully. Such a pattern already exists; it was set at the dawn of Creation by God Himself. But we are not following the Creator's directions.

Our twenty-four-hour day is based on the earth's rotation on its axis. Our twelve-month years are based on the revolution of our planet around the sun. But the only basis for the seven-day week that is used worldwide as a pattern for humanity's lifestyle is the Creator's example: "Thus the heavens and the earth were completed in all their vast array. By the seventh day God had finished the work he had been doing; so on the seventh day he rested from all his work" (Gen. 2:1–2). While God's week included rest on the seventh day, it also involved work for six days straight, giving us a pattern for the discipline of our lives.

### The Pattern for Discipline

Our society is increasingly becoming undisciplined. We work if we want to, show up on time if we can make it, and see a job through to the finish if we feel like it, all the while complaining about the pay or seeking more lucrative benefits. God worked persistently and consistently every day, all day long, until the job of creating everything was finished. God understands what it's like to begin each day in the morning, go to work, apply yourself to the project at hand, accomplish a portion of the goal day after day until you complete the job satisfactorily. God's weekly work was timely, orderly, precise, neat, thorough, planned, and goal oriented.

Our planet, as well as our lives, is the result of God's meticulous work and personal time and effort. How did He do it? Did He sit at some celestial computer in some universal central control room, computing the distance between stars and planets? How did He know just how fast to spin the earth? How did He know to place the sun at the exact distance from the earth so it wasn't so close that the earth would burn up or so far that the earth would freeze over? How did He figure out the exact twenty-three-degree tilt of the planet to give us four seasons to the year? How did He measure the distance of the moon from earth so that it would give us predictable ocean tides each day instead of the seas overflowing their boundaries and inundating us with water? How did He determine the depth of the ocean floors so that our atmosphere has the perfect mix of carbon dioxide and oxygen? And how did He keep the atmosphere at just the right density so that it prevents meteor bombardment of the planet?

God worked constantly for six days of the first week. What is your week like? What job have you done haphazardly in order to just get through? Are you slouchy and casual or serious and committed about your weekly work? Are you afraid of hard work? Often we tend to quit a job before it is finished because the job is too hard or we lose interest or we receive a better offer somewhere else. The Creator has built into each of us the capacity for tremendous satisfaction in work that is not only finished but well done. If we quit before we are finished, we miss out on the satisfaction that comes with completion.

Sometimes we think of not having to work as a luxury reserved for the lifestyles of the rich and famous. It is actually a deprivation! One reason unemployment is so devastating is because when a person is out of work, that person is outside the Creator's design for living and therefore denied the satisfaction that comes from working and from completing a job.

Johnny Evans was an All-American quarterback who played college football at North Carolina State University. When he graduated from college, he was drafted by the Cleveland Browns of the National Football League, where he played for three years before being traded to Buffalo. The Buffalo Bills released him after only six weeks, and Johnny spent the first fall in seventeen years not playing football.

At the time of his release from the Buffalo Bills, he had a wife and family responsibilities. While his college degree equipped him for a career, he could not immediately get a job in that field. Instead of feeling sorry for himself or accepting handouts from well-meaning friends or refusing to work unless the job was in his chosen profession, Johnny went to work selling shoes at a sporting goods store. His wife said that in the evenings when she would go to pick him up, she would find him vacuuming the store or kneeling at the feet of an eight-year-old, fitting the child with soccer shoes.

Within the year, Johnny received the opportunity to continue his football career in the Canadian football league, a position he held for three more years. He not only got back the job he wanted, but he had the satisfaction of maintaining the support of his family through his own work. While friends may have felt it was demeaning for someone of Johnny's stature to work as a shoe clerk, Johnny knew it was an honorable position. And he believed it was much more desirable than to disregard the Creator's pattern for the discipline of his life by not working at all.

Jesus Christ knew He had been sent to earth from heaven to save mankind from sin. Yet for thirty years He worked in a carpentry shop in Nazareth.[1] Talk about being overqualified for a job! And although the apostle Paul knew he had been sent from God to evangelize the world, establishing the church in the first century, he supported himself and others through tent making.[2] What job do you think is beneath you? Very often people refuse to work unless it's in a job that meets their qualifications and goals. All around us are men and women who, when they are laid off work because their company downsizes, just sit around, send out résumés, and complain that they are out of work. It takes only a glance at the classified ads in the newspaper to know there is plenty of work out there if we are just willing to take on a job we may be very overqualified for and one that doesn't match our lifetime career goals. You and I were created to work. Any honorable, respectable job is better than no work at all.

How closely does your weekly work follow the Creator's example? Are you disciplined enough to work hard at a job you don't particularly enjoy, you haven't personally selected, or you're professionally overqualified for? And not just work at that job, but work hard until the project is done? Sometimes the brokenness of our lives is self-inflicted because we are lazy, spoiled, and selfish in the way we spend our time. God's directions instruct us to be disciplined if we want Him to mend our brokenness. We are also to be devoted.

## The Pattern for Devotion

Like a boat that would be tossed endlessly and aimlessly and dangerously on the open sea without an anchor, we need to anchor our lives as well. That anchor is devotion to God. God worked for six days during that first "week," then rested on the seventh: "And God blessed the seventh day and made it holy, because on it he rested from all the work of creating that he had done" (Gen. 2:3). The word *holy* means "set apart," or different from ordinary things.

In the beginning, by His own example, God patterned our week to include not only the discipline of work but also one day out of every seven that would be "set apart," different from the other six days. Until the resurrection of Jesus Christ, Saturday was the Old Testament Sabbath—the one day in seven that was set apart for the Lord by His people. That "Sabbath rest" was fulfilled in Christ.[3] Therefore for most Christians today, the first day of the week, which is Sunday, has replaced Saturday as the day set apart for God because Sunday is the day of Christ's resurrection. However, the specific day, whether Saturday or Sunday, is not as important as the principle: that one day in seven is to be devoted as holy to the Lord.

From the law in Exodus we know one reason for this day of devotion is to ensure that we do not get too far away from God's pattern.[4] If one out of every seven days we are anchored by our focus on Him, we are less likely to drift from Him. On the other hand, if one day each week is not spent in giving Him our attention, we are more likely to put Him further and further away from our thoughts until we do not seriously think of Him at all, and we end up being tossed about on the sea of life only to wind up being smashed and broken on the rocks when a storm hits.

To be anchored in our devotion to Him by setting apart one day in seven for Him is to receive special blessing. "If you keep your feet from breaking the Sabbath and from doing as you please on my holy day, if you call the Sabbath a delight and the Lord's holy day honorable, and if you honor it by not going your own way and not doing as you please or speaking idle words, then you will find your joy in the Lord, and I will cause you to ride on the heights of the land."[5]

In many facets of our national life, we are not "riding on the heights"; we are sinking to the depths. As our society breaks apart and experts ponder how to curb inflation, stimulate the economy, and cut the deficit, they would do well to read and follow the Creator's directions. Could it be that not only individuals but corporations, companies, businesses, and governments need to break one day in seven from their routine for their own financial health? It may be that the economy is like a big engine that gets overheated if it is never given a proper rest. Perhaps God designed the economy to function at its fullest potential when it, too, is rested one day out of every seven.

Certainly the people in our society would operate more harmoniously, healthily, and happily if one day out of seven everyone's focus was on the God who created them and to whom they will give an account of their lives one day.

What about you? How much healthier mentally, physically, spiritually, and emotionally would you be if you followed the Creator's pattern of devotion for your life? For the majority of people today, there is very little difference between the way they keep Sunday and the way they keep Saturday. Sunday has become more of a holiday than a holy day. Sunday was not designed just so we could sleep late, meet friends for brunch, go shopping to take advantage of weekend sales, do extra yardwork or housework, attend the latest movie, or watch the playoff game on TV. Sunday was also not designed for us to gobble down breakfast while screaming at the children to hurry and get dressed so we can rush to church to get it over with so we can rush to a soccer match to rush to a swim meet to rush to the pizza parlor so we can rush off to Sunday evening worship so we can fall exhausted into bed, thankful that we made it through another Sunday! Sunday should be not only for physical rest and restoration but for spiritual refreshment and expression of our devotion to God.

Has the day that is supposed to be set apart fallen apart? Consider what you can do to keep Sunday special—different from the other six days of the week.

When I was a young girl growing up, Sundays were the most special days of the week. While there were many activities I was not allowed to be involved in, such as watching television, reading secular books and magazines, playing with friends, or doing homework, there were many things that were reserved just for this special day.

My mother began Sunday with Christian music played over the intercom so that my waking thoughts were on God. I was then called downstairs to the kitchen, where she had a special breakfast such as homemade whole-wheat pancakes and hot maple syrup waiting on the table. After dressing in clothes not worn the rest of the week, I went to Sunday school and church, sitting in the third pew from the front, nestled against my grandmother (who fed me Luden's cough drops during the service to keep me from fidgeting!).

Following Sunday school and church, I went home to a large family lunch, enjoyed at a table that had been set with the best china and silver as though company was expected. Sunday afternoon I was allowed one candy bar and soft drink to enjoy while listening to my father's weekly radio program, *The Hour of Decision*. Sometimes in the afternoon we would take a family hike on the mountain, going all the way up to the top where my mother explained the huge size of the trees was due to their strength developed as they resisted the strong winds that constantly buffeted the ridge. On Sunday evening, my grandparents usually joined my parents, brothers, sisters, and myself for a light supper, after which we sang hymns and played Bible games.

Sundays in my home were different from ordinary days of the week. And one of the results has been that God, true to His Word, has richly blessed my family. Although I had to make some adjustments when I got married, my husband and I also set apart Sundays for the Lord. Sundays are still special!

The basic guideline for my children, my husband, and myself has been that if something can be done Monday through Saturday—like shopping, housework, sports, yardwork, laundry, schoolwork—we do it then so we can keep our Sundays uniquely different from the rest of the week. And unless someone is physically incapacitated, we always go to Sunday school and church. That is a permanent commitment we have made so that we never have to decide on Saturday night whether we are going to church the next morning. It doesn't matter if we have a housefull of company or splitting headaches or if we've been up late the night before or if a huge midterm exam is facing one of the children on Monday, Sunday morning finds us in church. Even with the heavy speaking and travel schedule I keep now, I have a policy of returning from wherever I have been by Saturday night so I can be in church with my husband on Sunday morning. It helps keep me anchored in my devotion to God.

Examine the way you spend your Sundays; then make the necessary adjustments so that your weekly lifestyle reflects not only your discipline but also your devotion to God. As you do, the devotion to God that one day in seven was designed to help maintain will begin to mend the brokenness of your life as it permeates your home.

## FINDING MEANING IN A PLACE TO LIVE IN

The creation of man and the establishment of his home seem to be the object toward which all the information on Creation has been pointing. The change of focus between the first chapter of Genesis and the second is similar to the experience I have had in airplane travel. When flying long distances, the passenger jets I have flown in cruise at altitudes as high as thirty-seven thousand feet. The plane is so high that when I look at the horizon, I can almost see the gradual curvature of the earth. Then, as the plane approaches its destination, the earth that had looked hazy and blurred from a great altitude takes on more specific detail as roads, trees, streams, and houses can be distinguished. As the plane actually lands, much smaller details, such as the color and make of a car, the faces of the ground crew, and the writing on signs, can be clearly seen.

The description of Creation that began with a telescopic perspective in the first verse of Genesis was then viewed as though through binoculars in the rest of the first chapter. Chapter 2 gives us more of a microscopic focus as it zeros in on the details of man's creation.

One of the first details emphasized is that the earth was barren of real beauty and love and life until the home was established: "This is the account of the heavens and the earth when they were created. When the LORD God made the earth and the heavens—and no shrub of the field had yet appeared on the earth and no plant of the field had yet sprung up, for the LORD God had not sent rain on the earth and there was no man to work the ground, but streams came up from the earth and watered the whole surface of the ground . . . the LORD God had planted a garden" (Gen. 2:4–6, 8). The first time God is referred to as the Lord God is when He prepares a place for man to live in and establishes the home. He Himself was the first Homemaker—which in itself holds the key to mending broken homes and broken families.

In the first verse of Genesis, the Hebrew word Elohim is used for God. In chapter 2 His name is revealed as Jehovah Elohim, which is translated "Lord God."[6] Jehovah Elohim implies the concept of God revealing Himself to His people in a personal way. In other words, the first time God revealed Himself personally was in a home. Nothing could be more personal than God Himself planting and arranging the garden that would be the first home for the first man.[7]

On various occasions in the Old Testament, God appeared in human form as

He sought to reveal Himself personally to His people. This human form is implied when He brought the animals to Adam to be named[8] and by "the sound of the LORD God as he was *walking* in the garden in the cool of the day"[9] and later in the Lord's visit to Abraham's tent to discuss the impending birth of Isaac and the future of Sodom[10] and when Jacob wrestled with God in the Jabbok River[11] and when the Lord confronted Joshua at Jericho.[12] The ultimate and complete revelation of God as man was not when He came in human *form* but when He came in human *flesh*, the "exact representation of His being,"[13] in the person of Jesus of Nazareth.

Following the crucifixion of Christ, when Thomas, the disciple who tended to be very skeptical and therefore doubted much of what he was told, was confronted with the risen, living Christ, he exclaimed, "My Lord and my God!"[14] It was an astounding truth Thomas discovered, that the Lord God—*Jehovah Elohim*—of the Old Testament and Jesus of Nazareth *are one and the same*! What a blessed truth, then, to realize that it is the preincarnate Son of God, Jesus Christ,

who walked in the garden in the cool of the day . . .

who brought the animals to Adam . . .

who had lunch with Abraham in his tent . . .

who wrestled with Jacob in the river . . .

who confronted Joshua at Jericho . . .

who is the same Lord God who established the first home!

If you recently married and established a home for the first time or if you have just finished school and moved into your own apartment or if you have finally saved enough money so you can buy your own home, the Lord God understands

the fun and frustration,

the pressure and pleasure,

the responsibility and refuge,

the burden and the blessing

that establishing a new home can be!

Thinking ahead to the New Testament, the first time Jesus Christ performed a miracle, thus revealing Himself publicly, was in a home.[15] At the very beginning of His ministry, Jesus was confirming the elevated position He has given the home—a position that is fulfilled when the home reveals His presence.

Is God's presence in your home readily apparent to others? If a stranger walked in, would he or she be aware of God's presence through your family members' friendship toward each other? The consistency of prayer and Bible reading in your family times together? The frequency of God's name being lovingly, respectfully mentioned? The consideration and compassion shown to the hurting and helpless?

I have a dear friend whose home is not as large, lavish, or luxurious as she would like. In fact, at times she has felt embarrassed by its humbleness. But she has not only invited the Lord God to come in and make Himself at home, as the family in Bethany did;[16] she has offered it to Him for His use. She counsels troubled neighbors at her kitchen table, prays on her knees with friends in her family room, serves coffee and tea in her dining room to the unchurched, welcomes traveling missionaries to use her spare bedroom, and leads Bible studies in her living room! Her entire home is so permeated with the atmosphere of worship, reverence, and love for God that to walk through her front door is to be blessed by the reality of His presence within! Surely if the Lord God is really present, the life within our homes should reflect an unsurpassed quality of life.

God prepared the garden of Eden as the home for the first family: "Now the LORD God had planted a garden in the east, in Eden; and there he put the man he had formed. And the LORD God made all kinds of trees grow out of the ground—trees that were pleasing to the eye and good for food" (Gen. 2:8–9). We can imagine a wonderful picture of the Lord God . . .

> grubbing in the dirt,
> > preparing the soil,
> > > planting flowers,
> > > > transplanting trees,
> > > pruning shrubs,
> > cutting grass,
> arranging paradise as a home for His people!

What would the garden of Eden have looked like? With no pollution to dull the brilliant blue of the sky or the sparkling blue of the water, with no clouds to hide the glory of the sun or the twinkling of the stars, with no weeds or dead leaves or thorns or wilted blooms to mar the beauty of the landscape, it must have been breathtakingly, spectacularly, exquisitely perfect!

> Velvet grass like a plush carpet underfoot,
> lush fruit like oversized jewels waiting to be picked,
> emerald, variegated leaves like a living umbrella,
> a profusion of flowers like a multicolored garment softening the landscape,

clear blue water like a river of glass from which to drink,

soft dew glistening like diamonds to keep everything clean and fresh—

how can such a place even be imagined?

### A Place of Beauty

Recently as I prepared my house for a visit by my father, I was encouraged in my efforts as I remembered that man's first home was also prepared as a place that was pleasing to the eye. When I knew my father was coming, I began to clean and straighten my house. I even bought fresh flowers and plants to place around the rooms to make them seem more lovely. I wanted my home to look as inviting, comfortable, and pleasing to his eyes as I could make it. Then it struck me—if I felt this way about my earthly father's brief visit, how much more care I should give my home every day since my heavenly Father lives here.

I am not a good housekeeper. But motivated by the thought that my house is His home also, I try hard to keep my house clean and neat. It is not professionally decorated with all the latest gadgets, but it is as pleasing to the eyes as my time, energy, and budget will allow.

I want those who walk through my door to know that the Lord God lives here. And I hope the reality of His presence is evident to all by the beauty of the outward appearance and the quality of the inner atmosphere of warmth and love they find here.

When other people look at your home, do they see evidence of neglect or evidence that Someone special is not just coming for a visit but living there on a full-time basis? If our homes are clothed in the beauty of the Lord God, they will not only receive a blessing, but they will also be a blessing to others.

### A Place of Blessing

In the Bible, water often symbolizes blessing. A river of water not only flowed into and through Eden; it flowed *from* Eden. "A river watering the garden flowed from Eden; and from there it divided; it had four headstreams" (Gen. 2:10). In other words, the first home was a blessed place, and blessing flowed from it to the surrounding area.

In what way has your home been blessed by God? Has the river of God's blessing flowed into your home, then just trickled out to others? Or does the "river" that flows in seem to multiply into four times the blessing as it flows out?

Our homes have been blessed to be a blessing to others. One way we have sought to receive God's blessing in our home is through putting Him first, acknowledging Him in all we decide and do, loving Him with all our hearts, spending time with Him in His Word and prayer, talking about Him during the day—totally living our lives for Him. Then we seek to impart His blessing to others, not only by getting involved in church and community activities but through hospitality—inviting people in for meals or games or Bible studies and prayer.

When my youngest daughter became engaged this past Christmas, I invited forty friends to come celebrate with us. I asked the guests to bring with them a Bible verse written out on a card that would express their desire or wish for the young couple. Following a time of joyful conversation and dessert, the guests were gathered together, and each was asked to share his or her verse out loud.

Some guests gave gifts that illustrated the verse they shared. One friend shared Ecclesiastes 4:9–12, "Two are better than one, because they have a good return for their work: If one falls down, his friend can help him up. But pity the man who falls and has no one to help him up! Also, if two lie down together, they will keep warm. But how can one keep warm alone? Though one may be overpowered, two can defend themselves. A cord of three strands is not quickly broken."

Her gift to illustrate these truths was a beautiful, three-stranded gold cord from which hung a gold cross. I know as my daughter hangs the gold cord and cross in her new home, she will constantly be reminded of the strength God Himself will infuse into her marriage as she and her husband wind themselves around God and keep the cross central in their relationship. As one by one our friends read and explained their verses, I was consciously aware that the entire room was saturated in God's blessing! When the guests left later in the evening, without exception as they walked out of the door, they shared what a blessing they had received. The "river" had flowed through our home, to our children, and out to our guests.

We have used this same simple format on a variety of occasions, asking guests to share a verse that has been meaningful to them, and we have shared our verses with our guests. Sunday dinners, birthday parties, anniversaries, or any occasion when we have guests becomes richer and more meaningful as we place God at the center. The gatherings are prayerfully planned as we seek God's blessing on our home as well as on those who enter it that the "river" might flow fully and freely. Again and again, we have all been "drenched."

Many homes today seem to be preoccupied only with those who live within their walls. Parents either hover over their children, making sure they dress the right way, have just the right friends, and go to just the right parties, smothering them to the point that the children become so wrapped in selfishness they are not a blessing to anyone. Or children are totally neglected by parents who pursue their own selfish goals. Left to their own devices, very rarely do neglected children, who are not consciously aware of any blessings coming into their lives, become a source of blessing flowing out to others.

The first home in Eden was not only beautiful; it was blessed to be a blessing. The "river" flowed through it, and the river flowed from it. One of the blessings it carried was the benefit of moral instruction.

### A Place of Benefits

In the first home, the Lord God taught man the difference between right and wrong. "In the middle of the garden were the tree of life and the tree of the knowledge of good and evil. . . . And the LORD God commanded the man, 'You are free to eat from any tree in the garden; but you must not eat from the tree of the knowledge of good and evil, for when you eat of it you will surely die'" (Gen. 2:9, 16–17). Within the home, man was taught values based on the absolute authority of God's Word alone. Adam needed to know what his boundaries were, what was acceptable to God and what was not.

Today we are surrounded by a generation of people who have grown up living according to their own various moral codes, defying the boundaries. As a result, it is a generation with no peace or sense of security. Rather than inhibiting us, moral guidelines free us to live life in peace and security. The statistics on crime, divorce, abortion, wife and child abuse, drug addiction, alcoholism, and suicide give eloquent witness to the danger of living outside the boundaries as we assert our independence of God.

Can you imagine the chaos that would result if a multilane highway had no painted markings to give direction to the traffic? Motorists would not know how to proceed without getting in each other's way. Accidents and confusion would be the order of the day. No one complains about or resents the markings, because drivers know the painted boundaries exist for their own benefit and safety.

As we raise our children, even beneficial boundaries can be disputed and resented. Surely every loving parent who has brought home a baby has wondered,

*Will he be healthy? Will she be smart? Will he be athletic? Will she be popular and friendly and successful?* Our homes and our family life include a variety of ingredients and opportunities to encourage our children to develop into contributing members of society. But perhaps the most important question we ask ourselves is, "Will he be good?" If that question is to have a positive answer, we must establish boundaries that will benefit our children.

When a young teenage couple murders their newborn baby, when second-grade boys try to suffocate another child, when barefooted children in the inner city are the primary drug dealers, we need to examine how effective and beneficial the moral instruction is in our homes. Sunday school teachers, pastors, school-teachers, and government and educational institutions should not be relied upon as the sole sources of our children's moral instruction. God has ordained that ideally the wise, godly father should give his children the "commands," or principles, from His Word while the wise, godly mother helps teach the children the application of those principles.[1] But both mother and father are responsible before God to instill in their children moral values based on God's Word. How consistent and faithful are you in this God-given task?

Several years ago a friend struggled to fight back the tears as she told me about her husband, who thought nothing of subscribing to *Playboy* magazine, receiving it in the home, and reading it while drinking a beer, all under the watchful eyes of his sons. But he had become outraged at those same two teenage boys when they had come home drunk after being out all night with their dates, and he was baffled as to how the boys could have made such wrong choices. It was difficult for me to comfort the wife when she and I both knew her boys were making their choices as a result of observing their father's example.

Our homes are to be places of moral, spiritual, social, emotional, and physical benefit. If you think that what you do within the privacy of your own home is your own business, think again! God has made it His business, and you and I will experience serious consequences if we refuse to follow His directions for our homes.

Robert Coles, the psychiatrist and Harvard professor who won the Pulitzer Prize for literature about children, says, "Moral intelligence isn't only acquired by memorization of rules and regulations. . . . The child is an ever attentive witness of grownup morality."[18] The Bible puts it this way when it warns, "Only be careful, and watch yourselves closely so that you do not forget the things your eyes have seen or let them slip from your heart as long as you live. Teach them to your children and to their children after them. . . . Love the LORD your God with all your heart and with all your soul and with all your strength. These commandments that I give you today are to be upon your hearts. Impress them on your children. Talk about them when you sit at home and when you walk along the road, when you lie down and when you get up. . . . Know therefore that the LORD your God is God; he is the faithful God, keeping his covenant of love to a thousand generations of those who love him and keep his commands. But those who hate [or ignore or neglect or disobey] him he will repay to their face by destruction."[19]

The destruction and brokenness we have been warned about is all around us today. It is a brokenness that is directly related to denying our children the benefit of moral, spiritual, emotional, and social instruction. If we do not instruct our children about God and His "Manufacturer's directions" for living, they will develop their own standards and values based on what they feel, what they think, what their friends are doing, and what seems to work—and in one generation we will see the chaos and confusion that result from their "guessing" their way through life. God has given us directions telling us if we are to prevent brokenness, our homes are to be places of moral and spiritual benefit to those living within them.

## A Place of Bounty

The first home was filled not with negatives or things man could not do but with bountiful opportunities. "And the LORD God made all kinds of trees grow out the ground—trees that were . . . good for food" (Gen. 2:9). There must have been . . .

    apple trees
        and pear trees
            and orange trees
                and grapefruit trees
                    and cherry trees
                and coconut palms
            and banana trees
        and peach trees
      and plum trees
plus
    blackberry bushes
        and raspberry bushes
            and strawberry plants

and blueberry bushes
and cranberry bushes
and boysenberry bushes

plus

watermelons
and cantaloupes
and honeydews
and kiwis
and mangoes
and papayas
and pineapple
and star fruit
and grapes . . .

And the list is endless!

What an extravagant bounty of fruit! Every different type of hunger could be satisfied, and the individual needs of each family member could be met.

Does your home have "every kind of tree . . . for food"? Is there a bounty of food for emotional satisfaction as you offer love, discipline, forgiveness, a listening ear, and an understanding heart? Is there a bounty of food for spiritual satisfaction as you feed daily on God's Word and offer it to other family members? Is your home physically satisfying as it offers not only well-balanced meals but rest and peace and relaxation? In our morally, spiritually, and emotionally bankrupt and broken world, our families need a place of bountiful spiritual, emotional, and physical satisfaction.

While Eden abounded in literal fruit, the New Testament describes the characteristics of Christ that are to be revealed in our lives as spiritual "fruit." Love, joy, peace, patience, kindness, goodness, faithfulness, gentleness, and self-control is the fruit of the Spirit that ought to be bountifully present in our homes. Thus we need His fullness if these characteristics are to be found in abundance in our homes.[20] What kind of "fruit" are your children eating within your home? Does their "diet" consist of nagging, complaining, anger, bickering, gossip, impatience, meanness, selfishness, and rudeness? Or are they learning to be loving when someone is not lovable, to have joy when life is not fun, to have peace in the midst of pressure, to be kind when treated roughly, to be unselfish when they don't get their way, to forgive when they are wronged? How easy do we make it for our children to "eat healthy"?

Our homes should be places of rich, bountiful, moral, and spiritual teaching for our children. But that will not be possible if we ourselves are not moral and spiritual people, fulfilling God's purpose for our lives. If our broken homes are to be mended we must follow God's directions. The Lord God was not only the first Homemaker; He is man's Maker, and living in accordance with His purpose can prevent broken lives.

## FINDING MEANING IN A PURPOSE TO LIVE FOR

The crowning jewel of Creation was man himself. He was created for a distinct purpose. If the purpose is lived out, life is fulfilling. If the purpose is rejected or ignored, life will never be what it was meant to be.

A lightbulb is a simple glass globe. If placed on a desk or table, it is meaningless as well as useless. But if it is fitted into a lamp and plugged into a power source, it fulfills its purpose for existence, taking on meaning as a source of light that is useful for daily living.

Apart from the Creator's purpose, you and I are like the lightbulb lying in a meaningless, useless state. We need to fit into the Creator's original design, plugging into the power source—our relationship with Him—if our lives are to be what they were meant to be. God deliberately, personally planned for your existence when He decided to "make man in our image" (Gen. 1:26).

### A Life Uniquely Shaped by God

While the first chapter of Genesis gives us the brief yet profound statement that "God created man in his own image, in the image of God he created him; male and female he created them" (Gen. 1:27), the second chapter gives us more detail. We are given the most moving description of the Creator's personal involvement when we are told that "the Lord God formed man from the dust of the ground and breathed into his nostrils the breath of life, and man became a living being" (Gen. 2:7).

The Hebrew word for "formed" is *yatsar*, which means "to mold." It is the same word used to describe a potter molding and shaping clay. The description reveals that while God spoke

the worlds into space,

the planets into orbit,

the earth on its axis,

the seas within their boundaries,
the sun, moon, and stars to appear in the sky,
the trees and flowers to cover the earth,
the fish to fill the sea,
the birds to fill the sky,
the animals to fill the earth,
God personally shaped the physical characteristics of man with His own hands and breathed into man His own life! Such knowledge should cause us to pause and worship the Creator who molded man from the "dust of the ground." That doesn't mean we were formed from dust like the dust bunnies under our beds! Like the little boy who looked on the top of his mother's refrigerator and inquired, "Who is God making up here?" The dust from which man was formed refers to the smallest chemical elements that are seen only under a microscope, elements like calcium, iron, carbon, and nitrogen.

We can only imagine the concentrated thoughts that occupied the divine Mind and the gentle, skillful touch of the divine Hand as the dust took shape. Where did the Creator begin? Did He start with a skeletal frame? Did He then cover it with an outside layer of skin, which at no place is thicker than three-sixteenths of an inch, is packed with nerve endings to enable man to feel the outside world, and is virtually waterproof? Into the skin stretched over the frame did He next place the heart that pumps seventy-two times a minute, forty million times a year? When did He hang the lungs in their sealed compartments so that the rivers of blood necessary for life can deposit the carbon dioxide and pick up oxygen to be carried to every single one of the more than twenty-six trillion cells in the body? When did He place the brain inside the bony skull and program it to send messages that travel faster than three hundred miles an hour along the nervous system to the entire body? Were the eyes that can simultaneously handle 1.5 million messages at the same moment part of His finishing touch? What about the ears and nose and mouth and . . . ?[21] Truly, we are fearfully and wonderfully and lovingly and personally created![22]

Jesus Christ affirmed your creation by God.[23] The apostles Peter, John, and Paul also give clear testimony stating that God is your Creator.[24] While the world at large may have no qualms in calling Jesus Christ and His apostles liars by denying God as the Creator, are you prepared to say such a thing? Instead, consciously acknowledge that you were created by God, Who deliberately pre-thought your existence and brought you into being because He wanted you, because He loved you, because He has a purpose for your life. You are no accident! Your life was created and uniquely shaped by God.

While our bodies were formed from the dust—elements already present in the world—there was one notable addition that had never existed before. God created an eternal soul with a capacity to know Him in a personal, permanent relationship and placed it within man. Then God breathed His own life into man.

## A Life Uniquely Sacred to God

When God "breathed into his nostrils the breath of life, and the man became a living being" (Gen. 2:7), all human life became sacred because it came directly from God. Whether a person is a murderer on death row or the most beloved person in town, each one is to be treated with respect if for no other reason than human life comes from God.

Are you prejudiced toward someone? A person of a different race or educational background or economic level? Someone from another culture or denomination or religion? Someone with a different language or social status or skin color? There is absolutely no room for prejudice of any kind in a life that follows the Creator's directions. All men are created equal, not in abilities or opportunities, but in the eyes of God; because all men derive their lives from God.

God not only gave you His life once at Creation; He gave you His life again at Calvary. God the Creator became your Savior, dying on the cross to offer you forgiveness of sin that you might come back into the relationship with Him for which you were created. The apostle Paul said the only reasonable response to such an outpouring of divine life was to offer our lives back to God, totally yielded to His will as an act of worship.[25] Because you were also created for God.

## A Life Uniquely Satisfied in God

C. S. Lewis, in his testimony *Surprised by Joy*, described his growing awareness of the capacity within himself to respond with joy and delight in such a way that it gave him an insatiable desire for more joy and delight. The things he found so deeply satisfying left him with a craving for more and more satisfaction. He concluded that nothing in this world could ever give him lasting satisfaction, so therefore he must have been created for another world. And C. S. Lewis was right. Our very beings are created for God. We will never experience permanent, personal satisfaction and fulfillment apart from Him because, as Saint Augustine so eloquently stated, "our hearts are restless until we find our rest in Thee."

Our newspapers and magazines are filled with the examples of men and women today seeking satisfaction in

position,

power,

prestige,

popularity,

people,

programs.

They look for fulfillment in

educational achievements,

financial achievements,

professional achievements,

personal achievements.

Careers that began with aggressive energy,

relationships that began with starry-eyed commitment,

homes that were established with misty-eyed hope,

lives that were lived with single-eyed purpose,

crash into fragmented dreams when the company downsizes,

or the relationship is severed

or the home is broken

or the life is ended.

Apart from understanding the work of God in our creation, there is no real meaning to human existence. If there was no Creator, then you are some cosmic accident, having come from nowhere and on your way to nowhere. You are just a nobody with no ultimate accountability or eternal value. Now, that's depressing! Praise God, it's not true!

Where are you seeking lasting satisfaction? You may find temporary satisfaction in things and people, but permanent, deep, full satisfaction of your very being is only found in a tight relationship with God for whom you were created.

Not only is your being created for God, but your doing is created for God also. You and I were created for commitment to serve God. The garden of Eden was not only a place for man to live, but it was a place for man to serve.[26] Not only was it a place to be, but it was a place to do. "The LORD God took the man and put him in the Garden of Eden to work it and take care of it" (Gen. 2:15). The first home was a place of service to the LORD that reveals a fundamental aspect of man's design—man was created for commitment to God and His purpose.

One of the first responsibilities man was given was to name each of the animals God had created. "Now the LORD God had formed out of the ground all the beasts of the field and all the birds of the air. He brought them to the man to see what he would name them; and whatever the man called each living creature, that was its name. So the man gave names to all the livestock, the birds of the air and all the beasts of the field" (Gen. 2:19–20).

Names are very significant in the Bible because they denote the character, or the essence, of the specific person or animal. For example, God changed Jacob's name to "Israel" because it means "he struggles with God."[27] The angel told Joseph he was to name Mary's baby "Jesus" because the name meant He would save His people from their sins.[28] Jesus changed Simon's name to Peter because Peter means "rock."[29]

God brought the animals to Adam and assigned to him the task of naming each one accurately according to their various unique traits. Can you imagine the fun such a parade would be? God must have a sense of humor as well as a rich imagination just to have created some of the animals He did. What joy Adam's service to God would be as one by one the animals were brought to him. He very probably observed them carefully, discussed with their Creator the unique, individual characteristics of each, then named them accordingly:

giraffes

monkeys

koala bears

slugs

warthogs

hippopotamuses

penguins

anteaters

armadillos

cuckoo birds . . .

And whatever Adam called them, "that was its name," indicating he named them correctly the first time and did not have to change the name later. It seems like a fun, simple exercise, but in the beginning when everything was newly created, it would have required extensive wisdom and intellectual knowledge of the various species and individual animals in order to name them accurately. And because there would have been hundreds if not thousands of species, it would have required enormous commitment to finish the task.

What task has God assigned you?

Has He assigned you to

establish a home,

strengthen a marriage,

lead a family,

support a ministry,

travel to a mission field,

serve a church,

work a part-time job,

work a full-time job,

teach in a classroom,

or comfort in a sick room?

If you have been assigned to more than one of these responsibilities, check your attitude toward the assignment. Do you grumble and complain about it? Do you neglect and ignore it? Do you resent and reject it? Or do you enjoy fulfilling it as your service unto the Lord? God wants you and me to enjoy our service to Him, whatever it may be. And He also wants us to discuss each detail with Him as we do the work. One of His pleasures, as well as ours, is the joy of working together as we complete the task. Often, the more difficult the task, the greater the joy because it enables us to see the power of God and just what He can do in and through and for us. How committed are you to serving God? Are you committed enough to keep at the task He has assigned you until you finish the job, not just somehow, but triumphantly?

As we observe those around us in our homes, offices, schools, churches, and businesses, inevitably we see broken people whose lives are uniquely shaped, sacred, and satisfied in God yet who don't know the very purpose of their own uniqueness. They don't know the One for whom they have been created. They may know about Him, but if they haven't read His directions for themselves, they will live eternally meaningless lives as the purpose for their existence remains unfulfilled.

## Finding Meaning in a Partner to Live With

The *Washington Post* recently reported the release of a new poll by the Barna Research Group that found a higher divorce rate among those who professed to be born-again Christians than among those who did not.[30] As marriages break, people desperately need God's directions for living with a partner in marriage.

God was aware that man needed a partner and human companionship, but man was not aware of it. So God began to give Adam the desire for a mate. "The LORD God said, 'It is not good for the man to be alone. I will make a helper suitable for him.' Now the LORD God . . . brought [the animals] to the man to see what he would name them. . . . But for Adam no suitable helper was found" (Gen. 2:18–20). As the animals paraded before Adam for naming, I wonder if they came in pairs. Did he begin to get the picture that every single animal had a mate, but there was no one for him? Within Adam there must have been a deep yearning and heartache stirred up for someone who was like himself.

What deep emotional needs and desires do you have? Do you yearn for human companionship? Someone to love you and understand you and think of you and share life with you? God instructs us, "Delight yourself in the LORD and he will give you the desires of your heart. Commit your way to the LORD; trust in him and he will do this."[31] When you are living your life in commitment to God, He gives you the desires of your heart because they come from Him. God placed the desire for a companion and marriage partner within Adam's heart, then He fulfilled the desire.

In the beginning, Adam was single. Increasingly he longed for a true companion with whom he could share his life. He didn't have to beg God or beat the bushes or spend every Saturday night in a singles bar. He just went to sleep in God's will. I wonder if, as he drifted off to sleep, he was praying that God would somehow, some way, take away the strange ache in his heart and the loneliness he felt inside, especially when he had observed that every animal had a partner except himself. "So the LORD God caused the man to fall into a deep sleep; and while he was sleeping, he took one of the man's ribs and closed up the place with flesh. Then the LORD God made a woman from the rib he had taken out of the man, and he brought her to the man" (Gen. 2:21–22). In His wisdom, God knew exactly how to meet Adam's emotional needs—by presenting Adam with a wife.[32]

The primary reason for the woman's creation was not to produce children or provide sexual satisfaction or to keep the home but for the mutual happiness of the man and woman. Like the Father of the bride, God Himself brought Eve to Adam. We can only imagine the twinkle of delight in God's eyes as He gently awakened Adam to His gift. Adam's enthusiastic response was, "This is now bone of my bones and flesh of my flesh; she shall be called 'woman,' for she was taken out of man" (Gen. 2:23). Hebrew experts tell us that Adam's response was one of thrilling, joyous astonishment: "At last, I have someone who will be my true companion! A partner to share my life and work and hopes and dreams with. Someone who will take away my loneliness and be as dear to me as my own flesh. And God, she is perfect! In fact, she is spectacular!" The wording of Adam's response indicates Eve was received with loving, tender, enthusiastic affection.

As Eve gazed into Adam's adoring eyes, what did she think? Did she blush under the thrill of his attention and his touch? Did she rest in the security of his strength and protection? Did she relish the sound of his voice, hanging on every word he uttered as she learned from his advanced knowledge and wisdom? Did she get great delight in just looking at his perfect physique, listening to the sound of his laughter, and working beside him in the garden? The fact that Eve was created after Adam or that she was his designated companion and helper does not mean she was in any way inferior to Adam. As his partner, she was his equal.

### Equality in Partnership

The Bible clearly teaches there is to be an equality between man and woman, husband and wife. "In the image of God, . . . male and female he created them. God blessed them and said to them, 'Be fruitful and increase in number; fill the earth and subdue it. Rule over the fish of the sea and the birds of the air and over every living creature that moves on the ground'" (Gen. 1:27–28).

Dominion over everything was given to the woman as well as to the man. The woman was not inferior to the man; nor was the man greater than the woman. Men and women, husbands and wives, were and are equal.

The New Testament reaffirms the principle of equality when it says men and women are "heirs together of the grace of life."[33] And the apostle Paul, whose views of women are often misunderstood, said, "There is neither Jew nor Greek, slave nor free, male nor female, for you are all one in Christ Jesus."[34]

One reason for the rise in militant feminism is because our society has ignored this Creation principle. Perhaps only women can understand the humiliation they feel when their worth is based solely on the fact that they satisfy their husband's sexual needs, produce his children, cook his meals, clean his house, do his laundry, run his errands, supplement his income—receiving no respect or appreciation for their own gifts, abilities, and personhood. Women should not have to demand equality—it is their God-given right!

God in His wisdom created man and woman equal in His sight, and this equality is to be reflected in the marriage relationship. Husbands and wives are to give each other respect, appreciation, and understanding as equal partners. If your own heart and marriage are broken, you can begin now to mend them by following the Creator's directions for equality.

However, the fact that men and women are equal does not by any stretch of the imagination mean that they are the same! God created them male and female.[35] There is not only an equality but a diversity between men and women.

## *Diversity in Partnership*

Eve was as different from Adam as Adam was different from Eve. But the differences were complementary. Because of the emotional and physical differences, Eve would supply what Adam lacked, and Adam would supply what Eve lacked. Eve would complete Adam as a "helper suitable for him" (Gen. 2:18). The same Hebrew word used for "helper" in this instance is used again in Psalm 46:1 when it describes God Himself as being "our refuge and strength, an ever-present help in trouble." Rather than implying that Eve was somehow less because she was a helper, this term describes her godly characteristic of support for Adam.

The differences between my husband and myself have been the basis for many fights. My husband likes everything in its place while I never even notice when things are a mess. He is very outgoing, able to recall people's names easily. In contrast, I am almost a recluse and can't even remember the faces of people I've met. He is extremely athletic while I never played a sport in my life.

One day, following weeks of tension and fighting triggered by these differences, we began to make a study of the gifts of the Holy Spirit. We recognized our own particular spiritual gifts, and they were totally opposite from each other. This led us to recognize other differences, acknowledge those differences by name, learn to accept them in each other, and then grow to appreciate them for the balance they give to our marriage relationship. I cannot adequately convey the blessing this has been, the peace that has resulted, and the love that has increased between us simply because after years of doing it "my way," we finally followed the Creator's wise directions for diversity in our marriage.

Is someone trying to convince you that your marriage is doomed because of incompatibility with your spouse? Because you are so different? Recognize God's wisdom in creating male and female, two very different human beings. Sometimes very, very different! But the differences are meant to be a wonderful complementary balance as we follow the directions that include equality, diversity, and also unity.

### Unity in Partnership

Unity between the husband and the wife is expressed in a psychological commitment. "For this reason a man will leave his father and mother" (Gen. 2:24).

Much marital brokenness is the result of not understanding the psychological commitment required when the man leaves his family and the woman leaves her family and they establish their own family. For instance, the struggle can be as simple as the wife's inability to cook as well as the husband's mother cooks. Without realizing it, husbands may cling to their mothers and find fault with their wives when the wives do not measure up. Or maybe the husband is not the head of his company as the wife's father was head of his. By comparison, the husband doesn't seem as important as the wife's father. A wife may be inwardly critical of her husband because psychologically she's clinging to her father. This kind of psychological dependency becomes evident when couples face a major problem and one or both of them turn first to their parents for help rather than the spouse. Or maybe it's the parent who will not let go of a son or daughter, always calling, dropping by, giving unsolicited advice. Making a psychological commitment to our spouses means not only are we to leave, but we are to let go. We are to let go of our parents, and parents are to let go of their children.

We are to leave our own fathers and mothers and be united to each other, becoming "one flesh" (Gen. 2:24). The unity in marriage is to be expressed in a physical commitment between man and wife. Marriage unites husband and wife together as closely as Adam and Eve were united before they became separate individuals.[36]

Some people may consider the intimate side of marriage as somehow being "unspiritual." But if you stop to think about it, the first person who ever had a sexual thought was God. Love expressed in marriage in a mutually respectful sexual relationship is God's idea, and it is pure, holy, and pleasing to Him.

Dr. Ed Wheat, a prominent marriage counselor, has pointed out that if the physical side of marriage deteriorates, every other aspect of marriage will soon be affected.[37] When God commanded Adam and Eve to "be fruitful and increase in number" (Gen. 1:28), He seemed to be saying, "Make sex a priority in your marriage," not only for the procreation of the race but also in order to maintain the intimate physical unity with each other we were created for.

The commitment between a specific man and woman that we call marriage is not only psychological and physical, but it is to be permanent. This is implied when God said, "What God has joined together, let man not separate."[38] We are committed for better or for worse, for richer or for poorer, in sickness and in health, as long as we both shall live.

Many people go into the marriage commitment with an exit sign hanging over it. They get married with the idea that they will remain committed to their marriage only if things get better, if the financial situation eases, if the spouse gets healthier, if the spouse loses weight and looks younger. Even within the church, some couples seem to get married with the idea that "if this doesn't work out, we can always get a divorce." No, you can't! Not from God's perspective.

When Jesus was asked about divorce, He was reluctant to answer. Instead, He referred directly to these verses in Genesis as God's Creation principles for marriage. When He was pressured to answer, He acknowledged divorce was granted by Moses in accordance with God's law because of the hardness of man's heart. Then He gave the only specific basis for divorce in God's sight, which is adultery.[39]

If your spouse has committed adultery, the unity of your relationship has been broken in a unique way, and divorce is a biblical option. However, forgiveness is also an option. Peter said, "Lord, how many times shall I forgive my brother [or husband, or wife] when he sins against me? Up to seven times?" Jesus answered, "I tell you, not seven times, but seventy-seven times."[40] In other words, Jesus was saying, "Peter, as many times as the person sins or as many times as the memory of the sin returns to haunt you, you can choose to forgive. Forgiveness has no limits."

What limits have you placed on your forgiveness? It's frightening to see all of the divorces taking place today within the church when we realize God does not recognize divorce unless it takes place on biblical grounds. A person can obtain a piece of paper that says he or she is legally divorced in the eyes of the state, but that piece of paper is totally irrelevant if God does not recognize it.

When a person who has divorced without biblical grounds remarries, Jesus says that person is living in adultery.[41] This is exceedingly serious when we learn the Bible also says no adulterer will inherit the kingdom of God.[42] One reason divorce is so rejected by God is that it not only breaks God's Creation principles for marriage; it also mars the reflection of the relationship between Christ and the church, which is a permanent relationship.[43] God hates divorce.[44]

If you have been divorced without biblical grounds to do so and you have since remarried, what can you do? It's impossible to untangle the relationships you are now involved in. But you can acknowledge your present situation as the sin that it is in God's sight, confess it to Him, and ask Him to cleanse you through the blood of Jesus. Then commit your present marriage to Him. Choose from this day forth to follow His directions for your marriage. God will cleanse and forgive you and bless you by His grace.[45]

The first time I publicly taught on the subject of marriage and divorce, a young, newly married couple named Jack and Susan was in the audience.[46] I knew something of their story. Each had been married to another. Jack was married to his childhood sweetheart, Susan to a man she had met in college. After the first anniversary of her wedding, Susan met Jack, and they fell in love. Within weeks, both marriages were broken as their relationship intensified. Jack and Susan then married. In answer to many prayers, including those of Jack's first wife, Susan began attending a Bible study.

Several weeks later, when Jack and Susan sat in the audience and heard what God had to say about what they had done and how they were now living, they were devastated. Rather than rebel, defiantly trying to justify their actions, they broke down before God. They confessed their sin and asked God's forgiveness. For Susan, the experience was a complete recommitment of her life to the God she had known but had left. Jack was truly born again.

While they could not unscramble the tangled web of relationships involving former spouses and children nor erase the emotional scars inflicted on others as well as themselves, God graciously helped them to establish a Christian home filled with His blessing. I once asked Susan how she managed to cope. Eyes brimming with tears, she answered, "Anne, every time I look in the mirror, I see sin and guilt. But I choose to live in God's forgiveness."

Instead of living in despair or contemplating divorce, would you live in God's forgiveness? Choose to forgive yourself and the other persons involved, reconciling if they are willing, and committing yourself to live according to the Creator's directions for marriage.

As I spoke to various women following my Bible class one day, I noticed a beautiful woman who hung back from the rest, remaining in the sanctuary as others left. Finally, everyone else had gone. I walked over to her and asked if I could help in any way. With a chin lifted defiantly and eyes that flashed with anger, she told me she had just found out her husband was involved in yet another affair. Since their wedding over twenty years previous, he had had one adulterous liaison after another. She despaired, "He's sick. He's addicted to the pleasure of having all different kinds of women. I can't take it anymore. I'm going to divorce him this time."

My heart ached with compassion for her and with anger toward a man who had taken his marriage vows so lightly that he could repeatedly trample them in the mud of lust and selfishness.

But I looked her in the eye and counseled, "Nancy, you have the biblical right to divorce your husband. He has not only broken his vows but also the mystical, spiritual, and physical bond of unity between the two of you."[47] She looked a little astonished at my agreement with her. Her brow knit as she quietly waited to see if I had anything to add—which I did. "Nancy, you have the right to divorce Harold, or you have the option to forgive him. Again. And again. As often as he sins, you can forgive him. And while you continually forgive him, pray that the forgiveness and unconditional love you extend will break his wicked heart and his sinful habit and lead him to repentance."

Nancy left that day without making a decision. Several weeks later I learned she had exercised her option and forgiven Harold. Within a year of her decision, Harold did repent, and God restored their marriage. Their home has been blessed, their own lives are a testimony to God's power and grace, and both of their children are in full-time Christian service. To God be the glory for Jack and Susan, Nancy and Harold, and all the broken, shattered people who dare to take God at His Word and follow His directions, proving the Creator can mend our brokenness if only we will follow His directions!

"Therefore, what God has joined together, let man not separate."[48] Don't break up what God the Creator has put together in an equal, diverse, unified companionship we call marriage. God is the God of the impossible. It does not matter how bad the condition of your marriage is. Turn it over to God, follow His directions, and He can mend the brokenness.

God has created everyone. Whether you are from Africa, America, or Asia; whether your skin is white or black or brown; whether you speak English or Polish or Spanish; whether your religious affiliation is Baptist or Buddhist or Bahá'í everyone is created by God. The entire human race comes with the Manufacturer's directions for a pattern to live by, a place to live in, a purpose to live for, and a partner to live with. Isn't it time you followed directions?

THE OLD CLAY POT was cracked, shattered, and broken. So the man took it to the Potter, who broke it down even further, moistening the clay with water, making it soft and pliable before He put it on His wheel. Then He began to remake it into a vessel pleasing to Himself. He firmly applied pressure on some areas, touched lightly on other areas, added more clay to a specific spot that needed filling, and removed clay that hindered and marred the shape He had in mind. As He turned the wheel, His loving, gentle hands never left the clay as He molded and made it after His will. Finally, the Potter was finished. He took what had once been a broken clay pot off the wheel, but now it was unrecognizable. It had been transformed into a vessel of beauty. The Potter put it in His showcase that others might see the revelation of His glory in the work that He does. "This is the word that came to Jeremiah from the LORD: 'Go down to the potter's house, and there I will give you my message.' So I went down to the potter's house, and I saw him working at the wheel. But the pot he was shaping from the clay was marred in His hands; so the potter formed it into another pot, shaping it as seemed best to him. Then the word of the LORD came to me: 'Can I not do with you as this potter does? . . . Like clay in the hand of the potter, so are you in my hand.'"[49] "But we have this treasure in jars of clay to show that this all-surpassing power is from God and not from us. We are hard pressed on every side, but not crushed; perplexed, but not in despair; persecuted, but not abandoned; struck down, but not destroyed. We always carry around in our body the death of Jesus, so that the life of Jesus may also be revealed in our body . . . For our light and momentary troubles are achieving for us an eternal glory that far outweighs them all."[50] Live your life

57

according to God's pattern, establish your home as a place where God is central, fulfill the unique purpose for which you were created, and recommit your marriage partnership to Him . . . that the mended brokenness might be a dazzling display case for the Creator's glory!

# 3

## *I Forgive Your Sinfulness*

GENESIS 3

Three men were sitting on a park bench in Long Beach, waiting for the ferry to take them to Catalina. The first man was the town bum, a dirty, obnoxious beggar who shoplifted from the local supermarket, cursed those who passed him on the street, and was usually drunk. The second man was the town banker. He was elegantly dressed in his three-piece pinstripe suit, with his gold watch chain looped across his vest, his shirt cuffs monogrammed, and his wingtip shoes highly polished. The banker was known for his involvement in community affairs and had just given a large sum of money to be used for the local arts center. The third man was the Baptist preacher. He was loud and outgoing, with a big smile on his face and a strong clasp to his handshake, always ready to start up a conversation. Under his leadership, the church had established a soup kitchen for the hungry and a shelter for the homeless.

All three men began to get restless when the ferry was late. Finally the bum slurred, "I'm jush gonna jump to Cathalina." With that brief announcement, he stumbled down to the pier, walked off the end, and dropped into the water! The other two men looked after the bum in astonishment. Finally the banker found his voice, and as he reached up to straighten his tie, said in a rather arrogant tone, "I can't believe that bum jumped like that. He never even got a running start. I'm certainly better than he is, and I know I can jump farther than that." He gracefully got up, trotted smoothly down the pier, and leaped off the end, hitting the water about ten feet out.

By this time the preacher was all excited. He got to his feet, rubbing his hands together in anticipation. To no one in particular he exulted, "Boy, oh boy! Would

59

you just look at those two! Who would ever have thought the bum and the banker would try jumping to Catalina—and only make it ten feet! I can sure do better than either of them!" With that, he took off running as fast as any sprinter on the local university track team. When he came to the end of the pier, he gave a loud victory cry as he jumped with all his strength, sailed through the air, and landed thirty feet out in the water.

Within a few minutes, the ferry came into view. When the captain saw the three men floundering in the water, he slowed down and picked them up one by one. As the captain wrapped the dripping wet men in warm blankets, he asked them how in the world they happened to be in the water. The bum, who was now as sober as the preacher, said through chattering teeth that he had gotten tired of waiting for the ferry and had foolishly thought he could jump to Catalina.

The banker straightened his shoulders, lifted his chin, and huffed to the bum, "Well, I jumped farther than you did." The preacher, with the familiar grin back on his face, put his arms warmly around the shoulders of the bum and the banker and crowed, "I beat you both. I jumped thirty feet out." The captain, who had been observing and listening to the three men, shook his head in disbelief. Finally he exclaimed with consternation, "All three of you still missed Catalina by thirty miles!"

In the same way that it's impossible for anyone, no matter how good or religious or foolhardy, to jump from the mainland to Catalina Island, it's also impossible to jump from here to heaven. It doesn't matter whether a person is obviously bad like the bum or an outstandingly good and moral person like the banker or religious like the preacher, we just can't please God in ourselves. Some may get "closer" than others, but "all have sinned and fall short of the glory of God."[1]

What is sin? It has been defined as "not just that man is as bad as he could be but that he is not as good as he should be." The Greek definition of sin is of an archer who launches his arrow but "misses the mark." Sin is breaking God's moral law and therefore being unable to meet His standards of perfection.

Where does sin come from? Sin is a spiritual "disease" that has been transmitted to every single person in every single generation from the beginning of the human race. It infects the entire population of the world and is the cause of all the problems of war, greed, hate, prejudice, cruelty, corruption, and other ills that plague us.

While we all are born with a nature that has a strong tendency to sin, our lives bear the "fruit" of sin through the choices we make—which is where sin started in the beginning.

## FINDING MEANING IN THE CHOICES WE MAKE

From the time we make the choice to open our eyes and get out of bed in the morning until we make the choice to go back to bed and close our eyes in the evening, our days are filled with a series of choices. We choose

what we wear,

what we eat,

who we see,

who we talk to,

where we go,

what we do,

what we believe,

and how we behave.

Our own lives, reputations, relationships, careers, health, future, and values are shaped by the choices we make. The choice

to lie or to tell the truth,

to be cruel or to be kind,

to cheat or to be honest,

to hate or to love, to seek vengeance or to forgive,

to do the popular thing or to do the right thing,

to ignore God or to acknowledge God,

determines the type of person we are. Without question, the most important choice you will ever make involves your attitude toward God and your relationship with Him.

God brought Adam into existence from nothing, forming him with the gentle, compassionate, skillful hands of the Creator, giving Adam His own breath for life. He Himself prepared a place for him to live, making all the arrangements for his comfort as well as enjoyment. Then he satisfied the deep longings of Adam's heart by giving him a life's companion in Eve.

The longing of God's heart, if it can be expressed as such, is to be known, loved, glorified, and enjoyed by His creation. Although in His plural nature God has ultimate fellowship, love, and harmony within the Trinity, He also desired fellowship and friendship with Adam and Eve.

But early in their lives Adam and Eve made one choice that broke their relationship with God and cost them their happiness at the present and their destiny for the future, devastating their family for every generation to come. This devastation is inevitable because life is made up of relationships with God, with others, and with ourselves, and the choice to sin through disobedience destroyed all three relationships. Sin destroys our relationship with God through guiltiness. It destroys our relationship with others through lovelessness. It destroys our relationship with ourselves through meaninglessness. Adam and Eve destroyed their relationships when they chose to sin by disobeying God and by doubting His Word.

### The Choice to Doubt God's Word

Eve walked through her garden home one day, perhaps enjoying the tranquil perfection of the views around her as well as the satisfaction that was hers in being ruler over all. She probably felt the dew on the soft moss beneath her feet, smelled the fresh air that now and then carried with it the rich, heavy scent of blossoms, and enjoyed the warmth of the sun on her skin. Eve, newly created with the body of a woman yet the pure innocence and naivete of a baby, was totally relaxed. At ease. Off guard.

At that moment she was approached by what was possibly the most magnificent of all the created wild animals. He was also the smartest. The Serpent had planned his approach carefully, making contact with Eve when she was off guard and alone. "Now the serpent was more crafty than any of the wild animals the LORD God had made. He said to the woman, 'Did God really say, "You must not eat from any tree in the garden"?'" (Gen. 3:1). Eve's lack of surprise when the Serpent spoke to her indicates she was either so naive that she didn't know animals don't speak, or in the beginning, they did communicate in some way. In this case, Satan spoke through the Serpent. And Eve, without warning, was face-to-face with temptation.

It was springtime in Jerusalem when the Serpent attacked another prominent person, with devastating consequences. It was a time when kings went off to war, but this particular year, the king of Israel decided to stay home. He was lying in his bed in the early evening. Relaxed. Lazy even, to be in bed when it was still light outside. Comfortable. Secure. At ease. Off guard. I wonder what Satan did to stir the king out of his chambers and onto the balcony of the palace. There was no talking Serpent, just the balmy twilight with gentle breezes blowing in from the Judean hills—and a view of a nearby roof where Uriah's wife, Bathsheba, was taking her bath. And King David, without warning, was face-to-face with temptation.[2]

What temptation is facing you? When you are at ease, relaxed, off guard, secure, watch out! "That ancient serpent called the devil"³ is still crafty, subtle, and very smart in his approach. He knows exactly when you are the most susceptible to his tactics. He is no gentleman. He attacks when he senses you are the weakest. And you are the weakest very often when you think you are the strongest and most secure.

When the Serpent spoke, Eve was vulnerable because she did not know first-hand for herself what God had said. Before Eve was created, God had spoken very clearly to Adam when He instructed, "You are free to eat from any tree in the garden; but you must not eat from the tree of the knowledge of good and evil, for when you eat of it you will surely die" (Gen. 2:16–17). Eve's knowledge of God's command was therefore secondhand. Assuming Adam had taught God's Word to Eve diligently and accurately, she still knew it only through hearsay.

How have you obtained your knowledge of God's Word? Do you know it through your spouse? Or parent? Or friend? Or pastor? Or Sunday school teacher? Or radio Bible teacher? Or books and tapes about God's Word? In other words, is your knowledge secondhand because you have not actually read and studied God's Word for yourself? If so, you are vulnerable to the enemy's temptation to doubt the truth of it.

The first words of the enemy to Eve were, "Did God really say . . . ?" A contemporary paraphrase of his question might be something like this: "Eve, did God really say that? Are you sure you heard it accurately from Adam? Could there have been a mistake in the translation or transmission of the text? And even if that is what God said, don't you know you can't take Him literally? We all have our own interpretations of what He really means by what He said. You might have one interpretation, Adam another, and I have still another. Bless your heart. You're such an innocent, naive little thing. When you've been around longer, you will know that God's Word is not quite as black and white as you want to think it is."

Who has tried to make you feel ignorant and foolish and oh-so-naive for taking God at His Word? Whoever it is and whatever approach that person is using, the temptation to doubt God's Word is as old as Creation and comes straight from that old Serpent, the devil.

When I was a teenager, several of my Christian friends went to a college that was affiliated with a major religious denomination. They entered the school eager to learn, plunging themselves into their studies and campus activities. When they returned home for Christmas break, however, they were cynical, sophisticated, and faithless. One confided in me he could no longer even pray. When I inquired what had happened, he described a religion professor who had taught one of his classes. The professor began the semester by saying he felt it his responsibility to destroy any faith his students brought into his classroom so they could rebuild a faith of their own. Then he proceeded to destroy the faith of my friends, but he never rebuilt it. As a result they floundered for years in the twilight of doubt and unbelief.

As I thought through their experience, I became convinced that my friends had no real faith of their own before they left for school. What they took to college was their parents' faith and the faith of those in their church. But because they had not spent time in earnest Bible study for themselves, obeying God's commands and claiming His promises, they did not know by experience that His commands work and His promises are true. Their faith in God's Word was in essence based on hearsay; therefore it was weak, and they succumbed to the attack of the enemy.

Not only was Eve tempted to doubt God's Word; she was tempted to be dissatisfied with God's will when the Serpent smoothly said, "Did God really say, 'You must not eat from any tree in the garden'?" In other words, "Eve, God may have said that, but surely His will is for you to be happy. If God really loved you, He would give you anything you want. I can't believe He would say no to you."

### The Choice to Be Dissatisfied with God's Will

Satan focused Eve on the one thing God had said she couldn't have. I doubt the tree of the knowledge of good and evil was any more desirable than the other trees in the garden. The tree may have had a slightly different shape, the fruit a slightly different taste, the blooms a slightly different color, but there may have been many trees exactly like it in the garden. The thing that made the tree different from all the others was that God used it as a test of Adam and Eve's obedience to His Word and submission to His will. And it was God's will that Adam and Eve obey His Word. Period.

Have you become dissatisfied with God's will? Why? Because your attention is focused on the one thing you can't have? What is the forbidden fruit in your life? Someone else's spouse or job or house or position? An opportunity for revenge? A dishonest but profitable business scheme? Another drink? Are you letting the enemy convince you that surely God wants you to be happy and fulfilled and satisfied, and you can't possibly be really happy unless you have that forbidden fruit? Have you become intensely dissatisfied with God's will when God says no?

64

Once in a while I become intolerant of the extra pounds I seem to absorb from the very air I breathe in middle age, so I go on a diet. Invariably when I'm on a diet, I crave candy bars. That may not seem strange, except that I don't like candy bars and rarely eat them. The only time I ever even think about candy bars is when I'm on a diet and know I can't have them. The overwhelming attraction of candy bars that almost becomes an obsession lies in the fact that they are forbidden.

Eve became dissatisfied with God's will when Satan was able to focus her attention on the one thing God had said she could not have. She became preoccupied with the forbidden fruit. The temptation that confronted Eve intensified because she tolerated it by actually talking to the Serpent about it.

I wonder if Eve tossed her hair, rolled her eyes, and put her hands on her hips as she responded to the Serpent with an attitude of, "Well, I'm not as naive as you believe. I know more than you think I do," as she reported what she thought God had said: "We may eat fruit from the trees in the garden, but God did say, 'You must not eat fruit from the tree that is in the middle of the garden, *and you must not touch it,* or you will die'" (Gen. 3:2–3, emphasis added). Eve did not quote God's Word accurately. She added to it. She seemed to be gossiping as to her own opinions of what God's Word said.

But the basic problem was not what she said; it was that she said anything at all! As she conversed with the Serpent, she got into deeper trouble, because he responded, "You will not surely die" (Gen. 3:4). That was an absolute, deliberate contradiction of what God did say![4] Eve was confronted with Satan's word against God's Word. The choice had become very clear. Who would she *choose* to believe?

When Joseph was sexually tempted by Potiphar's wife, he ran from the temptation so quickly he actually left his coat in her hand.[5] Jesus said we are to cut temptation out of our lives by severing ourselves from whatever is causing us to be tempted.[6] The apostle Paul said we should run from it.[7] Nowhere in the Bible does it say we are to talk about it! Unless we do our talking with the Lord God.

How much better it would have been had Eve run back to her Creator and asked, "God, what did You say? I've been listening to someone who says what You said is not true. Just tell me again what You said. And by the way, I think this is harder than I can handle. Would You come with me and talk to the Serpent?" I would love to have seen the expression on that old snake's face if Eve had shown up with God at her side! But she didn't. She thought she could handle the temptation on her own. So the temptation intensified as Eve was confronted with doubt of God's Word, dissatisfaction with God's will, and denial of God's goodness.

### The Choice to Deny God's Goodness

Dr. Larry Crabb, a prominent psychologist, defines sin as "our effort to supplement what we think are limits to God's goodness. It is trusting our self instead of trusting God."[8] Satan led Eve into thinking that God was holding out on her. He persuasively argued, "God knows that when you eat of it your eyes will be opened, and you will be like God, knowing good and evil" (Gen. 3:5). In other words, "Eve, God knows this fruit is really good. But He's mean and doesn't want you to enjoy life to the fullest. Besides, He's also jealous and keeps all the best stuff for Himself."

Are you talking to someone about a choice that really is a temptation to partake of forbidden fruit? In talking with that person, do you find yourself rationalizing the truth? How has the person responded?[9] Is he or she trying to convince you that God is not good? That your heavenly Father does not have your best in mind? That He is holding out on you, and if you want to really enjoy life or get what you want out of life, you're going to have to get it yourself? We can hear the hiss of the Serpent in such reasoning!

Eve not only *talked* about the choice to disobey God; she *thought* about the choice. "The woman saw that the fruit of the tree was good for food and pleasing to the eye, and also desirable for gaining wisdom" (Gen. 3:6). Eve must have stood back and given her full attention to the fruit that had been forbidden. As she gazed at it, she must have thought that it looked so lush and tasty, she just knew she would enjoy eating it. "It was good for food." And besides, it was so beautiful, it would really enhance the loveliness of her home. "It was pleasing to the eye." The final thought that went through her mind was how impressive and important it would make her in the eyes of her husband and others (when others came along) because she would be smarter than anybody else. "Desirable for gaining wisdom." The more Eve thought about the forbidden fruit, the more attractive it became.

What temptation are you making more attractive than it is just because you are thinking about it so much? I may not (usually) like candy bars, but I love bakery birthday cakes, the kind with thick, white, lard-and-sugar icing. When I'm on a diet, I know the last thing I can have is a piece of birthday cake. Recently, when I was on another diet, a friend of mine who did not know I was dieting but does know of my love for birthday cakes brought over several pieces of her daughter's birthday cake to share with me. I thanked her, and she left it wrapped in aluminum foil on the kitchen counter. Instead of immediately throwing it out, I tolerated it. I left it right there where for two days I passed it every time I walked through the kitchen. I began thinking about what was inside that foil-wrapped package. I decided it wouldn't hurt just to open the foil wrapping and look at it. So I did. How moist the cake looked, how beautiful the pink roses of icing were on the top, how delicious I knew it would taste! After having resisted for two days, making the choice not to eat it dozens of times each day as I passed by, I rationalized that I deserved a taste for having resisted so long! Besides, it was going to spoil if someone didn't eat it. So I gave in and ate the entire portion at one time, aware when I was on my second piece that it wasn't nearly as good as I had thought it would be. I finished it feeling slightly nauseous from all that sugar, and very guilty for breaking my diet!

Temptation, whether in the form of a serving of birthday cake or the bed of your neighbor's spouse, intensifies through toleration. The toleration leads to a preoccupation of thoughts, and it's not long before we reach out to touch it. At that point, there is almost no turning back.

Maybe Eve thought, *I'll just test the situation. If I can reach the fruit and actually pluck it from the tree, that must mean I'm supposed to have it.* Have you convinced yourself that availability of the forbidden fruit means you can have it? Eve reached out and was able to pluck the fruit from the tree, letting it rest in her hand. I expect she examined it, turned it over, felt the smoothness of the skin and the softness of the flesh, and smelled the pleasing, ripe fragrance. Eve was playing with forbidden fruit. She was toying with temptation.

What temptation have you tolerated, thought about, touched, and toyed with? "It's just one more glass of wine." "It's just a little harmless flirtation." "It's just a magazine at the checkout counter." "It's just one date." Watch out! If you tolerate it, think about it, and toy with it, you are just a step away from actually doing it. Eve "took some and ate it" (Gen. 3:6). And in doing so, Eve disobeyed God.

### The Choice to Disobey God

The doubt of what God had said, the dissatisfaction with God's will, and the denial of God's goodness led Eve step by dangerous step to the choice of disobedience. She just did it! There must have been a moment of thrill as she dared to defy God's command and sank her teeth into the fruit. Amazingly, nothing happened! No lightning flashed, no buzzers went off, no whistle blew. So she turned and gave some of the forbidden fruit to her husband "who was with her" (Gen. 3:6)!

It's incredible to think that Adam apparently had stood by, knowing full well what was going on, and did nothing about it. He did not intervene and pull Eve away from the Serpent; nor did he protect her by interjecting that he knew first-hand what God had said. While Eve was deceived, Adam was not![10] He didn't doubt God's Word, but he did seem to doubt God's goodness and grace to be sufficient to get his wife out of the mess she was in.

Where had Adam been? When did he arrive on the scene? Had he seen his wife talking to the Serpent and gone over to listen to what was being said? Or was he not even really listening because while Eve was mesmerized by the Serpent and the forbidden fruit, Adam was mesmerized by Eve? One major problem for both Adam and Eve was that neither was focused on God!

As Eve offered the fruit to Adam, I wonder if she added her own testimony, "Adam, go ahead and have some. It's really delicious and quite an exciting experience. I ate it, and nothing has happened to me. You shouldn't take all this talk of sin and judgment so literally. God is a loving Father. He won't judge us." So Adam deliberately, consciously made the choice to sin and be with Eve, preferring her to God. He took the fruit, "and he ate it" (Gen. 3:6).

Whose advice are you taking and whose example are you watching? Is it someone who has sinned and seemed to get by with it? Someone you know who cheated on his tax statement and received more money on his return? Someone who cheated on her spouse and was never exposed? Someone who lied to the boss and then was promoted? Adam, who had been watching, listened to Eve and allowed himself to be talked into sin.

What sin have you allowed a loved one to talk you into committing? Disobedience of God's Word almost always affects someone else. Most tragically, it affects those we love the most. Eve's disobedience affected her husband and her children and her grandchildren and her great-grandchildren and every descendant since. Because the problem of sin doesn't stop with the choice. Choosing to sin leads to consequences.

## FINDING MEANING IN THE CONSEQUENCES AT STAKE

The Serpent never mentioned any consequences to Eve. And he does not mention them to you or to me, either. He fails to mention the psychological trauma that follows an abortion. He fails to mention the dirty feeling of being used after sleeping with your date, that haunts your marriage relationship years later. He fails to mention the panic and fear that continually grip you every time you go through your mail and every time you answer the phone after cheating on your tax return. He fails to mention the insatiable, unquenchable thirst for just one more drink—a thirst for which you would sell your own children to satisfy. There are serious consequences to sin. Always. Without exception. Adam ate the forbidden fruit his wife had offered, "Then the eyes of both of them were opened, and they realized they were naked; so they sewed fig leaves together and made coverings for themselves" (Gen. 3:7).

Satan had told Eve her eyes would be opened and she would be like God, knowing good and evil. In one sense he had been right. Eve's eyes were opened, but in a grotesque way. She knew good, but also that she was separated from it. She knew evil because now she was saturated in it. She knew good and evil in a way God never intended her to know—through her own experience. And she was deeply ashamed, which is the first consequence at stake in sin.

## The Consequence of Shame

Eve's shame must have been unbearably intense as she realized her guilt in her husband's eyes. She stood there, knowing she had been the one to offer him the fruit, and he now saw her in her sin and guilt. Adam's shame must have been even worse, because as her husband, he should have been guarding her. Had he just stood there while she talked to the snake? Where was the strength of his leadership in their relationship to say no to sin when she could not?

Adam and Eve stood before each other, dirty in sin and feeling very exposed. They were ashamed of themselves and ashamed of each other, but that didn't begin to compare with their feeling of shame before God. They were so ashamed that just the thought of having to face Him sent them scurrying for a cover-up. The fig leaves they chose to sew together were totally inadequate. God could see right through them.

What fig leaves have you sewn together as a cover-up for your sin and shame before God? Fig leaves . . .

of good works?

of religiosity?

of church attendance?

69

of community volunteerism?

of morality?

of philanthropy?

There are no fig leaves thick enough or big enough to hide your sin and shame from God. "Then the man and his wife heard the sound of the LORD God as he was walking in the garden in the cool of the day, and they hid from the LORD God among the trees of the garden" (Gen. 3:8).

Are you hiding from God? How? Have you stopped praying and reading your Bible? Stopped going to church? Do you tell your friends that your work schedule keeps you too busy when really you are hiding? Or perhaps you maintain the outward appearance of someone who lives in God's presence by going to church and calling yourself a Christian, but in your heart and mind you're closed to Him. Deep down you're afraid of being found out. And the last thing you want is to hear or read His Word.

How long have you been hiding? A week? A month? Years? A lifetime? Can you remember when you used to have sweet fellowship with God?

I would imagine that up until this point, whenever God would come into the garden, Adam and Eve would run to meet Him like excited children greeting a parent who had been absent for a while. Surely the primary joy of their brief lives had been talking with Him, listening to Him, learning from Him, watching Him, being with Him, and just loving Him! But when they harbored unconfessed sin in their hearts, His coming was a dreaded event, His Word was a loathsome thing, and the thought of His presence was terrifying.

Adam and Eve were overlooking the single greatest truth in the universe! *God loved them!* He loved them *in their sin* so much that He sought them out! He did not leave them quivering in fear, devastated by guilt, saturated in sin, hiding in the bushes. He came. "But the LORD God called to the man, 'Where are you?'" (Gen. 3:9).

God knew exactly where Adam and Eve were. He was not calling them to get information, but confession. He wanted them to confront what they had done so they could set it right and be restored in fellowship with Himself.

Is God calling you? "Where are you? I missed you in church this week." "Where are you? I missed meeting you for prayer this morning." "Where are you? You read your Bible but with such an absent mind." Where are you?

Adam emerged from his hiding place and responded to God's pleading, loving voice, "I heard you in the garden, and I was afraid because I was naked; so I hid" (Gen. 3:10). Adam's response was honest, but there was a lot between the lines he wasn't saying, such as, "Lord, I've got a guilty conscience. I was hiding because I didn't want You to find me out. I know I am not right with You, and I was desperately hoping You wouldn't notice me over here in this bush. And, Lord, I know judgment is coming. I just hope it won't be as bad as I think it's going to be." It takes courage to come into the Lord's presence when you have willfully disobeyed Him.

God doesn't let us get by with generalities. He wants us to pinpoint the sin. So He probed deeper, asking Adam, "Who told you that you were naked? Have you eaten from the tree that I commanded you not to eat from?" (Gen. 3:11). Instead of confessing their sin and admitting their guilt, Adam and Eve made matters worse when they rationalized what they had done by claiming to be victims. Adam blamed his Parent when he complained, "The woman *you put here with me*—she gave me some fruit from the tree, and I ate it" (Gen. 3:12, italics added). When God turned to the woman and reprimanded, "What is this you have done?" she said the devil made her do it! "The serpent deceived me, and I ate" (Gen. 3:13). While there was partial truth to what each one said, neither was willing to accept the full responsibility for their actions.

Like Adam and Eve in their effort to rationalize their guilt, our nation has become a society of victims. Everyone can find someone to blame for their behavior. We blame

poverty,

lack of educational opportunities,

job pressures,

the federal government,

big corporations,

immigrants,

parents,

siblings,

spouses,

coworkers,

the boss,

the weather,

the neighbor's dog . . .

anyone and anything except ourselves for our sin. How shameful! Adam and Eve's sin led to shame until all of Creation suffered the consequences.

## The Consequence of Suffering

What a scene that must have been! Adam and Eve cowering in their fig leaves, the snake wound into the smallest coil he could manage, and the Creator with a look of infinite tenderness and unfathomable suffering etched on His face by a love that would stretch all the way to the cross.

The sky would still have been cobalt blue, the river still sparkling clear, the grass still velvety green, the flowers still a profusion of scent and color. But I wonder if the animals froze in place . . . Did the deer lift its head with water dripping from its muzzle where it had been drinking and stand motionless, gazing at the shivering couple? Did the birds hush their singing? Did the swans stop their gliding? Did the squirrels stop their scampering through the trees and the bees stop their buzzing and the cows stop their grazing? Was all of creation suspended in time, poised to hear what the Creator—the Judge of all the universe—would say?

God first pronounced judgment on the physical body of the snake used as a channel for Satan's voice. "Because you have done this, 'Cursed are you above all the livestock and all the wild animals! You will crawl on your belly and you will eat dust all the days of your life'" (Gen. 3:14).

In this age of fascination with the occult, where seances are conducted in the White House and channeling is popularized by television talk shows and out-of-body experiences are big box-office draws, we need to heed the warning of judgment. Those who consciously allow Satan to use them are in danger of being cursed by the Judge of the universe.

God then turned and spoke sternly to Satan himself, "And I will put enmity between you and the woman, and between your offspring and hers; he will crush your head, and you will strike his heel" (Gen. 3:15). Although Eve had yielded to Satan's temptation, God was serving him notice that she would not belong to him. There would be enmity between Satan and Eve so she would not be his willing ally in his evil plan to thwart the purpose of God for the human race.

Not only would there be enmity between Eve and Satan but also between her offspring and his. Eve's offspring represented those who belong to God. Satan's offspring represented those who are in opposition to God and to His people. This prophecy has been fulfilled throughout human history in the repeated attacks on the Jews, God's chosen people, and in the persecution of Christians, the bride of Christ. At one point in His ministry, Jesus rebuked the religious leaders of His day as being the children of Satan who were at enmity with Himself, the Son of God.[11] This prophecy will climax in a day yet to come at the end of human history, when Satan's offspring, the Antichrist, will set himself against the Offspring of the woman, Jesus Christ.

Perhaps the most striking part of this prophecy is also the most difficult to understand, because God specifically speaks of the "seed" (KJV), not of a man but of a woman only. Throughout history, this unique wording has been accepted as a prophecy of the virgin birth of Jesus of Nazareth, Whose heel would be bruised by Satan on the cross. Yet Christ's death was temporary. On the third day He arose victorious from the dead, crushing the head of the devil, destroying his power forever.[12]

As a girl growing up in western North Carolina, I loved to hike in the mountains. But whenever I set out, my mother's admonition, "Watch out for snakes!" would ring in my ears. So while trying to climb higher or just enjoying the walk on the way up, I always had to keep one eye on the trail before me. Although I can remember killing only one snake myself, I was present at various times when snakes were killed by others. Each time I observed a fascinating phenomenon. After the snake was killed, its body invariably continued to twitch until sundown. Even though its head was crushed, rendering it powerless, the dead snake's writhing body was enough to keep me at a distance. After sundown it would finally lie still, and its death was more believable.

You and I need to remember that ever since the resurrection of Jesus Christ, Satan has been a defeated foe. His head has been crushed. As you and I seek to climb higher in our faith and service and knowledge of God, or as we simply enjoy the walk with Christ, what we are confronted with is merely the twitching of his defeated body. But sundown is coming! One day even the twitching body of that old Serpent, the devil, will be destroyed.[13]

With what surely was a heavy heart, the Father God turned to the beloved jewels of His Creation and pronounced judgment on Adam and Eve. To Eve He said, "I will greatly increase your pains in childbearing; with pain you will give birth to children" (Gen. 3:16).

Does God's judgment on Eve seem unfair to you, since Eve herself had not known God's Word firsthand? It is an awesome, solemn truth that God held Eve accountable for the truth she had opportunity to know.

When Jesus Christ was subjected to His first religious trial, the former high priest, Annas, asked about His disciples and His teaching.[14] His interrogation must have been condescending and self-righteous as he inquired, "Tell the court, Jesus, what, who, when, where have You been teaching." Jesus looked him coolly in the eye as He replied, "I have spoken openly to the world . . . I always taught in synagogues or at the temple, where all the Jews come together. I said nothing in secret. Why question me? Ask those who heard me. Surely they know what I said."[15] As a former high priest, Annas should have known what was being taught on the temple grounds and to whom it was being taught. Jesus held Annas accountable for the truth he had had opportunity to know.

You and I are also held accountable for the truth we have opportunity to know. Recently I was in California on a Sunday morning. I turned on the television at 7:00 a.m. and caught two excellent worship services with outstanding expository, biblical teaching—one was on the will of God, and one was on the water of life. I don't know what the viewing audience of those programs is, but I do know God holds the thirty-two million people living in California with access to television sets accountable for the truth they had opportunity to hear whether they did or not. That's awesome! That's frightening! Because in America, we have opportunity to hear and know so very much.

Every daughter of Eve has felt the consequences of Eve's judgment as God held her accountable for what she had opportunity to know. Since the garden of Eden, women have suffered literal pain associated with childbirth. The physical labor that preceded the birth of my own children lasted more than twenty-four hours in each instance. Yet as excruciating as the physical pain was, it doesn't touch the emotional pain endured in the process of raising children. Every hurt, disappointment, rejection, failure, pain, or heartache they experienced I experienced to an even greater degree than they did. Eve herself not only knew the pain of childbirth but also the severe emotional pain of watching her first two sons grow up with distinctly different natures that clashed with each other, until her eldest murdered her secondborn. I wonder how many times she whispered to herself in the black of the night, "If only . . ."

There was another interesting aspect to God's judgment of Eve's sin. He said, "Your desire will be for your husband, and he will rule over you" (Gen. 3:16). Does this mean women were to have a strong tendency to control, manipulate, and manage, yet their position in society and in the family would put them in subjection to their husbands?"[16] The greatest oppressor of women is not government policy or male chauvinist attitudes or a "good old boy" hierarchy or unfair wage laws. It's just sin!

At the end of this tragic scene, the Father God turned His full attention on Adam. Unlike Eve, Adam not only had opportunity to know the truth, Adam knew the truth! And God held Adam accountable for the direct disobedience to the truth of His Word.

Do you know someone who says God is such a loving Father He will not judge that person's sin? God is a loving Father. He is also a righteous and just and holy Father. He cannot be less than Himself, and His justice demands judgment. So in a voice ringing with His authority as the righteous Judge over all creation, He pronounced the consequences of Adam's sin: "Because you listened to your wife and ate from the tree about which I commanded you, 'You must not eat of it,' Cursed is the ground because of you; through painful toil you will eat of it all the days of your life. It will produce thorns and thistles for you, and you will eat the plants of the field. By the sweat of your brow you will eat your food until you return to the ground, since from it you were taken; for dust you are and to dust you will return" (Gen. 3:17–19).

Adam's work had been a delight and joy as he was taught and trained under the loving supervision of the Creator. Each challenge he had faced was an exciting opportunity that he had met consistently with success. Now, as long as he lived, he would be resisted. His life would be filled with struggle and sweat, frustration and failure, disappointment and discouragement.

The consequences of Adam's sin are easily seen around us in our work situations. Nothing comes easily.

In what way is your suffering today linked to Adam's sin? Have you worked hard to maintain your physical health through exercise and good eating habits only to be hindered by old age and the painful limitations it brings? Have you invested days and months and years into a family that has disintegrated in divorce and despair? Have you worked endlessly to further your education only to have the latest technology move you out of your job opportunity? After struggling to work as diligently, faithfully, and heartily as you know how, your work will "produce thorns and thistles." In the end, all you and I have to show for a lifetime of hard work is death and dust.

I will never forget rushing to the hospital in response to an urgent call telling me that a dear friend was close to death. She was my age and in perfect health. I had talked with her twelve hours previously, and nothing had been wrong. When I arrived at the hospital, I was told she had apparently breathed in a type of virus that had reacted like an internal hand grenade, and all of her bodily functions had shut down. As I wept and prayed and talked quietly with the family members and friends who had gathered, I was horrified to learn she had been disconnected from the life-support system and was dead. I slipped into the chapel where her husband and children were crying and praying, and to this day I can hear the echo of her son's agony as he angrily said over and over, "It's not right. It's not right! *It's just not right!*"

And her son was right! Such death and destruction and tragedy are *not right!* It was never meant to be! Next time you are at the graveside of a loved one, instead of blaming God, remember, "the wages of sin is death, but the gift of God is eternal life in Christ Jesus our Lord."[17] God created you and me to live with Him in His heavenly home, enjoying fellowship with Him and glorifying Him forever! Death was not part of His plan. It was through Adam's sin that death—temporal and eternal—entered the human race.[18] And death entered creation as well.

Flowers fade. Grass withers. Birds sing in minor key. Trees lose their leaves because "creation was subjected to frustration, not by its own choice, but by the will of the one who subjected it, in hope that the creation itself will be liberated from its bondage to decay and brought into the glorious freedom of the children of God. We know that the whole creation has been groaning as in the pains of childbirth right up to the present time."[19] Because of man's sin, creation has been in a cycle of death and decay. The greatest threat to our environment is not fluorocarbon or nuclear testing or the burning of tropical forests in the Amazon River region or toxic waste. The greatest threat to our environment has been and is sin!

As bad as they are, shame and human suffering are not the worst consequences of sin. The worst consequence is separation from God.

### The Consequence of Separation

There was no reverberating sound of a steel door clanging shut or even the click of a garden gate swinging back on its hinges. There was only the spine-chilling, irrevocable verdict of the Judge: "'The man has now become like one of us, knowing good and evil. He must not be allowed to reach out his hand and take also from the tree of life and eat, and live forever.' So the LORD God banished him from the

Garden of Eden to work the ground from which he had been taken. After he drove the man out, he placed on the east side of the Garden of Eden cherubim and a flaming sword flashing back and forth to guard the way to the tree of life" (Gen. 3:22–24).

Adam and Eve were driven from their garden home, driven from security and safety and serenity and success and satisfaction, separated from God! The loneliness and desperate agony of loss must have been overwhelming. As they looked back, they could see at the entrance to what had been their home a powerful angel standing guard with a sword swirling like a mad dervish, preventing any thought of return. Even though God had explained His reasoning, that in mercy He was protecting them from the temptation to eat of the tree of life and so live forever in their sin, the finality of their separation from all they had been created for must have been devastating.

Since there was only one entrance into the garden and it was guarded carefully and constantly, it was not just hard to get back into God's presence—it was impossible! God Himself prevented it. Neither Adam nor Eve, nor you nor I, nor anyone ever born into the human race could ever get back into God's presence. The garden of Eden, God's heavenly home, can never be regained through human effort. Paradise has been lost!

GOD IS righteous and just. But God is also loving and merciful. He cannot be less than Himself. Satan, in his temptation of Adam and Eve and in his plan to defeat the purpose of God, failed to take into account the very character of God. He failed to realize one very important thing—how much God loved the man and woman He had created and the depths to which His grace would go in order to bring them back to Himself. It never entered Satan's wicked, self-centered imagination that God would commit the fullness of His eternal, divine nature to bring man back into a right relationship with Himself. It never occurred to Satan, who ever seeks his own preeminence, that the Creator of the universe would lay down His own life in atonement for man's sin. But that's exactly what happened. The solution to the problem of sinfulness is the cross of Jesus Christ.

The cross is very subtly pictured when, following His judgment for their sin,

"The LORD God made garments of skin for Adam and his wife and clothed them" (Gen. 3:21). In order to clothe Adam and Eve with skins, the Lord God had to kill an animal, which introduced the Old Testament system of sacrifice.

Under the law of Moses, when someone sinned, that person was required to bring a lamb without blemish to the priest at the temple.[20] The sinner had to grasp the lamb with both hands and then confess his sin. It was as though the guilt of the sinner was conveyed through his arms, down to his hands, and transferred to the lamb. Then the sinner took the knife and killed the lamb, so the lamb died as a direct result of the sinner's action. The priest then took the blood of the lamb and sprinkled it on the altar to make atonement for the person's sin. Based on the sinner's confession of sin, obedience to God's instructions, and faith in the blood sacrificed to make atonement, the person was forgiven.

When John the Baptist observed Jesus of Nazareth walking beside the Jordan River, he exclaimed, "Look, the Lamb of God, who takes away the sin of the world!"[21] John was acknowledging that the sacrifices in the Old Testament—all the millions of animals that had been slaughtered and all of the oceans of blood that had been shed—were like an audiovisual aid that pointed to Jesus Christ.

The sacrifices were like IOU notes. When someone sacrificed for sin, it was as though God said, "I owe you forgiveness. I owe you redemption. I owe you atonement." The blood of lambs and bulls and goats could never atone for man's sin,[22] because it was symbolic. It pointed to God's sending of His own Son in the person of Jesus Christ. And when Jesus Christ died on the cross, His sacrifice for sin was accepted by God, and all the IOU notes were paid in full. Including Adam and Eve's! There is no other payment for the IOUs. There is no other salvation God accepts. There is no other answer to the problem of sinfulness. None other than Jesus Christ, and Him crucified.

Today, when we grasp the Lamb of God with our "hands" of faith and confess our sin, the guilt of our sin is transferred to the Lamb. Although the Romans physically crucified Jesus, it was your sin and mine that was responsible for putting Him to death. He died as my personal sacrifice—and yours. His blood was sprinkled on the altar of the cross for my sin, and God accepted the sacrifice, granting me atonement, redemption, forgiveness, and a way back into His Presence through the substitutionary death of Jesus Christ.[23]

Adam and Eve had had the right idea when they tried to cover themselves. They needed a covering for their sinfulness, guilt, and shame in God's eyes. But fig leaves were woefully inadequate, so the Lord God provided forgiveness of their sin through the blood of the Lamb. Isn't it time you stopped clutching at fig leaves? You can receive forgiveness for your own sinfulness by claiming Jesus Christ as God's Lamb, sacrificed for your sin. Right now, wherever you are, bow your head, and pray this simple prayer by faith:

> *Dear God,*
> *I confess to You that I am a sinner. Not only do I have a strong tendency to sin, inherited from my parents, Adam and Eve, but I have specific sins in my life. I do not blame anyone else but take full responsibility for the sin in my own life. I am willing to stop sinning if You would come into my life and help me.*
> *I believe Jesus Christ is Your Lamb who was sacrificed to make atonement for me. I ask You to cleanse me from my sin with His blood. I believe He rose from the dead to give me eternal life. Would You now give to me eternal life? I open up the door of my heart and invite Christ to come into my inmost being, surrendering the control of my life to Him. From this moment on, I will seek to know and serve You. In Jesus' name, amen.*

As you come out of your hiding place in the bushes and shed your fig leaves, thank your heavenly Father for providing you with His own robe to wear.

"I delight greatly in the Lord; my soul rejoices in my God. For He has clothed me with garments of salvation and wrapped me in a robe of righteousness" (Isa. 61:10).

# 4

## *I Uproot Your Bitterness*

GENESIS 4

One evening at dinner, my youngest daughter, Rachel-Ruth, came to where I was seated at the table and whined, "Mommy, something bit me." I pulled up her shirt and saw a little red bump. I searched the rest of her shirt and clothing but could find nothing there, so I told her whatever it was had gone. A few minutes later, she wriggled up to me and complained she had been bitten again. I examined her tummy, and sure enough, there was another little red bump. This time I took her shirt off and examined the rest of her but saw nothing else, so I put a clean shirt on her and told her to go back and play, everything was all right.

A few minutes later she came running into the kitchen, her blonde curls bobbing around her frightened face and tears glistening in her eyes, whimpering, "Mommy, Mommy, whatever it is, he's biting me all over!" I lifted up her clean shirt and was shocked to see that her tummy, chest, and back were covered with little red bumps. Rachel-Ruth had the chicken pox! While the first little red bump had indicated Rachel-Ruth's body was riddled with the disease, I didn't know enough to diagnose it accurately until she had broken out all over.

Every descendant of Adam and Eve has been born with his or her "body" infected with the disease of sin, but until it breaks out all over in wrong habits and attitudes and actions and decisions, it can be difficult to diagnose. However, the New Testament tells us that

the first spot of sin—

the first worry

or little white lie

or selfish thought

80

or flash of anger

or proud look

or angry word—

indicates our entire lives are riddled with it.[1]

The disease of sin entered the human race through Adam and Eve's choice to disobey the Lord God. It was easily diagnosed in Cain, the very first child born to them, when he broke out in bitterness rooted in resentment.

## Bitterness Rooted in Resentment

What was it like to wake up the morning after having been banished from the garden? I would imagine Adam and Eve had been lying on the cold, hard ground, covered in smelly animal skins. After a fitful night's sleep, did they have a moment in between unconsciousness and full alertness when they thought everything they had been through the day before was just a horrible nightmare, only to come fully awake and face-to-face with the cold, hard consequences of their choice to disobey God? There would have been no comfort in each other on that first night after the way Eve had initiated Adam's involvement in sin and the way Adam had blamed Eve when convicted of it. They may not even have been speaking to each other!

Thomas Merton, a solitary monk, expressed his own similar alienation from God in an eloquent description of despair: "I sat there in the dark, unhappy room, unable to think, unable to move, with all the innumerable elements of my isolation crowding in upon me from every side: without a home, without a family, without a country, without a father, apparently without any friends, without any interior peace or confidence or light or understanding of my own—without God, too, without heaven, without grace, without anything!"[2]

In utter loneliness, separated and alienated from God, their minds must have been initially preoccupied with reliving those awful moments that had led to their disobedience. "If only I hadn't talked to the snake." "If only I had prayed first." "If only I had intervened to protect her." What are you wishing "if only" you had done differently?

The most tragic day in all of human history could not be relived. The only hope for Adam and Eve and the entire human race to come was the promise of God that one day He would send an Offspring, a Savior, who would destroy the power of the Serpent and in some way restore them in a right relationship with their Creator.

Life outside the garden was much harder than it had been in paradise. After months of struggle, sweat, and frustrating toil with the elements and the unyielding ground, Adam and Eve were given their first child, a son they named Cain. As Eve gazed on the miraculous bundle of life in her arms, she exclaimed, "With the help of the LORD I have brought forth a man" (Gen. 4:1). An alternate translation of what she said is, "I have gotten a man, even Jehovah." Apparently Eve thought her firstborn was the fulfillment of the Lord's promise of an Offspring who would take away her sin, reestablish her in a right relationship with her Creator, and restore her to the garden of Eden. She was wrong. Cain was not the promised Offspring. His life would be an added nightmare in itself. But the seeds were sown for deep-rooted grievances within the home.

## Resentment toward Grievances

Adam and Eve must have already been experiencing overwhelming grief as a consequence of their disobedience. The birth of their son, although physically painful, was surely the single greatest joy of their lives since being banished from the garden. They must have thought their firstborn would be the beginning of the end of their long nightmare. Assuming this was Eve's thought behind her exclamation, consider how her attitude could have affected Cain as he was growing up. At the very least, he would have been raised by someone who had very high expectations of him, expectations he couldn't possibly live up to. Was Cain inadvertently programmed to go through life feeling like a failure because he could never measure up to his parents' unrealistic expectations?

What expectations did your parents place upon you? Did they expect you to be very musical and artistic, but you are athletic instead? Did they expect you to come into the family business, but you decided to enter an entirely different field of work? Did they expect you to get married and have a family, but you have remained single and devoted to your career? In what way have you failed to live up to your parents' expectations? Sometimes this kind of failure sows seeds of resentment in our lives that bear the fruit of bitterness.

If Cain failed to meet his parents' expectations of him, they also failed to meet his expectations of them. I doubt they were the kind of parents he wanted. His parents were failures, making one "mistake" that cost him a high standard of living and an easier lifestyle within the garden.

How have your parents failed you? Is their failure still affecting you, even in adulthood? Did your father file for bankruptcy just as you needed a college education, so you are still struggling to get by without a degree? Did your mother die just as you entered your teenage years when you needed her the most, so that even now you feel emotionally deprived? Did both of your parents work full-time, with no energy or time left over for you? Was one of your parents an alcoholic or abusive physically or verbally? Sometimes we feel at a disadvantage today because of the past failure of our parents.

Our parents' failure can affect our attitudes as it inflicts inner pain and emotional scars. Such grievances are common in life, but they can become a devastatingly destructive force if they are tolerated and even nurtured into resentment and bitterness.

Perhaps your grievance is unrelated to your parents but caused by someone else—a pastor or friend or ex-spouse or neighbor or client.

For nine years I taught a Bible class in the church my husband and I attended. For reasons that are still not completely clear, the ruling board closed the church to the class. From one day to the next, I found myself, along with five hundred class members, without a facility in which to meet. When a reporter from the local newspaper called she inquired bluntly, "Anne, there was no reason for the church's decision. Aren't you bitter?" And I knew I was confronted with the choice to allow my feelings of hurt to blossom into bitterness.

On another occasion I was a state witness to the execution of Velma Barfield, the first woman to be executed in the United States in more than twenty-two years.[3] I had developed a friendship with her about six months prior to her execution as a result of her correspondence with my mother. I had grown to love her as a sister in Christ and was greatly blessed by the testimony she maintained within the maximum security facility where she was incarcerated. Following the 2:00 a.m. execution, another newspaper reporter called me, probing my reaction. "Anne, how are you going to get back at the state? Aren't you bitter?" Once again, I knew I had the opportunity to allow the grief over my friend's death to go a step further and become a grievance that would become bitterness.

By God's grace, in both cases, I chose to take my reaction to the cross of Christ. In prayer, I had to "crucify" the anger and bitterness I felt was justified, leaving it with the One who said, "It is mine to avenge; I will repay,"[4] understanding that the Judge of all the earth does right.[5] I was also motivated by the conviction that my anger and bitterness, though justified by what had been done by others, was as sinful in God's sight as the actions and attitudes of those who had provoked it. More than I wanted to indulge in the sin of anger and bitterness—and I did want to indulge—I wanted to be right with God. So I laid my grievances at the nail-pierced feet of One who understands firsthand what it feels like to be deeply wounded by the sin of other people. He understands what it feels like to be treated unjustly through no fault of His own. I knew He could cleanse me of my wrong attitudes, take the sting out of the emotional pain and anger, comfort and strengthen me to let them go, and then bring blessing from them. I never want to forget that after

>the pain
>
>>and suffering
>>
>>>and humiliation
>>>
>>>>and injustice of the cross
>
>comes the glory
>
>>and the power
>>
>>>and the victory
>>>
>>>>and the blessing of the resurrection!

God rewarded my submission to Him by pouring out His blessing. In the case of the class, within a week of being removed from my own church's facility, another church warmly welcomed us into theirs. Because of the publicity surrounding the incident, I was also given several strategic opportunities to give testimony to God's faithfulness in the midst of difficulty. The class continues to flourish to this day in that same facility, enjoying a blessed relationship with the church staff and membership.

And a month following Velma Barfield's execution, the warden of the women's correctional facility opened the entire prison up for an evangelistic service. My father came and preached to about 250 inmates at one time, with dozens responding to his invitation to get right with God by placing their faith in Christ. Then he and I were escorted to every cell in maximum security and in lock-up, where he spoke to every single prisoner, telling her personally that God loved her and would forgive her if she asked.

Within three months of that wonderful evening that brought such healing after the horror of the execution, we were able to establish a Bible Study Fellowship class within the facility. The class is continuing today, stronger than ever, with more than 150 inmates enrolled. To God be the glory! He can and will do great things if you and I will release the bitterness so that we might receive His blessing.

On the other hand, if we do not release our bitterness to God, He warns us that it will take root and grow up to defile our entire lives.[6] The Bible describes defilement as that which renders us unacceptable or displeasing to God.[7] In other words, the defilement caused by bitterness could cost us God's pleasure in everything else we do. Regardless of how energetic and busy we are in Christian service, regardless of how loving and thoughtful we are in personal relationships, regardless of how gifted or respected we are by others, the root of bitterness will so defile our lives that they are wasted in God's sight, with no eternal value and therefore no hope of eternal reward at the Judgment Seat of Christ.[8]

Is it worth it to trade God's pleasure and your eternal reward for the momentary sweet taste of bitterness? Let it go!

Adam and Eve had another son they named Abel (Gen. 4:2). When he was born, Eve said nothing. That's what his name meant—emptiness, nothingness. It may be that Eve was so focused on her oldest son and what she dreamed he would become that she neglected her secondborn. Or although their third son, Seth, was yet to be born, perhaps Eve had already slipped into the mentality of viewing Abel as the middle child. Was Abel just ignored? Or by the time of his birth, was Eve so disappointed and disillusioned in Cain and his failure to live up to her expectations that there was no real joy in having another son? Whatever the reason for her recorded silence, Abel was born into a situation that was fertile ground for bitterness in his own life.

Like his brother Cain, Abel was born to parents who were failures. He also had to live outside of the garden of Eden, toiling by the sweat of his brow. And he, too, experienced a lower standard of living and a decreased quality of life. He had the added stress of an older brother who was increasingly consumed by resentment and a hair-trigger temper. But there is no evidence of bitterness in Abel's life.

Apparently, Adam and Eve had instructed their sons on where to approach their God. There must have been a specific place where they could meet with Him, as indicated by the fact they "brought" their offerings to the Lord (Gen. 4:3–4). Later we are told that "Cain went out from the LORD's presence," as though he left a particular physical place (Gen. 4:16).

We can also assume that having provided the clothing of animal skins after His judgment for their sin, God taught Adam and Eve the symbolism of those skins, revealing to them that the way out of judgment and back into a right relationship with Himself would be through the blood of a prescribed sacrifice.

It was at that meeting place, seeking the presence and blessing of God through sacrifice, that the domination of the "disease" of sin in Cain's life can be clearly diagnosed. It broke out, not only in resentment toward grievances, but in resentment toward God.

*Resentment toward God*

Cain's resentment was evident in his apparent refusal to bring a blood sacrifice, revealing his attitude of arrogance toward God: "Now Abel kept flocks, and Cain worked the soil. In the course of time Cain brought some of the fruits of the soil as an offering to the LORD. But Abel brought fat portions from some of the firstborn of his flock. The LORD looked with favor on Abel and his offering, but on Cain and his offering he did not look with favor. So Cain was very angry, and his face was downcast" (Gen. 4:2–5).

Perhaps not only the place and sacrifice were specifically designated but the time for sacrifice also. I wonder if the place was a carefully constructed altar of stone under a large spreading tree near the entrance to the garden of Eden. Were the cherubim with the flaming, swirling swords visible from that special place as a constant reminder that the way back into the garden was closed? Would the place of sacrifice intensify the conviction and sorrow for sin and judgment to those who approached God there?

Abel thoroughly examined his flocks until he found the best animals. Then he sacrificed to God the best of the best—the fat portions of the firstborn. His attitude is one of genuine worship and gratitude to the Lord his God, expressed through his conscientious obedience. He was rewarded with an overwhelming awareness that God was pleased, and his sacrifice was accepted.

Cain, on the other hand, had an attitude of arrogance. I suspect he deeply resented the place of sacrifice since he hated being reminded of sin and judgment and the garden home from which he was banished. Because his heart wasn't in it, he decided to sacrifice some fruit that was convenient and comfortably within his reach, fruit that cost him as little time and effort as possible.

Maybe Cain, as Eve's firstborn, was just a spoiled brat who was used to getting his own way. Maybe he was so accustomed to having everything done the way he wanted, with others serving and pleasing him, that he could not bring himself to do what someone else wanted. Maybe he was raised to totally live for himself by parents who doted on him and tried to satisfy his every whim.

However spoiled he might have been, the writer to the Hebrews informs us that Cain's sacrifice was not accepted by God because it was not offered in faith.[9] If the term faith as it is used here means specific faith in the blood of a proscribed sacrifice to atone for sin and gain acceptance by God, then Cain was pridefully insisting that God accept him on his own terms. He was asserting his right to approach God any way he chose. He must have concluded that God ought to be pleased because he was at least making some effort to keep the "letter of the law," even if he wasn't keeping the spirit of it.

Do you know people who are arrogantly insisting that if their good works outweigh their bad works, God is somehow obligated to accept them? As you look around, what "fruit" do you see others insisting is sufficient by bringing it to the place of sacrifice instead of humbly approaching God through the blood sacrifice of His Son? The "fruit" of

religious activity,

good works,

ethics,

morality,

or philanthropy?

Many people do not want to come to the place of sacrifice, the cross of Jesus Christ, because it intensifies the conviction of their own sin and judgment and is a constant reminder that heaven's gate is closed to sinners. God warns that "a man is not justified by observing the law,"[10] because "without the shedding of blood there is no forgiveness" of sin.[11] Jesus clarified the necessity of coming to the cross when He asserted that He Himself was the only way back into God's presence because there is salvation in no one or nothing else.[12]

Cain's attitude of arrogance produced an attitude of apathy indicated when he brought the sacrifice "in the course of time." He brought whatever he could spare when he felt like it. He was very casual in his approach to God as he gave his leftover fruit, his leftover time, his leftover attention, his leftover effort. God hates leftovers![13]

Is your sacrifice and service to God something God hates? Are you offering Him the leftovers in your life? If you had time yesterday after doing everything else and weren't too tired before going to bed, maybe you prayed. Or if you had time last week in the midst of your busy work schedule, perhaps you read your Bible. If the weather was bad so you couldn't get out on the golf course, you might have gone to church on Sunday. Do other things come before God in your life? He refuses to accept second place—and that refusal made Cain "very angry."

When God rejected Cain's arrogant, apathetic attitude in worship, Cain's disease of sin—his true nature—broke out all over as he reacted with an attitude of anger.

If his sacrifice of fruit was just a misunderstanding, when it was rejected he might have said, "God, I am so sorry. Abel always seems to do the right thing. He's just more religious than I am. But I do want to be right with You. Please teach me how to sacrifice in a way that is acceptable to You." But that wasn't what Cain said.

Obviously, the attitude in Cain's heart had been wrong all along or it would not have boiled out in anger that rose up to consume him. He was angry that Abel's sacrifice was accepted and his was not, angry that the labor of his own hands was not enough to please God, angry that God refused to lower the standards for him.

What is your attitude when you sense God's displeasure in what you're doing while those around you—in your home or church—seem be filled with His joy, get answers to prayer, make an impact on the lives of others, and receive His blessing? Do you react with angry resentment, feeling God is just too hard to please? Actually God is impossible to please if you and I try to do it our own way, through our own efforts. But that truth can be a difficult pill to swallow when your heart, like Cain's, is filled with pride.

King David testified from experience that "the sacrifices of God are a broken spirit; a broken and contrite heart, O God, you will not despise."[14] God has never refused anyone who has come to Him humbly, in faith, by way of the cross. Cain just refused to come. His bitterness became deeply rooted in resentment toward grievances and toward God, and then toward the guilt that began to envelop him.

*Resentment toward Guilt*

God, in His infinite love and mercy, reached out to Cain. Like a Father, He initiated contact by appearing to Cain in some type of visible form in a process that would be similar to His speaking to us through our consciences, convicting us of sin. He asked Cain, "Why are you angry? Why is your face downcast? If you do what is right, will you not be accepted? But if you do not do what is right, sin is crouching at your door; it desires to have you, but you must master it" (Gen. 4:6–7).

The Father God loves His people so much that He does not leave them consumed by anger and riddled with guilt but clearly shows the way to successfully deal with dangerously destructive attitudes. God's inquiry should have caused Cain to reflect on the unreasonableness of his attitude that had already robbed him of his joy and peace, a loss reflected in his downcast face. The fact that Cain knew right from wrong was also made clear, as well as the warning that if he refused to do what he knew to be right, the sinful attitudes would begin to dictate his choices and dominate his life. The real problem in his life was neither his brother nor the sacrifice but the attitude crouching within himself.

What sin is crouching at the door within your heart?

Pride?

Unforgiveness?

Revenge?

Anger?

Jealousy?

Lust?

Lies?

Selfishness?

Resentment?

Bitterness?

You must master it. You must get control of it by confessing it to God, asking Him to cleanse you and release you from its power through the blood of Jesus Christ. If you do not, it will have you in its control. It will rise up to dominate your life and dictate not only the choices you make but the person you become; it will determine your eternal destiny and reward. Wrong attitudes have enormous power in our lives. That's why God has placed within each of us a conscience that begins to feel guilty when our attitudes and actions are wrong.

Many of the later-model cars are equipped with theft alarm systems. The more sensitive ones can be annoying to the general public as the least bit of motion by a passerby or the lightest touch to the car body can send off an earsplitting siren accompanied by flashing lights and honking horn. But that obnoxious sensitivity is purposefully designed to be a protection against unwanted entry.

God has built into each of us an alarm system to warn us of the unwanted entry of sin into our lives. The alarm system is called guilt. Guilt is our friend. Without it we would go on in sin until we were dominated and defeated by it.

In our pleasure-seeking, anything-goes, feel-good society, guilt is anathema. We run from it through frantic activity, drown it in alcohol, drug it with Prozac, escape it through entertainment, talk about it to a therapist, blame it on someone else, suppress it through mental gymnastics, but we can't rid ourselves of it! It's like a stain that won't come out of our clothes no matter how many wash cycles we put it through or what kind of detergent we use because the stain has become part of the fabric! The only thing that can "wash away" our sin and guilt before God is the blood of Jesus Christ. So God has given us a conscience with a guilt alarm that goes off when sin enters so that we might go to Jesus Christ for cleansing.

Apparently Cain shut his ears to the guilt alarm blaring away in his conscience. He just ignored God, not saying a word. His bitterness, which had been rooted in resentment toward grievances, God, and guilt, now climaxed in resentment toward anything and anyone who was good and right with God.

*Resentment toward Good*

Because he was right with God, there must have been a peace and joy in Abel's life that would have been obvious to his older brother. There must have been a quiet confidence that came from knowing God was pleased with him. And every time Cain saw Abel, it must have triggered conviction and set off the alarm of guilt in Cain's conscience. For this reason, Cain despised his brother Abel.[15]

Jesus gave His disciples insight about this kind of attitude as He was preparing to leave them. He revealed that the world loves its own kind, those who are living in sin, separated from God; but the world hates those who are different, those who have reconciled with God. The righteousness of the godly leaves the world without any excuse for its attitude of sin and rebellion.[16] With such similar backgrounds and grievances, Abel and the right choices he had made left Cain without excuse for the wrong choices he had made. So Cain hated Abel. One day the hatred that had been crouching at the door of Cain's heart rose up and took control of his life because he had refused to heed the Creator's warning and master it.

The day when the line of hostility was drawn between the righteous and the unrighteous that would stretch until the Millennium must have been very much like every other day. When his brother invited him to walk out into the field, Abel had no warning that it was anything other than an opportunity to view his brother's harvest. Since Abel was a prophet, maybe as they walked under the clear

90

blue sky and viewed the straight rows of crops in the field, enjoying the crisp air and bright sunshine, he tried to reason with Cain.[17]

I remember walking down the beach with a friend who was struggling with her husband's unfaithfulness to her. Although her husband had confessed his sin, broken off the wrong relationships, and sought to reconcile with my friend, she could not resolve the pain and anger and resentment that were crouching at her heart's door. I tried to feel her pain while at the same time warn her about the bitterness that was beginning to take root in her heart. I reasoned with her to the best of my feeble ability, trying to convince her that the only power strong enough to master the crouching sin was the cross of Christ. I told her God would deal with the sin in her husband's life, but she had to deal with the sin in her own by confessing it and crucifying it on the cross, an act that would include the decision to forgive her husband. Although she didn't say so at the time, she could not forgive her husband because in her mind that meant she would be letting him get away with his sin. Later she rationalized that she had forgiven him as a Christian brother but could never forgive him as a husband. The forgiveness she extended was not genuine biblical forgiveness because it did not offer reconciliation when her husband repented. And so, to my utter, helpless despair, she cut me out of her life.

Was Abel trying to reason with Cain in a similar fashion? "Cain, if you don't master the bitterness in your life that is rooted in resentment against grievances, against God, and against the guilt you are feeling, you will never experience life the way God created it to be lived. Cain, your choices are destroying your life. I love you, and I can't bear to see you living in such miserable unhappiness."

Even as Cain lifted his hand to slay his brother, I wonder if he said through clenched teeth, "Who do you think you are to sit in judgment over me? How can you be so self-righteous and judgmental? I'm sick and tired of your goody-goody attitude, and I won't stand for it anymore." The Bible says only, "And while they were in the field, Cain attacked his brother Abel and killed him" (Gen. 4:8).[18]

What a shock it must have been, even to Cain in his anger! To struggle with his own flesh and blood, to wrench the life from his younger brother, to see the still and crumpled form on the ground at his feet, lying in a growing pool of blood—surely it would have caused Cain to fall on his knees and cry out to God, "What have I done? God help me! I'm so sorry! Sin mastered me, just as You said it would, but I don't want to live enslaved by it. Oh, God, help me; forgive me. How can I face my parents? Show me what to do to get right with You."

But Cain didn't react with any evidence of regret or repentance at all. He went from bad to worse. He went from bitterness rooted in resentment to bitterness that grew into rebellion.

## BITTERNESS ROOTED IN REBELLION

Cain hardened his heart and turned a deaf ear toward the alarm of guilt that must have been sounding shrilly and incessantly within his conscience. He chose to embrace his resentment until it blossomed into rebellion. He must have thought he deserved to be angry and bitter. He must have felt he had to ignore his own guilt because he perceived others to be guiltier than he was.

Do you have that same attitude that believes you, too, have a right to feel resentful and bitter because life has been so unfair and unjust? Why is it that we seem to think we can control the unfair, unjust grievances in our lives through bitter resentment and rebellion? We seem to be afraid that if we forgive and reconcile with those who have mistreated us that somehow they will "get away with it." We try to control their judgment by seeking to hold them accountable through our harsh attitudes.

Cain's life testifies that seeking revenge by withholding forgiveness won't work. You have the power to hurt the other person, but in the end you will destroy yourself.

How long was it before God came to Cain and confronted him with his action? Was it minutes or hours or days or weeks of misery such as King David described when he cried out, "When I kept silent, my bones wasted away through my groaning all day long. For day and night your hand was heavy upon me; my strength was sapped as in the heat of the summer"?[19] David knew the agony of rebellion against God.

Whenever it was, sometime after the murder, God approached Cain and inquired, "Where is your brother Abel?" (Gen. 4:9). God knew where Abel was. He wanted Cain to tell Him where he was. He wanted Cain to confess his sin, but like King David, in his rebellious condition, Cain resisted.

### Rebellion that Resisted Confession

Cain boldly questioned God's right to inquire by flippantly retorting, "I don't know. . . . Am I my brother's keeper?" (Gen. 4:9). In today's terms, Cain's response sounds very familiar: "What gives You the right to question me? Why should I confess my sin to You? Besides, Abel was making my life miserable, and it's my right to choose to end my misery."

With infinite, loving patience, the Creator gave Cain another opportunity to confess his sin, challenging him to reveal what he was hiding: "What have you done? Listen! Your brother's blood cries out to me from the ground" (Gen. 4:10). Surely Cain was squirming inside. Yet he still resisted confession.

The New Testament teaches us that we are not to "make light of the Lord's discipline, and do not lose heart when he rebukes you, because the Lord disciplines those he loves, and he punishes everyone he accepts as a son."[20] God, as our loving Father, confronts us with our sin and convicts us of it in order to get us to confess. Because He knows if we do not confess and correct it, our misery will envelop us and we will live life at a very low level in comparison with the life He created for us.

What have you done that you resist confessing? Something you don't even recognize as sin? When Cain retorted, "Am I my brother's keeper?" he was making light of what he had done. And perhaps because you haven't committed "big sins" like murder or adultery or stealing, you're making light of "little sins" like temper, gossip, worry, exaggerations, and jealousies.

If you and I resist confessing our sin when God brings it to our attention through our own Bible reading or through a spouse or a child or a friend or a pastor or just our own consciences, we harden our hearts. And a hardened heart is an impenetrable barrier in our relationship with God, our enjoyment of His blessings, our emotional and spiritual security, and our eternal reward. A hardened heart is the core of a miserable life.

Cain's life proceeded to increase in misery. He not only resisted confession; he refused correction.

### Rebellion that Refused Correction

Although we may not acknowledge and confess the sin, there will be judgment for it. The only hope is to turn to God, confess the sin, and submit to His correction, because our Creator is also our Judge. Cain was accountable to his Creator for his actions whether or not he acknowledged his accountability. And the Judge rendered the verdict: "Now you are under a curse and driven from the ground, which opened its mouth to receive your brother's blood from your hand. When you work the ground, it will no longer yield its crops for you. You will be a restless wanderer on the earth" (Gen. 4:11–12).

Cain lost his peace. He lost real meaning to his life. His inner security and contentment. His satisfaction and sense of fulfillment. The ground would no longer produce for him, forcing him to wander from place to place as he tried to make a living in some other way. And while he wandered, the alarm of his conscience would be constantly screaming his guilt so that he could never escape what he had done. He would be on the run all of his life—running over the next hill, through the next valley, to the next town. Anytime he found a place he thought he liked and could call home, the restlessness would fall on him like a thousand bee stings, and he would run again. Anytime he met someone he thought he could call a friend, the relationship would disintegrate, and he would run again. Anytime he thought he had found a job that would make him a living, it would fall through, and he would be on the run again.

Running, running, running—
  away from God,
    away from love,
      away from peace,
        away from joy,
          away from contentment,
            away from fulfillment,
              away from meaning . . .

Are you on the run? Not outwardly, perhaps—although a workaholic schedule can be an emotional and spiritual marathon—but inwardly? You can choose to repent instead of to run!

Cain chose to run instead of repent. But before he left the starting blocks, he had to express a final word of grievance as he whimpered, "My punishment is more than I can bear. Today you are driving me from the land, and I will be hidden from your presence; I will be a restless wanderer on the earth, and whoever finds me will kill me" (Gen. 4:13–14). His complaint is peppered with the use of seven personal pronouns! All Cain cared about was himself. There was no fear or reverence for God, no regret for the loss of innocent life, no sorrow for sin, no thought for his parents who had lost one son tragically through murder and would be losing another through rebellion. There was only a preoccupation with himself.

Yet God still cared about Cain! In compassion for the son of Adam, who would be the first of many who would choose to run rather than repent, God announced, "'If anyone kills Cain, he will suffer vengeance seven times over.' Then the LORD put a mark on Cain so that no one who found him would kill him" (Gen. 4:15). Perhaps one reason God spared Cain's life was to use him as an example to the people of his own day and ours—an example of the destructive defilement of bitterness in one person's life.

The most tragic consequence of the bitterness that rose up and defiled Cain's life was his separation from God. Through his parents, he had been banished from the garden of Eden. Now he was banished from God. "So Cain went out from the LORD's presence and lived in the land of Nod, east of Eden" (Gen. 4:16).

### Rebellion that Rejected Communion

Cain had been created by God. He had been created with life from God. He had been created for God. And now he was separated from God. Unconfessed sin and rebellion makes a person so miserable in the presence of a holy, righteous God that the sin must either be confessed and cleansed or the sinner must leave God's presence. But God also warns us that if we forsake Him, He will forsake us.[21] Cain made his choice when he resisted confession and refused correction so that his heart was hardened to reject communion with his Creator. Therefore his Creator rejected communion with him.

Several years ago a new minister took over a large church in our city. He was young and dynamic, with an apparent love for God's Word and a heart for the gospel. Under his preaching people were saved, and the church quickly grew in size. A few years later, many members of his congregation noticed a change in his preaching. It was subtle at first, then more obvious; there was a decreasing power and conviction. At one point, the minister went so far as to poll his congregation on whether or not they believed the Bible was true. When 60 percent responded they did not think the Bible was all true, he accepted their conclusion as a mandate to cease preaching the gospel and to begin actually deriding the Word of God. Not too long afterward, the front page of the local paper carried the news of his resignation following his admission of an affair with a married woman in his congregation.

Although the congregation had no way of knowing, the sin in the minister's life had put him at a distance from God and His Word, which was the real reason he had ceased to preach with power and conviction. He apparently resisted confession; the later public reports said that he had wound up being admitted to a psychiatric hospital.

Cain's tragic life illustrates the hard lesson that guilt is our friend if it drives us to God. However, if we refuse to turn to God in repentance and confession, guilt will drive us away from God to our own destruction. Cain's bitterness that was rooted in resentment and rebellion bore wicked fruit in his family for generations to follow. Cain's sin, left to take its own natural course, intensified with each generation until the entire civilization of the world in his day was ravaged by it.

*Rebellion that Ravaged Civilization*

Life without God can be attractive. It can involve lots of money, successful business ventures, exciting travel, and pleasurable entertainment. Cain's world evidently had all of these things. Superficially, he led an interesting life. He married[22] and had children whose descendants were progressive and aggressive. They built cities, raised cattle, produced literature and other expressions of culture, developed technology, and generally did some amazing things.

Does life apart from God look attractive to you? Could it be that the outward attractiveness of such a lifestyle is blinding you to its reality?

The North Carolina Correctional Center for Women looks quite attractive when you drive up to the front gate. A small collegiate-type campus features low brick buildings, huge oak trees, well-trimmed lawns, and an abundance of flowers. It requires a close look to see the guards, the barbed wire, the towers, and the guns, and even closer scrutiny to see the ravaged lives of those who live there.

As we take a closer look at Cain's civilization, we see in Cain's activities the restlessness that characterizes someone on the run from God. Genesis 4:17 says Cain "was then building a city"; as the world's first real estate developer, his opportunities must have seemed limitless! Did he pore over topographical maps, make convincing presentations to the county commissioners, research the local zoning laws, walk off the land to determine the best building sites, meet with the architects, then supervise every phase of the actual construction? Once the streets were laid out and the sewer, water, and electrical lines connected, did he begin the construction of homes, offices, shopping centers, schools, hospitals, civic centers, and sports arenas? Was a church even built for those who wanted to worship God in their own way? Cain's civilization was characterized by booming construction.

In reality, while we can imagine all sorts of ways Cain would be involved today as a developer, a city in his day wouldn't have been much more than a few houses surrounded by a wall for defense against a common enemy. But it reveals Cain's need to stay busy as a cover-up for his own life that was in the shambles of destruction.

Everywhere I go in the world today, someone is building something! In Hong Kong, the shoreline has been extended so that buildings now stand on what used to be the harbor. The hotel in which I have stayed six or eight times used to be on the water's edge. But the last time I stayed there, the water could barely be seen from the highest floors because a high-rise hotel, shopping mall, and cultural center have been squeezed in front of it on newly deposited landfill.

When I was in Paris, the Champs Élysées was so torn up by construction "improvements" that pedestrians could not safely walk down the world-famous tree-lined boulevard. The sidewalk cafés had jackhammers for music instead of violins. Even the Louvre was partially closed off due to construction of a multilevel parking deck under the central plaza.

In London, Prince Charles has taken up the banner of outrage against out-of-control construction that shows no thought to the beauty of the historic old landmarks. And in Germany, road construction has backed up traffic for mile after frustrating mile on the autobahns.

Zermatt, Switzerland, is one of the most secluded, serene, and beautiful spots on planet Earth I have been privileged to visit. It boasts a picturesque alpine village nestled amongst chalets and cow pastures with a spectacular view of the Matterhorn. Two summers ago I revisited the little village with my daughters, excited to experience once again the beauty of creation in such a unique setting. We drove to a little village at the foot of the pass, then took a train that wound up through the mountains to Zermatt. What I had remembered as a train ride through alpine forests and farmland as scenic as a *National Geographic* tour was instead a firsthand look at Swiss construction and strip mining! The river that had tumbled down from the glaciers and snow-covered Alps had been dredged for miles, turning the water into gray sludge and the river banks into a scarred gravel pit.

Everywhere I go there is construction. My own city has been rated as one of the fifteen "boom towns" in the United States.

Roads,
airports,
streets,
shopping malls,
more shopping malls,

schools,

office complexes,

auditorium expansion,

civic center expansion,

a new sports arena—all are under construction!

Is the booming construction progress? Or is it a cover-up for the fact that, generally speaking, our lives are in rebellion against God? The majority of people in this world are living lives that are not right with God, and they get busier and busier, running faster and faster, without realizing they need to stop running and repent of their rebellion against Him.

Cain's civilization was marked not only by construction but by the corruption of moral values that would, in the end, provoke the judgment of God. Cain's son Enoch had a family: "To Enoch was born Irad, and Irad was the father of Mehujael, . . . the father of Methushael, . . . the father of Lamech. Lamech married two women, one named Adah and the other Zillah" (Gen. 4:18–19). Within a few generations, God's Word, which had clearly stated His principles for the bedrock of any society—marriage and the family—were not only ignored but seemed to be publicly flaunted by Lamech's taking of two wives (Gen. 4:23).

That disregard for God's principles continues to this day, when many couples live together outside of marriage,

> when one in every four marriages ends in divorce,
>
> when abortion is used as a form of birth control,
>
> when the gay rights lobby is one of the wealthiest and strongest
>  in Washington,
>
> when entertainers boast of their sexual conquests,
>
> when the blockbuster movies are those that portray explicit sex scenes,
>
> when sexual impropriety by top government officials is front-page news,
>
> when we march to claim our right to sin, flaunting it in the eyes of the world,

our days are numbered and our doom is sure.

Could it be, in the midst of all the moral corruption in modern society, that people are looking for the happiness, pleasure, and joy they lost when they rebelled against God, for whom they were created?

Cain's morally corrupt civilization was a time bomb ready to self-destruct. Interestingly, it was also very cultured. One of Cain's descendants, Jabal, "was the father of those who live in tents and raise livestock. His brother's name was Jubal;

he was the father of all who play the harp and flute. Zillah also had a son, Tubal-Cain, who forged all kinds of tools out of bronze and iron" (Gen. 4:20–22).

Cain's civilization found expression in music even as ours does today.

Symphonies,
　　　operas,
　　　　　rock concerts,
　　　　　　　choirs,
　　　　　　　　　orchestras,
　　　　　　　vocalists,
　　　　　recitals,
　　all on tapes
　　　and CDs
　　　　　and videos
　　　　　　　and MTV
　　　　　and radio,
　　listened to in live concert,
　　　　　on boom boxes,
　　　　　　　from headsets,
　　　　　in the car,
　　　while jogging . . .

From morning to night our civilization is polluted with noise! Could it be the noise is trying to drown out the sound of God's still, small voice calling us to get right with Him?

Just think of all
　　the bronze
　　　and iron
　　　　and silver
　　　　　and gold
　　　　　　and steel
　　　　　　　and plastic
　　　　　　　　and fiberglass
　　　　　　　　　and aluminum . . .

out of which we forge
　cars
　　and trucks

99

and planes
and ships
and trains
and art sculptures
and skyscrapers
and computers
and bridges.

Could it be that our preoccupation with education and technology and science is a cover-up for our lack of wisdom because we have lost our fear and reverence of God?

Cain's civilization was characterized by construction, corruption, culture, and, not surprisingly, crime. Lamech boasted, "I have killed a man for wounding me, a young man for injuring me" (Gen. 4:23). How could the people in Cain's civilization know anything of compassion when they had separated themselves from the One who is love?[23] How could they extend forgiveness to someone who had injured them when they themselves had not experienced forgiveness? If Lamech was a typical representative of his day, and the record indicates he was, the entire population was selfish, thoughtless, rude, cruel, vengeful, sadistic, unforgiving, and with a totally arrogant attitude toward the Creator that was expressed in Lamech's defiant boasting, "If Cain is avenged seven times, then Lamech seventy-seven times" (Gen. 4:24). It was as though Lamech, a mere dust person, shook his little dust fist in the face of God and said, "God, I don't need You in my life. I can take care of myself. Just see how well I can get along without You."

Our nation is like Lamech. We don't want God or His name mentioned at school, in the workplace, in government, or in society circles. With our advances in technology and science and knowledge in every area, we have become our own gods, defying Someone who would threaten the high esteem in which we hold ourselves. Those who seek to live according to the Manufacturer's directions are told by the majority that they are offensive, exclusive, narrow-minded, intolerant, and divisive.

In September 1996, Hurricane Fran hit our state's coast and then moved inland. When the storm struck our city, 120 miles from the ocean, it still packed hurricane-force winds. Fran left us with more than a billion dollars' worth of damage, thirty thousand homes devastated or destroyed, a thousand miles of downed telephone cables, and one and a half million homeowners without power. As I was talking with a friend about her home, which is directly on the coast, she said the downstairs level was untouched while the second floor was flooded, with windows blown out and water and sand inside. The experts who examined it have concluded that a sixteen-foot ocean wave actually went over her home!

Our nation has watched, horror-struck, as a crime wave has rolled over our society. Drive-by shootings, date rape, serial killings, thefts, carjackings, and kidnappings make the gun battles of the old "Wild West" look quaint and almost preferable to the sophisticated mayhem of today. Yet society seems to flaunt its sadistic violence,

> applauding Jack Kevorkian, the "Doctor of Death," as an angel of mercy,
> cheering when an accused wife abuser mocks the law,
> burning churches in which African Americans worship,
> insisting on a woman's right to destroy the next generation,
> emulating the lifestyle of those who live rudely, selfishly, immorally,

and the list goes on . . .

The blame is placed on

> easy-to-get illicit drugs,
> > alcohol,
> > > poverty,
> > > > lack of education,
> > > > > the Democrats,
> > > > > > the Republicans,
> > > > > > > or politics in general

when the primary reason is that those in our society, like in Cain's civilization, are operating without the Manufacturer's directions. In fact, they don't even acknowledge there is a Manufacturer but have convinced themselves they have simply evolved, with no purpose or reason for being and no accountability at the end.

Cain's civilization provoked the judgment of God and was washed away in the Flood. All the culture and construction, all the plans and progress, had no value in God's sight. He did not even record the years of their lives. It had no lasting, eternal value at all except as a warning to you and me.

Cain's bitterness that was rooted in resentment toward grievances, God, guilt, and good grew into a rebellion that resisted confession, refused correction, rejected communion, and in the end, ravaged the civilization of his day. It rose up and defiled not just his entire life but the lives of his children and grandchildren and great-grandchildren. In fact it defiled his entire world. When he was an old man, dying without peace and love and hope and happiness—without God—did he wonder, *Was it worth it?*

☙

THE INSTRUCTION is plainly given: "See to it . . . that no bitter root grows up to cause trouble and defile many."[24] We "see to it" by confessing the rebellion and resentment that has caused it, asking God for cleansing.

The way to uproot bitterness was discovered by the minority of those living in Cain's civilization: "At that time men began to call on the name of the LORD" (Gen. 4:26).

Jesus gave a powerful illustration of this when He told the story of a young man, very much like Cain, who was also reared in a good home. He, too, decided to go out from the presence of his father to enjoy all that the civilization of his day had to offer. He lived totally for pleasure and popularity—for himself. When he became sick of himself, his wasted life, his resentment and rebellion, he decided to go back to his father and confess, "Father, I have sinned against heaven and against you. I am no longer worthy to be called your son. Make me like one of your hired men."

So the young man returned to his father, but while he was still a long way off, his father, who had obviously been waiting for him, saw him, and was filled with compassion for him. He ran to meet his son, threw his arms around him, and kissed him. And the son said, "Father, I have sinned against heaven and against you. I am no longer worthy to be called your son."

But the father said to his servants, "Quick! Bring the best robe and put it on him. Put a ring on his finger and sandals on his feet. Bring the fattened calf and kill it. Let's have a feast and celebrate. For this son of mine was dead and is alive again; he was lost and is found." And so they celebrated.[25]

Your heavenly Father has been waiting for you to come home to Him, waiting for you to confess your sin of resentment and rebellion, waiting to celebrate the joy and love and pleasure He wants you to have in relationship with Him. Don't make excuses; don't rationalize your bitterness. Go to God; ask Him to cleanse you of your sin. Ask Him to uproot your bitterness. Invite Him into your life to take control of everything, including past memories of abandonment or abuse or adultery, present circumstances of injury or injustice, and future dreams and disappointments.

Follow the example of the psalmist, who wrote, "Then I acknowledged my sin to you and did not cover up my iniquity. I said, 'I will confess my transgression to the Lord'—and you forgave the guilt of my sin."[26]

"Blessed is he whose transgression is forgiven, whose sin is covered."[27]

Wouldn't you rather be blessed than bitter?

# 5

I AM THE GOD OF COMPASSION

*I Redeem Your Wastedness*

GENESIS 5

When my children were younger, my husband took them each weekend to various University of North Carolina sporting events. The kids were fascinated, not only because they, like my husband, are quite athletic, but because of the thrill of watching skilled athletes and outstanding teams compete.

One of the most exciting events they watched was the one-mile relay race, in which four runners compete as a team. As a relay race begins, the first runner from each team crouches at the starting block, gripping the baton in his hand. When the signal to begin is given, the runner explodes out of the starting blocks and runs the first quarter-mile as swiftly as he can. As he completes the lap around the track, he is met by the second runner on his team. In full stride, the first runner shifts the baton to his right hand, stretches out his arm, and as his teammate starts running full speed alongside of him, he passes the baton into the outstretched hand of the second runner. The second runner then runs his quarter-mile lap and passes the baton to the number three runner, who takes it in full stride, and so on until the fourth runner crosses the finish line, tightly clutching the all-important baton.

Winning a relay race depends not only on the speed of the runners but also on their skillful ability to transfer the baton. If the baton is dropped, precious seconds are wasted, and the race may be lost. If the runner fails to pass the baton, he is disqualified from the race altogether.

In the race of life, the "baton" is the truth that leads to personal faith in God. Each generation receives the "baton" from the previous generation, runs the race to the best of its ability, then passes the "baton" smoothly and securely to the next generation.

The genealogy in Genesis 5 reminds me of a relay race. Each of the ten gener-ations is represented by an individual who is named. These ten men lived in the midst of Cain's civilization, which was as progressive and sophisticated as any our planet has ever known. In fact, the *Wall Street Journal* once made the fascinating suggestion that Cain's civilization could have been the long-lost golden age of Atlantis![1]

Yet it was Cain's civilization that was so wicked and rebellious against God that it provoked His judgment, resulting in the Flood. And despite its supposed great-ness, this civilization was ultimately so meaningless the only record we have of it is in the Bible.

Any knowledge,
> any culture,
>> any science,
>>> any technology,
>>>> any development
>>>> any society,
>>>>> any art,
>>>>>> any literature,
>>>>>>> any family legacy
>>>>>>>> has been washed away.

In contrast to the surrounding members of this society, the ten men listed in Genesis 5 stood out like giants in the midst of spiritual dwarfs:

In the midst of ungodliness, they were godly.

In the midst of wickedness, they were good.

In the midst of rebellion, they were righteous.

In the midst of bitterness, they were blessed.

In the midst of those running from God, they walked with God.

In the midst of a wasted world, they lived lives that were worthy of eternal honor.

They were like a ten-man relay team. From those who had preceded them, they received the baton of truth, which leads to faith in God. They ran their own race with diligence and perseverance, then they relayed the truth to the next generation.

Our civilization today is even more progressive and sophisticated than that of Cain's day. New discoveries are occurring in science and technology at such a rapid pace that today's breakthrough quickly makes yesterday's obsolete. We have flashed from slide rules to calculators to computers to cyberspace so fast that the average person has yet to learn how to even access such technology, much less use it. Every day we see advances bringing better health care, longer life spans, and ever-expanding knowledge. We have the capacity to ensure everyone has a meal on the table, a car in the garage, a microwave in the kitchen, a PC in the office, and a TV in the den. And many of us have leisure time to develop our interests in art, music, and literature.

But underneath all the progress and sophistication, our civilization is experiencing a bankruptcy of moral and spiritual values that threatens to erode our very existence. Our society is just as wicked and rebellious against God as Cain's civilization was.

The flashing-red-light warning for you and me is to beware getting so caught up in the way everyone around us is living that we get swept away by the current of wickedness and waste our own lives in a meaningless existence. In the midst of spiritual dwarfs, we must strive to be giants by receiving, running with, and relaying the baton of truth that leads to personal faith in God that has been handed down to generation after generation since Creation.

## FAITH IN GOD WAS RECEIVED FACE-TO-FACE

Adam and Eve received personal faith in God through a face-to-face relationship.

They knew what it was to talk with God.

They knew how attentively He listened to them.

They knew the expressions on His face.

They knew the sound of His voice.

They knew the light that glowed in His eyes when He saw them.

They knew the touch of His hand.

They knew what it was to walk with Him in the cool of the day.

They knew the power of His presence as they worked side by side.

Adam and Eve had an intimate, personal, loving relationship with their Creator—in the beginning. And even after being banished from the garden of Eden, they clutched the baton they had received from Him face-to-face. That baton, which has been passed down through the centuries, is available to anyone who is a physical descendant of Adam and Eve—and that's all of us human beings on the face of the earth!

*Our Physical Descent from Adam*

Who were your parents? How would you describe your mother and father? Which of their physical characteristics do you share? Do you have the same hair or eye color? Do you have the same laugh or sense of humor? Do you have something of their shy or outgoing temperament? Do you have their shared ability in cooking or counseling? In athletics or accounting? In sewing or selling?

Each of us has inherited certain characteristics from our parents. I inherited my mother's love of cooking and reading, her strong will and sensitivity, and the texture of her hair. I inherited my father's love of sunshine, his enjoyment of animals, a tendency to worry, a zeal in service—and his long legs.

You and I also have inherited many things from our first parents, although those characteristics may not include Eve's natural beauty, Adam's perfect physique, their love for the outdoors, or their fascination with fruit! I'm sure I didn't inherit Eve's poise that let her keep her composure when the snake slithered up to her and started speaking! But we did inherit something very significant. As members of the human race, each of us inherited from Adam and Eve a sinful nature that results in death.

The historical accounts of all but two of the men whose names are recorded in Genesis 5 ends with the phrase "then he died." It is the only genealogy in the entire Bible in which you can hear the drumbeat of death: "Adam lived 930 years, and then he died. . . . Seth lived 912 years, and then he died. . . . Enosh lived 905 years, and then he died. . . . Kenan lived 910 years, and then he died. . . . Mahalalel lived 895 years, and then he died. . . . Jared lived 962 years, and then he died. . . . Methuselah lived 969 years, and then he died. . . . Lamech lived 777 years, and then he died" (Gen. 5:5–31). It reads like a funeral dirge.

Why is that phrase included again and again? Perhaps it's to emphasize an important truth. God had told Adam and Eve if they ate of the tree of the knowledge of good and evil, they would surely die (Gen. 2:17). The Serpent had contradicted God's Word when he stated emphatically to Eve, "You will not surely die" (Gen. 3:4). The drumbeat of death underscores the truth of God's Word: "The wages of sin is death."[2]

John Horgan, senior writer for *Scientific American*, has been quoted as saying, "Science . . . has given us vaccines and birth-control pills and jets and laptop computers. But we still cannot comprehend ourselves. We still get cancer and become depressed. We still grow old and die. Far from becoming God-like, we are as mortal as ever."[3]

When have you heard the drumbeat of death? Have you recently been to a funeral? Has your eye been caught by the name of a friend in the newspaper obituaries? Regardless of how productive life has been, in the end it is meaningless as it returns to the dust from which it came, just as God said it would. Every time you and I hear the drumbeat of death, we should be reminded that what God says is so.

But the drumbeat of death is muffled by the even louder roll call of life. While the phrase, "and then he died" is repeated eight times, the phrase "and he lived" is repeated seventeen times![4] God, in His grace and mercy, has said, "The wages of sin is death, but the gift of God is eternal life."

When have you heard the roll call of life? Do you know of someone who recently gave birth to a baby? Have you just celebrated the birthday of a loved one? Such milestones should remind us of God's grace. The only reason we live is because He says so! Our lives are like the morning mist, like a vapor, so temporary that everything is meaningless apart from the eternal value God can give it.[5]

Life and death are constant reminders that we have descended from Adam and Eve physically. But there are also reminders that we have a spiritual heritage from them as well.

*Our Spiritual Descent from Adam*

Just as certain physical characteristics are passed from one generation to another, so truth that leads to faith in God is passed from one generation to another. This is subtly revealed by the fact that Adam's life is not recorded in the genealogy of his firstborn, Cain, but in the genealogy of his third son, Seth. It was Seth's descendants who relayed faith in God while Cain's descendants rebelled against Him and therefore wasted their lives. The list of men in Genesis 5 is not only a list of physical descendants of Adam but of spiritual descendants whose lives, even though they ended in death, were not wasted from God's perspective.

The list of spiritual descendants continues to be kept by God today.[6] John the apostle explained the reason for the heavenly bookkeeping when he described what he saw take place at the end of time: "Then I saw a great white throne and him who was seated on it. Earth and sky fled from his presence, and there was no place for them. And I saw the dead, great and small, standing before the throne, and books were opened. Another book was opened, which is the book of life. The dead were judged according to what they had done as recorded in the books. . . . If anyone's name was not found written in the book of life, he was thrown into the lake of fire."[7] The Book of Life is the "genealogy," or registration, of the righteous remnant of people who, throughout human history, have placed their faith in God; a name listed in this book is the final proof of a life that has counted.

Are you a spiritual descendent of Adam as well as a physical descendant? If the books were opened today, would your name be found there? How does one register in the Lamb's Book of Life? Is registration based on water baptism? Church membership? Confirmation classes? Holy Communion? Good works?

Registration in the Lamb's Book of Life is similar to registration for marriage. With two daughters engaged this year, I well remember the thrill and excitement of the first love I experienced thirty-one years ago with their father. When he proposed to me rather shyly in the living room of my parents' home, I couldn't say yes fast enough! But his proposal and my acceptance didn't register me as his wife. Then he gave me what I thought was the most spectacular ring I had ever laid eyes on; he slipped it on my finger with the promise of a lifetime commitment. But that beautiful ring didn't register me as his wife, either. After several months of being engaged, we selected the day we would be married, I bought a wedding gown, and my parents sent out hundreds of wedding invitations, but I still was not registered as his wife.

Finally, the wedding day dawned. I dressed in my bridal gown, put on my wedding veil, and accompanied by friends as witnesses, walked down the aisle of the chapel, took Danny Lotz by the arm, looked up into his adoring eyes . . . but I still was not registered as his wife!

The only way I could be registered as Mrs. Danny Lotz was to say my vows of commitment to him. In the eyes of those present, in the eyes of the state, and in the eyes of God, I vowed to surrender my life and join myself to him. He, in turn, vowed to commit himself to me. At that point we were married, and my father, who was the attending preacher, pronounced us man and wife. Then we each signed a certificate that recorded us officially as being married.

You and I are registered in the Lamb's Book of Life when we "marry" the Lord Jesus Christ[8] by coming to the marriage altar of the cross, renouncing our old lives of being single and self-centered, and vow to love, honor, and obey Him as long as we live.[9] At that moment, the heavenly Father pronounces you to be the bride of His Son and registers your name in the Book of Life. That registration validates you as an authentic child of God, a member of the righteous remnant whose life will count for eternity.

If the genealogy in Genesis 5 continued all the way through the Old and New Testaments up until the present time, would your name be in it? When did you deliberately, with your adult conscious mind, say your vows of commitment to Jesus Christ, accepting His invitation to be your Lord and Savior?

If you have been validated as an authentic child of God, your life has great meaning and value in His sight. Age is not mentioned in the list of Cain's descendants while in Adam's genealogy the years of each man's life are carefully recorded. God lovingly counts the years of those in the righteous remnant, because they glorify Him as evidence that His plan of redemption has been worth it and therefore have eternal meaning.

Our life's meaning is partially fulfilled when we pass the baton of faith to someone else. Nineteen times in Adam's genealogy the phrase "he became the father of," or "and he begat" (KJV) is repeated. While this phrase refers to passing down physical life to the next generation, it also implies that faith in God was passed on since each man listed was considered part of the godly minority who lived in the midst of Cain's civilization.

From whom did you receive the truth that led to your faith in God? Regardless of the specific person or means that passed it to you, it originally came to you from Adam and Eve, who had seen God and talked to God and heard God speak and felt God's touch and been in God's presence. Their faith was based on sight, face-to-face, then relayed through the generations.

### Faith in God Was Relayed Faith to Faith

Following their sin of disobedience and banishment from the garden, Adam and Eve were restored in their relationship to their Creator through sacrifice (Gen. 3:21, 4:3–7). Having experienced the freedom of living in God's presence twenty-four hours a day, what would it then have been like to have to approach Him only at a designated place through a designated sacrifice? What would it have been like to wake up every morning, work throughout every new day, and go to bed at night constantly aware of a great gulf fixed between you and the One for whom you had been created? A gulf that could only be spanned by carrying a bleating lamb to an altar of stone, slitting its throat with a knife, spilling its blood over the wood piled high on top of the altar? And how did that give Adam and Eve an assurance of God's forgiveness and blessing? Did He send fire down to consume the sacrifice so they would know it had been accepted?[10] Did He suddenly appear to speak with them?

After years of approaching God through His prescribed sacrificial system, the people knew the rivers of blood shed at the altar did not take away their sin. The sacrifices simply served as a wretched reminder of their sin and pointed them to the necessity of a Lamb yet to come who would fulfill all the symbolic sacrifices, forgive them of their sin, and save them from God's wrath for sin through His own sacrificial death.[11]

While Adam and Eve understood by firsthand experience the destructive power of sin and its penalty, they did not know the details of exactly why the sacrifices were necessary to atone for their sin. We assume they just knew God had given the instructions to them, and they obeyed. The system worked as the only way to God. And so they were the first of hundreds and thousands and millions of people who followed to walk by faith. Their faith in God, which had been received face-to-face, was relayed to their children and grandchildren, great-grandchildren and great-great-grandchildren from generation to generation, faith to faith. And the relay began as they passed the baton to their second son, Abel, whose life was a powerful witness.

*Through Witnessing of God*

There is no record of Abel teaching or preaching to anyone else. Instead, he seemed to have a silent witness of living a righteous life that was different.

What caused Abel to choose to be a righteous man?[12] I wonder if it was the positive example of his own father within the home. Was it Adam's absolute confidence in the reality of God that impacted his son? Surely, although he was now separated from Him, Adam would never forget the touch of God's hand, the sound of God's voice, the expressions on God's face, the authority of God's Word. His faith in who God is and what God said would have been unshakable because He knew God firsthand, for himself.

The baton of truth was relayed to me by that same positive example within the home. My parents were so confident in who God is and what God has said through His Word that it genuinely never crossed my mind, nor to my knowledge the minds of my siblings, to doubt God! When I was a child, I told my mother I wanted to know God personally for myself, and she lovingly gave me the instructions about how to approach Him. So I followed her instructions and went to the designated place at Calvary, to an altar of wood called the cross, and took my sacrificial Lamb. The knife of my sin and guilt was responsible for His death, and His shed blood

111

made atonement for me. When I walked away from that altar, not only was I reminded of my sinful condition; I had the deep peace and assurance that my sins were forgiven and I was no longer separated from God but accepted by Him, because my sacrifice was the Lamb of God who is my Creator who became my Savior!

Who has impressed you with the confidence of his or her faith in God? Are you acquainted with someone who knows God is real? What a blessing to have parents who are people of confident faith. What a blessing to be a parent with confident faith like that!

Whether or not it was Adam's example that inspired Abel to lead a righteous life, we know Abel made his own decision to live in contrast to the rest of the world of his day, a fact that was evidenced by the sacrifice he brought to God (Gen. 4:3–4). His action of bringing a blood sacrifice when others gave God whatever they felt like giving revealed a submissive attitude toward God's Word. And his attitude toward the grievances in his life, when others reacted with anger and bitterness, revealed a sweet acceptance of God's will, even when it included hardship and suffering. While everyone around him rebelled against God, Abel turned to Him. As a result, his life was different from Cain's life and the civilization that followed.

Jesus described the powerful witness of a life that is different when He illustrated it as "the light of the world."[13] The primary value of light is that it is so different from the darkness. And Jesus described a powerful witness as being like "the salt of the earth."[14] The primary value of salt is that it is so different from anything it is placed on. When Jesus then informed His disciples, "you will be my witnesses,"[15] it was clear that one primary value of the apostles' witness would lie in the difference of their lives from those who lived around them.

How much of a contrast is there between your life and the life of your neighbor who doesn't know God? Are you so afraid of offending those around you that your salt has lost its savor, your light is hidden under a bushel, and you are basically denying who you are? One impact of our fears is that they greatly affect our children in the next generation. For example, some parents are so afraid their children will not be popular at school if they are different that the parents encourage them to be like everyone else—doing the same things, dressing and talking the same way, seeing the same movies and television shows, reading the same magazines and books, belonging to the same clubs, and going to the same places.

A witness that is lived can be as powerful as one that is spoken. It's not what you say but who you are that catches the attention of those around you—which is one reason God allows grievances, crises, sufferings, injustice, and hardship to come into our lives. Because problems offer us the opportunity to give silent, relevant witness to the difference faith in God can make.[16] The problems enable us to become a showcase so that the world can look into our lives and see the glory of God revealed.

Abel's choice to let his "light shine" in the darkness—his choice to live a life that was different from those around him because he lived by faith in God—was a silent witness that effectively relayed the baton to the next generation.

Although to our knowledge Abel never married or had children, he did have a younger brother born to Adam and Eve after he was murdered. When the younger brother was born, Adam and Eve named him Seth, signifying "God has granted me another child in place of Abel, since Cain killed him" (Gen. 4:25).[17] Surely, as little Seth grew up, he was told about his two older brothers, the lives they had lived and the choices they had made. As a result, the witness of the difference in Abel's life impacted others even after his death—not only Seth but a multitude who would follow. It was for this silent witness that the writer to the Hebrews singled out Abel for commendation, saying, "By faith Abel offered a better sacrifice than Cain did. By faith he was commended as a righteous man, when God spoke well of his offerings. And by faith he still speaks, even though he is dead."[18] Abel's life, although brief, was not wasted because of his faith in God, expressed through his witness.

Have you ever wondered what people will think of you when you're gone? What will your grandchildren know about you? Will your great-grandchildren even know your name? And if they do, what will they be told about you? Wouldn't it be wonderful, if, like Abel, you are remembered throughout all the generations to follow as one who lived by faith in God?

Abel passed the baton of truth that leads to faith to the next generation, which was represented by his little brother, Seth. If you are single or childless, you are not exempt from the privilege as well as the responsibility of relaying the baton. While unable to relay it to your own children, you can relay it to someone else's—your siblings, your siblings' children, your neighbors' children, your friends' children. The possibilities are limitless.

Seth received the baton of faith and relayed it to his son Enosh, who is remembered primarily for the expression of his faith through worship.

*Relayed through Worshiping God*

To worship God means to attribute worth to God through obedience to God, pre-occupation with God, and praise of God. The Samaritan woman at the well in Sychar said, in essence, "Oh, well, I worship God." And Jesus corrected her, "You Samaritans worship what you do not know." Why was her worship invalid? Because she was substituting the traditions and rituals of her religion for a personal relationship with God through faith. So Jesus explained, "God is spirit, and his worshipers must worship in spirit and in truth."[19]

What does it mean to worship "in spirit and in truth"? To worship God in spirit means to worship Him in deepest sincerity from the heart as one who is indwelled by the Spirit of God. To worship Him in truth means to worship Him honestly, without hypocrisy, through faith in His Word, both living, which is Jesus, and written, which is the Bible.

It was after Enosh was born that "men began to call on the name of the LORD" (Gen. 4:26). Although the Bible doesn't clearly state that Enosh was responsible for the return to worship, let's assume he was.

What could have motivated Enosh to worship God? I wonder if it was the negative example of his uncle Cain, who would still have been alive in Enosh's lifetime. Did Enosh see the misery of his uncle who lived with a guilty conscience? Did he see the bitterness that had taken root in resentment then blossomed into full-blown rebellion against God, destroying everything in society that was noble and kind and decent and good?

Has someone served as a negative example for you? Do you have an "Uncle Cain"? Someone who has rebelled against God and is living an interesting life but has no real peace or joy or fulfillment or lasting satisfaction? Such an example can be a powerful motivation to get your own house in order by giving real worship of God priority in your life.

While Cain set a negative example for Enosh, Enosh's father, Seth, set a positive one. But God has no grandchildren! While Enosh could inherit a godly heritage from Seth, he could not inherit a personal, right relationship with God. That had to be his own choice. And living in the midst of Cain's civilization, Enosh made that choice. When he did, others followed his lead. I wonder if they worshiped individually or joined Enosh in corporate worship.[20]

Surrounded by a rebellious civilization, the implication is that a small group of men separated from the crowd, following Enosh's example. They must have drawn strength and encouragement from each other. They must have been renewed in their commitment to live by faith in God every time they met. They must have known they needed each other if they were to live lives that were pleasing to God in the midst of such godlessness. They worshiped God together.

Many people are sporadic in their corporate worship because they say they don't see the need for it. That reasoning is similar to the young man who grew up in a church under the leadership of a pastor whom he loved and respected as a man of God. The young man went off to college, and when he returned home for Christmas after the first semester, he went by to see his beloved old pastor. He visited the old man in his book-lined study, with a fire blazing on the hearth. During the course of the conversation, the old pastor looked intently at the young man and asked, "Where do you go to church?"

The young man replied that he found college life much too demanding to be able to take time out to go to church on Sunday. Besides, he had many new friends who didn't go to church, and he didn't really feel the need to go, either.

The old pastor leaned down to stir the fire in the fireplace, then took one of the blazing logs from the fire and put it on the hearth. He gazed at the log so long the young man thought he had either forgotten he was there or had slipped into a nap. So the boy cleared his throat and began to rise from his chair. The old pastor quickly turned his head with an understanding smile and looked at him from underneath his bushy, white eyebrows. With his hands folded on the top of his cane, he leaned over and gently inquired, "Did you think I was dozing? I was just watching that log. Did you notice? It was blazing when it was with the other logs in the fire. But when I removed it and placed it on the hearth, the fire began to go out. Now it's cold." Then he proceeded to instruct the young man on the necessity of corporate worship and fellowship with others on a regular basis if he wanted to maintain the fire of his faith in God.

You and I do need to be involved in regular corporate worship of God. Living in the midst of a wicked, godless, rebellious, hostile civilization, we must—it is not an option, we must—worship God with those who also worship in Spirit and in truth if we want to maintain:

the fire of our faith,
the strength of our commitment,
the zeal of our love,
the faithfulness in our service,

> the consistency of our obedience,
>
> the depth of our surrender.

However and whatever God actually used to motivate Enosh to worship, Enosh did make that choice. His life was not meaningless. He received the baton of faith, expressed it during his lifetime through worship of God, then relayed it to his son Kenan, who received and relayed it to his son Mahalalel, who received and relayed it to his son Jared, who received and relayed it to his son Enoch, who went one step further in expressing his faith.

*Relayed through Walking with God*

Enoch made the choice to walk with God when he was suddenly confronted with the awesome responsibility of parenting a baby: "After he became the father of Methuselah, Enoch walked with God" (Gen. 5:22). The challenge of being a godly parent and seeking to raise a godly son in the midst of Cain's civilization must have been overwhelming to Enoch.

When have you been confronted with more responsibility than you could handle? Have you suddenly been confronted with the responsibility of supporting yourself and your family because of a death or divorce? Have you just been fired from your job and have no reserve resources to carry you over to the next one? Has your unmarried teenager told you she is pregnant, wants to keep the baby, and asked you to help care for it? Have you been confronted with the needs of elderly parents who can no longer take care of themselves? Have several staff members quit at the same time, leaving a mountain of work in your office, with no one to do it?

As Enoch held his firstborn baby in his arms and looked at those chubby, flushed cheeks and rosebud mouth and curling eyelashes and little fist wrapped tightly around his finger, he must have been overcome with an intense awareness that it was his responsibility to care for this child's physical, emotional, and spiritual well-being. So Enoch began walking with God. Spending time with God. Talking with God and listening to God and learning from God and depending upon God.

And Enoch kept on walking with God every day, one day at a time, 365 days a year, for 300 years! What a walk!

Every morning that I'm home, weather permitting, I walk with two friends for two and a half miles. We have to abide by two basic rules when we walk, or we can't

116

walk together. The first rule is that we must walk at the same pace. The second rule is that we must walk in the same direction. The same two rules apply when walking with God.

To walk with God, Enoch had to walk at the same pace, which meant a moment-by-moment obedience to God's Word. Disobedience, neglect, or ignorance of God's Word would cause him to get out of step. And he had to walk in the same direction God was walking, which would have meant a moment-by-moment surrender to God's will. He couldn't go off in a direction of his own. He had to stop insisting on his own way, or he would find himself on a different path from the one God was on. And Enoch must have discovered God doesn't adjust His pace or direction for anyone. Enoch had to adjust his pace and direction to God's if he wanted to walk with Him.

What adjustments do you need to make so you can walk with God? Adjustments in your daily and weekly schedule? Adjustments in your attitude and ambition? Adjustments in your personal habits of prayer and Bible reading? You and I cannot walk with God if we don't know what His pace is or the direction in which He is going. And the only way we can know His pace and direction is to prayerfully read His Word.

Are you too busy to make time for prayer and Bible reading on a daily basis? Jude tells us that Enoch had something of a full-time lay ministry; he was a preacher.[21] Not only that, Methuselah was the first of "other sons and daughters" born to him (Gen. 5:22), which meant he had many responsibilities in the home. In addition, he must have had a full-time job so he could provide for his family. Surely Enoch knew what it was to be stressed-out, yet he still made time every day to walk with God, one step at a time.

I wonder what Enoch and God talked about as they walked together each day. Perhaps Enoch commented on the beauty of the sunrise that morning and how much he had enjoyed listening to the sound of the birds calling to each other as they awakened before dawn. Or perhaps he told God how grateful he was for the evidence of His faithfulness when he saw the sun come up every morning. He may have spoken in awe of God's power as he observed the rivers rushing out of Eden, flowing into the wilderness.

Did he thank God for meeting him each day so they could walk together? Did he talk to God about his children's friends and the peer pressure they were being subjected to at school? Did he ask God to prepare other godly young people who would not only be friends to his children but one day to their spouses as well? Did he ask for wisdom to know how to steer them into the right youth groups that would encourage them in their faith? Did he express heartfelt concern for the spiritually lost members of his family? Did he ask God to enable him to pass the baton smoothly and safely to the next generation? And did he ask God to increase his wife's love for him, and his for her, that their marriage might be the standard that would determine their children's marriage standards? Did he ask God to give him opportunities to witness to those in Cain's civilization who lived in rebellion against God? Did he tell God how much he loved Him and needed Him for everything?

What did Enoch and God talk about as they walked every day for three hundred years?

Think of the blessing those walks were to God! Since Adam and Eve had been banished from the garden of Eden, God must have longed for the human companionship He had created man to share with Him. How empty the garden must have seemed when He walked there in the cool of the day. There were no happy voices calling to Him, no "children" to instruct in the ways of the animals, no one to impart His wisdom to, no one to share the specially prepared garden home with, no one who would know Him.

What was different about Enoch, not just different from the world around him but also different from Abel and Seth and Enosh before him? Maybe it was just that he had a heart for God Himself. Maybe God had found someone who loved Him with all of his heart, soul, mind, and strength.[22]

Whatever the reasons, we know Enoch walked with God until increasingly he became aware of God's presence and love in his life. As he walked with God on a daily basis, he didn't grow weary of walking. It was never drudgery to meet with God. It wasn't something he felt he had to do; it was something he wanted to do. In the process, he must have grown in an ever more intimate, loving, personal knowledge of who God is. He gave God his undivided attention, spent more and more time with Him, gained a greater and greater depth of understanding, allowed fewer and fewer interruptions until there were no interruptions at all and his walk of faith became sight! "Enoch walked with God; then he was no more, because God took him away" (Gen. 5:24).

Enoch's friends looked for him, but "he could not be found, because God had taken him away" to be with Himself![23] Enoch's life wasn't wasted; it was wanted by God Himself!

What is keeping you from taking a "walk" with God?

Enoch received the baton of faith, grasped it firmly in hand as he walked with God, then relayed the baton to his son Methuselah, who received and relayed it to his son Lamech, who received and relayed it to his son Noah. Noah received the baton and, praise God, he worked to express his faith in God. He built an ark.

*Relayed through Working for God*

Have you ever stopped to think what would have happened had Noah been too busy to work for God? Or too tired? Or too apathetic? Without his work, you and I wouldn't be here today! His work for God is of legendary proportions. Even those unfamiliar with the rest of the Bible are familiar with Noah and his work.

What motivated Noah to work for God? I wonder if it was his father's prayers. When Noah was born, Lamech prayed that his son would "comfort us in the labor and painful toil of our hands caused by the ground the LORD has cursed" (Gen. 5:29).

Lamech must have been a man of prayer. I wonder if he prayed that his son would receive and relay the baton of faith. I wonder if he prayed that his son would be different from the wicked world around him, that he would lead others to live lives that were different also—the difference of a righteous, blameless life. Did Lamech increasingly have the impression that the world was becoming so wicked that God would have to intervene? And that God's intervention would occur in the lifetime of his son, who would be used by God as a comfort in some way during the time of judgment? Lamech prayed for his son—that his life would not be wasted, but that it would count for God.

A few years after I was married, my husband and I wanted to have children. After months of trying to get pregnant, I wasn't. None of the standard medical procedures was effective. After a year and a half, I ceased the medical treatments and instead set aside one day a week to fast and to pray for a child. I studied women in the Bible who had also struggled with infertility—Sarah, Rebekah, Rachel, Hannah, and Elizabeth—as well as the children they eventually conceived.

A year later I was praying and fasting when the Lord seemed to impress on my heart that He was going to give me a son. That day I stopped praying and fasting and began to thank the Lord. The next month I found out I was pregnant. And sure enough, I gave birth to a boy! That baby boy, Jonathan, is now twenty-seven years old, six feet ten inches tall, and in full-time Christian ministry. Many of the prayers I prayed the year before he was conceived are being answered today.

As Jonathan and his sisters were growing up, rather than pressuring them to be first in their class, to make the "right" socially acceptable friends, to choose a "respectable" career, to acquire certain material things that would reflect my status as a parent, I just wanted them to find God's will for their lives and live in the center of it. My prayer for them was not only that they be Christians but that they would be Christian leaders, bringing others to faith in Christ. Those are the same prayers I have for them today.

When have you prayed for your children? If you are not praying for your children, who is? If you have not been praying for your children, start praying for them today!

What do you pray for your children? Do you want them to be healthy, happy, prosperous, problem free only? Do you pray that they will be wealthy, successful, famous, educated only? Do you think it's possible for your children to live up to your expectations and still lead a wasted, meaningless life? Without prayer, how will you know whether or not your expectations for your children are in line with God's will?

> As you and I prayerfully seek to teach our children God's Word and
>    the necessity of obedience to it,
> as we encourage them to love the Lord their God wholeheartedly,
> as we instruct them to put God first in their time and tithe,
> as we help them establish godly priorities and practices,
> as we help them develop Christian relationships and responsibilities,

God willing, He will raise up some Noahs from among them.

Lamech's prayers seemed to motivate Noah to work for God when no one else did. In fact, he worked for God when everyone must have thought he was crazy for doing so.

As the last man listed in this relay of faith, Noah could have said, "Well, look at who my father is—that great prayer warrior, Lamech. And look at who my grandfather is—Methuselah, who lived longer than anyone in history. And look at who my great-grandfather is—Enoch, who was so spiritual he just disappeared right into heaven. Work for God? I don't think so. I can coast along on my family identity. I don't need to work for God." With an attitude of overconfidence like that, Noah would never have built the ark! His life would have been wasted.

On the other hand, Noah could have said, "I can never work for God because I can't be the prayer warrior my father Lamech was. And I'll never live as long as Methuselah did. I'm much too practical to be as spiritual as Enoch was. I can't work for God because I can't serve Him in the way others have." That attitude of feeling overwhelmed by other servants of God wouldn't have built the ark either, and he would have risked living a wasted life.

Are you either overwhelmed or overconfident when confronted with God's work because you are comparing yourself to His other workers? Someone once asked my younger sister what character in the Bible she identified with the most, and she said, "Andrew." When asked to explain, she said, "Because Andrew was always known as Peter's brother. He was always known for his identity with someone else."

Then she was asked, "Does it bother you to always be identified with someone else?"

"No, because Andrew used that identity to bring people to Jesus," she replied.

Noah seemed to draw motivation and inspiration from his identity with his ancestors, those great men of God. As a result, he was obedient to God's unique call to work, and life on this planet was preserved.

Who will be saved because of your work for God? What excuse do you have for not working for God? Do you say you can't work for Him because you can't work the way your mother or your father did? I understand that kind of intimidation, I assure you! But God doesn't accept it as an excuse. Do you say you don't have to work for God because your spouse is working for Him? God didn't accept that excuse when I gave it to Him, either. Do you say you will work for Him at a more convenient time—when you're married? When your children go off to school? When you get established in business? When you retire? There will never be a convenient time to work for God. The enemy will see to it. You have to make the choice to just do it!

Why would you and I work for God? So our lives will not be wasted. Noah's life counted because he "was a righteous man, blameless among the people of his time, and he walked with God" (Gen. 6:9). He was "righteous"—he chose to worship God. He was "blameless among the people of his time"—he chose to witness through a life that was different from those living in the world around him. Noah walked with God, and he worked for God. Noah received the baton of faith in God that was initially relayed by Adam and Eve; he preserved it then relayed it

121

successfully to the next generation. He was truly a gold medal winner in the race of faith.

Adam and Eve received the baton of faith from God, face-to-face. They then relayed it to Abel, who received and relayed it to

Seth,

Enosh,

Kenan,

Mahalalel,

Jared,

Enoch,

Methuselah,

Lamech,

and to Noah.

Noah then relayed the baton to Shem, who received and relayed it to

Eber,

Terah,

Abraham,

Isaac,

Jacob,

Joseph,

Moses,

Joshua,

Deborah,

Gideon,

Samson,

Ruth,

Samuel,

David,

Solomon,

Josiah,

Hezekiah,

Elijah,

Elisha,

Ezra,

Haggai,

Zechariah,
 Nehemiah,
  Malachi,
to John the Baptist, who received the baton of faith and relayed it by bearing witness to "the Lamb of God, who takes away the sin of the world!"[24] And for a short while, once again, man's faith became sight as he gazed on God face-to-face! Jesus of Nazareth is the Son of God, the Seed of the woman, who came to take away our sin and reconcile us to His Father, just as God had promised Adam and Eve He would! John the apostle rejoiced as he exclaimed, "We have seen his glory . . . full of grace and truth," the only begotten of the Father, "which was from the beginning, which we have heard, which we have seen with our eyes, which we have looked at and our hands have touched—this we proclaim concerning the Word of life."[25]

John the apostle received the baton of faith face-to-face from Jesus Christ. He then relayed it by faith to Polycarp, an early church leader who heard John say he had seen God in Christ. Polycarp received the baton and relayed it to
 Ambrose,
  Augustine,
   Anselm,
    John Wycliffe,
     John Huss,
      Martin Luther,
       John Calvin,
        John Knox,
         John Bunyan,
         Jonathan Edwards,
       John Wesley,
      George Whitefield,
     Francis Asbury,
    William Carey,
   Charles Haddon Spurgeon,
  Dwight L. Moody,
 I. M. Haldeman, Billy Sunday,
Billy Graham, and
Anne Graham Lotz, who relays it to you. Now it's up to you: Receive the baton of faith in God and run with it by worshiping God and witnessing for God and walk-

ing with God and working for God. Then relay it to someone else until your faith becomes sight and you see God face-to-face.

❦

ALAN REDPATH recalled that as a young man he worked for a large accounting firm in London. He was not a Christian at the time and was doing his best to work his way up to a senior position. One day the firm hired a new accountant and within a short period of time, everyone in Alan's office recognized that this man was different. He did not use profanity or tell dirty stories or get drunk after work or cheat on the number of office hours he worked. All the other workers assumed he must be very religious, and therefore no one liked him. They frequently made fun of him behind his back and occasionally to his face. He seemed to take it with good humor.

Shortly after the new man arrived in the office, the president of the firm called Alan into his office and informed him that he was being sent on an assignment to the north of England. It would involve a promotion and a substantial salary increase. Alan was elated to have been selected for the job and readily agreed to the challenge.

Then his boss said, "And by the way . . . I'm assigning the new man to you for training." Alan did not let it show, but he was mortified that he would have to spend three weeks with a man he considered to be a religious fanatic.

Before Alan and his coworker left on their trip, everyone in the office laid bets as to who would have a greater impact on whom. Would the fanatic turn Alan into a religious person? Or would Alan turn the fanatic into a wicked person? With a raucous send-off, Alan and his companion left for the northern district. Within three days, the "religious fanatic" had led Alan Redpath to salvation through faith in Jesus Christ! During the rest of the job assignment, the young coworker taught God's Word to Alan, prayed with him, and served as a Christian friend. Alan's life was transformed!

When he returned to the London office, Alan was peppered with questions. Everyone wanted to know how his or her bet had turned out. "Alan," they taunted, "have you got religion?"

"No."

"Alan, are you any different? Did the fanatic get to you?"

"No." He shrugged off further curiosity.

So they suggested, "Alan, come to the pub with us after work."

"No, thank you."

They persisted. "Alan, come on. We're only going for a little while. Come to the pub with us like you always do."

"No, thank you. I really don't feel like going."

"Alan, are you sick or something?"

"No, I'm not sick. I simply don't want to go to the pub."

"Alan, come on. Just come to the pub for a few minutes. We want to hear how our bets turned out."

"No, I don't want to go to the pub today."

"Alan, have you got religion?"

"Okay, I'll go, just for a few minutes."

So Alan went to the pub with the workers from his office. When they arrived, they all ordered drinks and invited Alan to do the same. He refused.

"Alan, come on and have a beer."

"No, thank you."

"Alan, just one beer."

"No, I really don't want a beer."

"Alan, are you sick or something?"

"No, I'm not sick."

"Then just have one beer."

"No, I don't feel like having one beer."

"Alan, have you got religion or something?"

"All right, I'll have just one beer."

Alan Redpath said that one moment of weakness cost him seven years of his Christian life—because he didn't have just one beer. He had another one and another one until he was drunk. As a result of his compromise, he became so discouraged and defeated by failure that he went right back to living the way he had been living before he had put his faith in Christ. For seven years, no one could tell the difference between Alan and any of the other workers in his office.

At the end of those seven years, the "fanatic," who had led him to Christ and had since moved away, came back to visit. He spent about an hour with Alan, talking about how he was doing. Then as he left, he turned, looked Alan in the eye, and said, "Alan, did you know that it is possible to have a saved soul and yet live a wasted life?"

Then he left.

Alan played rugby, and he had a match out of town that night. As he rode the train to the match, he related later that every time the wheels clacked on the tracks, it was as though he could hear those words: *Saved soul, wasted life. Saved soul, wasted life.* When he got to the rugby match and the band came out on the field to play, every beat of the drum seemed to say, *Saved soul, wasted life. Saved soul, wasted life.*

It rang like a refrain in his mind. He knew he was a saved soul living a wasted life. He came back home, got on his knees, and surrendered in prayer, saying, "Lord, I want to live for You. I repent of the waste in my life."

That moment of surrender lasted all of his life. God redeemed his wastedness as he grew deeper and deeper in his commitment to live a life worthy of Christ. He became one of the greatest Bible teachers of his generation, passing the baton of truth to many who placed their faith in Jesus Christ.

Don't drop the baton! Pick it up! Run with it! And pass it on!

# 6

I AM THE GOD OF SALVATION

*I Share Your Loneliness*

GENESIS 6

In May 1989, my mother took my two sisters and me on a five-week journey to visit her birthplace in Huaiyin, China.[1] The last week of our trip found us in Beijing. We stayed in a small hotel on the Avenue of Eternal Peace that was jammed with hordes of demonstrators who seemed to march endlessly twenty-four hours a day. The constant procession included students with banners held high, trucks jammed with workers spilling out from all sides, buses overflowing with children, and pedestrians of all shapes, sizes, and ages walking down the long avenue to Tiananmen Square.

The second day in Beijing, Mother wanted to rest, so my sisters and I quietly put on our sneakers, picked up our umbrellas, slipped out of the hotel, and joined the throngs of Chinese who were demonstrating for democracy. The carnival-type atmosphere was like a Fourth of July parade. People were laughing and singing and waving while they walked steadily to the center of Beijing. We fell in step with their pace and in spirit with their cause. When we had been walking about a mile, a thunderstorm broke over us with torrential rain and lightning that zigzagged through the sky, seeming to flash, crackle, and pop from building to building. We folded up our umbrellas, fearing they would attract the electricity we could feel in the air.

Thoroughly drenched, we finally arrived at Tiananmen Square outside the Forbidden City, which used to be the palace of the Chinese emperors. The square was immense, bordered on one side by the intimidating, fortresslike walls of the Forbidden City itself, plastered with huge poster pictures of Chairman Mao. The side of the square facing us was fronted by the imposing Great Hall of the People.

127

Almost in the center of the square stood a homemade statue that was somewhat dwarfed by the size of the square and buildings that surrounded it. It was the Goddess of Liberty that had been erected by the students for democracy.

As we stood there in the pouring rain with the thunderstorm continuing to rage, taking our pictures and exchanging greetings through sign language with those around us, we had no way of knowing the real storm that was brewing. One week later, Chinese government tanks rolled up the Avenue of Eternal Peace and into Tiananmen Square and crushed the democracy movement along with those who had supported it. The Goddess of Liberty was demolished along with the lives and hopes and dreams of an entire generation.

Stuart Franklin was a photojournalist who captured the essence of what was taking place when he snapped a picture that took the story immediately around the world. The picture is of a long line of Chinese government tanks halted in their advance on Tiananmen Square by a single Chinese man who boldly stood three feet in front of the first tank. With nothing more than the conviction of his cause, one man stood against the entire Chinese army, which was backed by the Communist Chinese government and estimated to be three hundred million strong. Just one, lonely man taking a stand against his entire world. But the image of his stand has become a rallying symbol for millions around the world who courageously stand alone, not only for freedom and against oppression, but who stand alone against overwhelming odds.

What long line of "army tanks" are you confronting by yourself? Bribery at work? Hypocrisy at church? Infidelity at home? Dishonesty at school? Is the loneliness of such a stand overwhelming you? What difference does your stand make?

What difference did the stand of the solitary Chinese man make? Perhaps none, if the effectiveness of his stand is judged by the fact that the tanks were not halted permanently. But if the effectiveness of his stand is judged by the impact he made around the world as he clearly communicated the heart and the will of the average Chinese citizen, then it made a huge difference.

What difference does your stand for righteousness and against wickedness make? When you stand alone against the tide of public opinion or the erosion of spiritual principles or the decay of personal morality, what difference can you make? You and I will never know the answer to that until we are willing to be one person, standing alone.

There was another man in history who took a lonely stand against the evil and wickedness of his day. His example emphasizes to you and me the power of one. Because if he had not stood against the wickedness of his day, the entire human race would have been totally eradicated by the Flood. His name was Noah, and he lived in the midst of Cain's godless world.

## FINDING MEANING WHEN LIVING IN THE WORLD

Cain's civilization, characterized by its construction and its culture, crime, and corruption, became more and more openly, blatantly rebellious against God with each generation. Noah lived in the midst of the final generation, which provoked the judgment of God. He just didn't fit into the totally godless generation that the Bible describes in a somewhat mysterious picture: "When men began to increase in number on the earth and daughters were born to them, the sons of God saw that the daughters of men were beautiful, and they married any of them they chose. . . . The Nephilim were on the earth in those days—and also afterward—when the sons of God went to the daughters of men and had children by them. They were the heroes of old, men of renown" (Gen. 6:1–2, 4).

A close look reveals that Noah's world has some striking similarities to our own day. While no one knows exactly what these verses may be referring to, it is clear they are describing a unique, intolerable wickedness in God's eyes since He warns of His thinning patience and His judgment to come: "My Spirit will not contend with man forever, for he is mortal; his days will be a hundred and twenty years" (Gen. 6:3).

### A Wicked World

What was the world's wickedness that was pushing the patience of God to the limit? First, it may be that it was rooted in a dilution of God's principles. It could be that the "sons of God" were the sons of Seth, the remnant who had placed their faith in God, seeking to pass the "baton" to the next generation in the midst of Cain's civilization. The "daughters of men" may have been the daughters of Cain, therefore an integral part of the rebellious society. Could it be that these two groups of people intermarried, compromising faith in God? Could it be that they then produced children who were raised to believe that God was not very important, nor was He to be feared and obeyed?

One of God's principles for marriage is that those who have established a right relationship with God through faith in Jesus Christ are not to marry those who are not in a right relationship with God.² The reason for this principle was explained logically by Amos when he said, "Do two walk together unless they have agreed to do so?"³ For someone who has real faith in God to marry, or "walk with," another person who is in rebellion against God would mean a lifetime of compromise on everything from how to spend time and money, to setting priorities and standards. If there is no basic agreement on an issue as significant as a person's relationship with God, then there can be no agreement on lesser issues, and a compromise would have to be made to preserve the marriage. That compromise would inevitably lead to neglect of God's Word.

On one of my travels, a woman shared with me the hard consequences of her compromise. She was a beautiful woman who was raised in the church as a "nominal" Christian. While in college, she fell in love and married an outstanding leader on campus who was religious but without a personal, right relationship with God. In order to maintain harmony in her marriage, she had to compromise on the church she attended, the lifestyle she lived, and the activities she was involved in. Her personal faith in God blossomed when she began to earnestly study the Scriptures for herself, but within her home she was discouraged from sharing what she was learning. As a result, her family never prayed together, nor did they ever gather together for a time of Bible reading, nor did they seek God's will involving matters that faced them. Although she experienced her husband's support and blessing as she became a social leader in her community, she experienced his displeasure whenever she sought to give expression to her faith through serving the Lord. The constant need to balance her life between two "lords" led to the continual compromise of her faith and the dilution of God's principles in her family so that God was not taken seriously in daily, practical matters. Today, three of her four grown children express no faith in God at all.⁴

What compromises of faith have you felt forced to make within your marriage and family by an unbelieving spouse? In what way have you seen those compromises impact your children? What a tragedy if the great wickedness in the world of Noah's day was caused by parents who compromised their faith in God by marrying spouses who were in rebellion against God and therefore produced children who were raised by the very example of their parents to be indifferent toward God!

Jesus pinpointed the root of wickedness in Noah's day as indifference to God: "For in the days before the flood, people were eating and drinking, marrying and giving in marriage, up to the day Noah entered the ark; and they knew nothing about what would happen until the flood came and took them all away. That is how it will be at the coming of the Son of Man."[5] Nothing was really wrong with any of the activities described by Jesus, except that God was left out of all of them.

Who do you know who is leaving God out?

Out of decisions?

Out of activities?

Out of attitudes?

Out of business?

Out of the home?

Out of the marriage?

Out of leisure time?

Out of plans?

Out of life?

Much that is in our world today is not wicked in that it is criminal; it is wicked in that it is godless!

What are you doing to ensure that God will not be neglected by your family? Are you focusing attention on Him through family times of prayer, Bible reading, and church attendance? Are you instructing your children in His principles, especially as they relate to marriage?

One way my parents instructed me was to hold up before me the high standards God set for marriage by applying some of those same standards to dating. They understood that I would eventually marry someone I had dated. Therefore, as a guard against compromising God's principle of not being unequally yoked to an unbeliever in marriage, I was not allowed to date someone who was not a Christian.

Have you ever given similar instructions to your children? Apparently, many Christian parents today have not taught their children God's principles, either through their words or example, because God is becoming less and less important and more and more neglected within our society.

The wickedness of Noah's day may well have been due to the dilution of God's principles, which led to neglect of God within marriage, the home, the family, and the society. Or it may have been due to a bizarre form of demon possession.

The "sons of God" may have been fallen angels who came to earth and married "the daughters of men," or human women. The children that resulted from such an unnatural union may have experienced a unique form of demon possession.

The New Testament speaks of "the angels who did not keep their positions of authority but abandoned their own home" and were therefore "bound with everlasting chains for judgment."[6] It goes on to say that God's judgment came upon these angels because of some great sin they had committed.[7] Although Jesus told us that angels do not marry,[8] it may be that when they left "their positions of authority" and became Satan's demons, they may have married, producing the great wickedness in Genesis 6 that provoked the judgment of God.

While this viewpoint is dubious among some scholars, it has valid application for you and me today. We are living in a world of increasing demonic activity. Demons operate through "slasher" movies, pornography, and heavy metal music, all designed to arouse the human emotions to violence and destruction. Channeling that allows "imaginary" people of a former age to speak through a human vessel as well as outright satanic cults with witchcraft, black-and-white magic, and animal sacrifices are also evidence that our society may be more similar to the fiendish atmosphere of Noah's day than we would like to think.

One evening in Durban, South Africa, I was driven from my hotel to a meeting where I was to speak. In the car was a lovely woman who began to describe her sister to me as an educated, well-to-do woman who attended a "spiritualist" church where the people talked to the dead. When I asked her to describe what the "dead" seemed to be saying, she related "messages" that were blasphemous against God. I told her that the "talking dead" were not former relatives and loved ones at all but demons in disguise.

In another setting, when I concluded my weekly visits in the North Carolina Correctional Center for Women, I always led in prayer. Before the prayer, as I conversed with the inmate, I would be aware of a general hum of activity in the background. But invariably, as we bowed our heads to pray each week, the hum of activity would become a roar of bloodcurdling screams from other inmates that literally raised the hair on the back of my neck! She and I both knew the screams were coming from demons within those incarcerated women, demons that violently protested our communication with the One whose very name causes them to tremble.

Tarot cards, Ouija boards, horoscopes, channeling, transcendental meditation, heavy metal music, and seances may seem harmless, but they are the tip of the devil's long tentacles, reaching out to pull our society away from God's Word toward himself and destruction. The Bible prophesies that demonic activity will thrive and increase in the days preceding God's final judgment on earth, just as it did in the days preceding His judgment on the world of Noah's day.[9] Yet those who have placed their faith in God are not to fear or be timid, because "the one who is in you is greater than the one who is in the world."[10] But there is no mistaking the fact that the devil is in the world, drawing it into willful wickedness.

### A Willful World

Cain's civilization was headstrong in its rebellion and determination to live life as it chose, with no fear or reverence for God. "The LORD saw how great man's wickedness on the earth had become, and that *every* inclination of the thoughts of his heart was only evil *all the time*" (Gen. 6:5, italics added). Was the permeation of evil throughout society due primarily to depravity and perversion or to just plain selfishness? Whichever it was, there was

> no goodness,
> > no kindness,
> > > no wholesomeness,
> > no thoughtfulness,
> no gentleness,
> > no humbleness,
> > > no niceness,
> > no faithfulness,
> no righteousness,
no holiness,

in anyone at any time in any way at any place in all the world!

Can you imagine a world where every member of a family would fight over the biggest piece of pie? Where no one would allow anyone else to merge into a line of traffic? Where abortion would be as accepted as a tooth extraction? Where the killing of the elderly and the infirm would be honored as an act of mercy? Where lawsuits would be as common as traffic tickets? It's easy to imagine a world totally given over to selfishness because you and I are living in a world that increasingly revolves around itself. We don't call it a willful world; we call it humanistic. A world where man is without God. But the world that ignored and neglected God had His undivided attention.

*A Watched World*

Instead of being indifferent or inattentive or uncaring about what took place on planet Earth, "the LORD saw how great man's wickedness on the earth had become.... God saw how corrupt the earth had become" (Gen. 6:5, 12). God saw

> the deals made behind closed doors,
> > the whispers uttered behind backs,
> > > the agendas hidden in political posturing,
> > > > the spin doctors misinforming the public,
> > > > > the destruction of the pristine environment,
> > > > the preoccupation with perverted pleasure,
> > > the exploitation of the human body,
> > the abuse of innocent children,
> the spoiled goods sold as fresh,
> > the dangerous chemicals labeled as safe,
> > > the covenants broken by whim,
> > > > the truth exchanged for a lie,
> > > the glory given to the obnoxious,
> > the honor given to the blasphemous,
> the legalized acceptance of abomination.

God saw it all! And it broke His heart! "The LORD was grieved that he had made man on the earth" (Gen. 6:6). The word *grieved* is a love word. You don't grieve for someone unless you love that person.

The God who created the heavens and the earth as an environment for man, the crowning glory of His creation . . .

The God who brought Adam into existence because He wanted to be known by him . . .

The God who personally planted a garden eastward in Eden as a home for the man He had created . . .

The God who tenderly gave Adam the desire of his heart when He created woman to be his true companion . . .

The God who had supplied all of Adam's needs over and above what he could have thought to ask for . . .

God was ignored and neglected by Adam's descendants, "and his heart was filled with pain" (Gen. 6:6). God was emotionally involved in the indifference of Noah's world.

Do you think He cares less about the indifference of our world today? Do you think the indifference of our world has caught Him by surprise? Do you think God has to wait until the evening news to see what has happened each day? If He sees what happens when it happens and is fully informed of what is going on down here, do you think because He has not yet judged our world that He is tolerating its wickedness and willfulness?

The Bible tells us God watches our world with patience, "not wanting anyone to perish, but everyone to come to repentance."[11] But don't mistake His patience for toleration. Or His love for acceptance. Or His grief for weakness. There is a limit to God's patience with the world, but He never sneaks up and delivers judgment by surprise.

*A Warned World*

God warned Noah's world that judgment was coming: "I will wipe mankind, whom I have created, from the face of the earth—men and animals, and creatures that move along the ground, and birds of the air—for I am grieved that I have made them" (Gen. 6:7). His warning carried with it the implied opportunity to repent so the people could avoid judgment; otherwise He wouldn't have bothered to warn the world. But no one seemed to be listening. It was as if God were speaking to Himself.

If our world, like Noah's, is provoking the judgment of God, how is He warning us today? In the Old Testament, when a nation slipped so far away from God that its people no longer read His Word or heeded His prophets, He warned them of impending judgment through national or natural disasters such as an invading army or a locust plague.[12]

Today, He warns us in the same ways. When we hear

of a nation invading another nation

or a country self-destructing into civil war

or a volcano erupting

or a tidal wave sweeping villages away

or an earthquake leveling entire cities

or a forest fire devouring hundreds of thousands of acres of woodlands

or a flood covering roads and homes and businesses

or a drought shriveling millions of acres of farmland

or an epidemic threatening to wipe out a nation's entire population, are we hearing the warning of the Creator demanding, "Repent! Judgment is coming! I am holding you accountable for your wicked, willful ways"? Who is listening?

God also warns the world today through the conscience of each person. When the warning-alert system, which we call guilt, is activated, shattering our inner serenity and tranquillity and peace of mind, we know we need to get right with God. But we silence the alarm with

    drugs,

        alcohol,

           busyness,

                parties,

                    sports,

                        entertainment,

                            therapy sessions,

                                self-help seminars,

                                    sex, and

                                        just plain denial.

God is warning us, "Repent! Judgment is coming! I am holding you accountable for your wicked, willful ways!" But who is listening? God warns the world through godly men, women, and young people who stand in the pulpits,

    who work in the marketplace,

        who live in the neighborhoods,

        who teach in the schools,

            who coach on the field,

            who tend the sick,

                who sit in the classroom,

taking a bold stand for the Lord God and proclaiming the truth of His Word all over the world. As they live out their testimony among their peers, shining the light of their lives into the darkness, God is warning, "Repent! Judgment is coming! I am holding you accountable for your wicked, willful ways." But who in the world is listening?

Judgment is coming. If not in a worldwide flood, it's coming for each of us when we face God, either at death or at the second coming of Jesus Christ. The Bible says, "Man is destined to die once, and after that to face judgment."[13] Are you listening?

In the midst of a wicked, willful world that was watched and warned by God, there was one man who was listening. One man who "found favor in the eyes of the LORD" (Gen. 6:8). One man who found meaning in the midst of chaos. That one man was Noah.

## FINDING MEANING THROUGH LISTENING TO THE LORD

Noah made time to listen to God's Word when no one else did. Think of the loneliness of his life. Outside of his own immediate family, he would have had no one to talk to who would understand his viewpoint, no one who would agree with his decisions, no one who would share his goals and priorities, no one to whom he could turn for wisdom or counsel or encouragement or even fellowship. No one in the whole wide world.

When have you felt all alone? Not just physically but emotionally and spiritually? I wonder if Noah ever felt uncertain or insecure in being the only one in all the world who ever prayed or even acknowledged the existence of God. Genesis tells us, "Noah was a righteous man, blameless among the people of his time, and he walked with God" (Gen. 6:9). Noah was right with God when everyone else was wrong. Noah was blameless among the people of his time when every other person was to blame for every kind of evil. Noah walked with God when the entire world followed in Cain's rebellious footsteps and ran away from God. Yet Noah's attitude seemed to be so confident it was as though he considered the whole world to be crazy while he was the only one who was sane! Surely he received much-needed strength and encouragement from his wife and three sons, but his confidence came from listening to what God had to say.

Danny Wuerffel was the quarterback at the University of Florida when he was named *Playboy* magazine's 1996 National Scholar Athlete of the Year, a very prestigious award. When the honor was announced in the media, Danny was invited to receive his award along with a trip to an exclusive resort and a five-thousand-dollar gift in his name to Florida's scholarship fund.

But he politely refused. His reasoning was based on his faith in God and his conviction that his appearance in and association with such a magazine would hurt his testimony, which he often gave at area churches and youth group meetings. When he declined the award he was derided, criticized, called names, and pretty much left to stand alone against a tide of public opinion while another athlete received the honor.

Where did his strength come from to take such a courageous stand? It came from talking to God twice a day, keeping his Bible in hand, and praying on his knees before going to bed each night.[14] It came from listening to God! Not a popular habit in today's world, yet it is the timeless key that gives us courage to stand alone. And God shared Danny's loneliness. At the end of the 1996 football season, Danny was named the nation's most outstanding football player of the year and given the coveted Heisman Trophy.

Like Danny Wuerffel, Noah listened to God as he walked with God, cultivating the awareness of His presence in the midst of his loneliness.

*Listening as You Walk with God*

Like Enoch before him, Noah made the time to walk with God. Perhaps for Noah, who lived in the vicinity of the garden of Eden, walking with God involved literally spending time in His physical presence.

Did Noah knock on the garden gate after offering the prescribed sacrifice on the altar, asking if God would walk with him?

Perhaps Noah didn't even have to knock, because God was there waiting to meet with him. Or perhaps God came to Noah's house, knocked on his door, and invited him to go for a walk. Maybe they shared a power walk with arms swinging energetically, or was it a stroll, with their hands clasped behind their backs as they thoughtfully conversed together? And what would they have talked about? Would they have enjoyed pointing out the beauty of the world to each other? Would they have discussed Noah's neighbors and what could be done to draw them to the truth? Did Noah ask God for advice as a father about how to raise his three boys in such a wicked world? Did He ask God's help in meeting the emotional needs of his wife, who seemed to feel more and more alone in her circle of friends? I expect Noah talked with God about everything that was on his mind. Increasingly, Noah must have grasped the true meaning of his loneliness. Increasingly he must have realized the entire world was out of step with God, and therefore as he walked with God, he was out of step with the world. But as Noah walked with God, God shared his loneliness.

When do you walk with God? Is there a specific time when you draw aside from your busy day and just enjoy His presence? You and I will never have the strength and courage to take a lonely stand and maintain it if we don't first spend time with God.

God seemed to come to my door one day and ask if I would start walking with Him by getting up early in the morning for prayer and Bible reading. At first I thought it was something I had to do. I dragged my feet because I found I didn't want to sacrifice the extra few minutes of sleep! He was so patient as He waited for me to understand that it wasn't something I had to do; instead it was a personal time of fellowship where I could just grow in my love relationship with Him. What a difference it made in my whole attitude and approach to the early-morning hours when I became consciously aware that my heavenly Bridegroom was waiting to meet with me at that designated time!

Although the struggle to get out of bed will always be a battle I fight, the early-morning times with my Lord are so exceedingly precious I will never eliminate them from my day. The time with Him each morning begins with reading a few verses from the Bible, not to gain information or to study for deeper truth but just to hear His voice. When a verse seems particularly meaningful or appropriate for my day, I slip down on my knees and talk with Him about it. I always begin by telling Him at least one thing I love and respect Him for. After a little while I resume my sitting position and discuss with Him my family, my friends, my responsibilities—anything or anyone who comes to mind. I do not always have the feeling that He is there with me, but by faith I know He is.

Walking every day, day after day, year after year, takes time. One reason I have maintained my walk with God is that no one else, not my beloved husband and children or my precious mother and father or my close and loyal friends, really understands me. No one else truly knows my fears and longings and hurts and dreams and failures. But He shares my feelings, my loneliness. Spending time with God as I "walk" with Him meets needs that are in the deepest part of me. He Himself is the solution to the loneliness of the human spirit.[15] I know.

And in some way I don't understand, I believe walking with me satisfies His heart. It brings Him pleasure to be loved and enjoyed and known just for who He is. He is enthralled with the beauty of your character and mine as increasingly it reflects His own, and He rejoices over you and me.[16] What could be more humbling or more thrilling than to walk with the Lord God, Creator of the heavens and earth?

Walking with God helps to insulate us against the world. Many years after Noah, this insulation was experienced dramatically by three young men who found themselves in a crowd of people, all of whom were commanded to conform to the tolerant, religious standard of the day and bow down in worship to a statue of gold.

I can imagine[17] it was a warm, clear day, with occasional gusts of wind stirring up little dust devils that danced across the vast, endless plain of Dura. Thousands of people, each one a leader or government official or person of influence, congregated around a golden statue of a man so tall it reduced the appearance of the crowd to a sea of ants swarming at its base.

Suddenly an announcement blared out that all who had gathered were to bow and worship the statue of gold when the musical signal was given. If anyone refused, he was to be thrown into a fiery furnace. Surely a ripple of consternation swept through the throng of people. As they exchanged glances, many must have shrugged in a complacent, resigned gesture, because they had been taught to value toleration of all types of religious expression. Three young men in the crowd also exchanged glances—not of indifferent resignation but of comprehension, conviction, and courage.

The hum of conversation would have ceased as the music played, and like pilgrims thronging the shrine in Mecca during Ramadan, the entire sea of people fell on their faces in outward obeisance to the statue. All except Meshach, Shadrach, and Abednego, who stood with their backs straight, their shoulders squared, their chins lifted, their eyes clear, refusing to even bend.

Their lonely stand was quickly obvious to everyone because they literally stood out from the crowd around them. They were immediately reported to King Nebuchadnezzar, who furiously subjected them to intense interrogation, finally threatening, "If you do not worship it, you will be thrown immediately into a blazing furnace. Then what god will be able to rescue you from my hand?"[18]

The answer they gave is a classic response of God-fearing, God-honoring, lonely courage: "O Nebuchadnezzar, we do not need to defend ourselves before you in this matter. If we are thrown into the blazing furnace, the God we serve is able to save us from it, and he will rescue us from your hand, O king. But even if he does not, we want you to know, O king, that we will not serve your gods or worship the image of gold you have set up."[19]

And so Shadrach, Meshach, and Abednego were roughly seized, tightly bound, then viciously thrown into the furnace that was so hot it incinerated the guards who threw them into it. As the king and his counselors gathered to peer into the furnace and gloat over the destruction of the three uncompromising young people who had dared defy the king's order, the king exclaimed hysterically, "Weren't there three men that we tied up and threw into the fire? . . . Look! I see four men walking around in the fire."[20]

The three young men who had refused to compromise their convictions, who had refused to worship anything or anyone other than the one true living God, who had refused to "love their lives so much as to shrink from death,"[21] those three young men not only experienced God's deliverance from the fire but God's presence in the midst of it as He shared their lonely position. And the entire world of their day gave God the glory! How much more accurately the world would perceive God if you and I simply abandoned ourselves totally to live for Him.

Why do we care what others think as long as we know God is pleased? Why do we get our feelings hurt when no one seems to understand us—as long as God understands us? How can we feel shunned and left out when God seeks to spend time with us? How can we feel unloved when we are basking in His love? And how could we possibly sin deliberately when we know it would hurt the One we love? Would you be willing to "lose your life" in order to find it?[22] To walk with God and keep walking until increasingly your satisfaction, fulfillment, happiness, and purpose in life are centered in Him?

Our walk with God naturally progresses to our work for Him, because as we spend time with Him, He reveals to us what is on His heart and mind. He begins to impress upon us the need to get involved in drawing others to Himself—which means we need to spend time quietly listening to what He has to say.

We know Noah walked quietly at times, just listening to his Friend share His concerns and what was on His heart, because it was at such a time that God revealed to Noah the meaning of what was taking place in the world around him: "I am going to put an end to all people, for the earth is filled with violence because of them. I am surely going to destroy both them and the earth. So make yourself an ark" (Gen. 6:13–14). As Noah listened to the heart cry of God, he felt compelled to get involved, because God didn't want him to be just a listener but a doer of His Word.[23]

*Listening as You Work for God*

God told Noah exactly what work He wanted him to do: "'So make yourself an ark of cypress wood; make rooms in it and coat it with pitch inside and out. This is how you are to build it: The ark is to be 450 feet long, 75 feet wide and 45 feet high. Make a roof for it and finish the ark to within 18 inches of the top. Put a door in the side of the ark and make lower, middle and upper decks. I am going to bring floodwaters on the earth to destroy all life under the heavens, every creature that has the breath of life in it. Everything on earth will perish. But I will establish my covenant with you, and you will enter the ark—you and your sons and your wife and your sons' wives with you. You are to bring into the ark two of all living creatures, male and female, to keep them alive with you. Two of every kind of bird, of every kind of animal and of every kind of creature that moves along the ground will come to you to be kept alive. You are to take every kind of food that is to be eaten and store it away as food for you and for them.' Noah did everything just as God commanded him" (Gen. 6:14–22).

Wow! What an assignment! There was no large body of water nearby, and it's doubtful that Noah had ever even seen a boat, much less one the size of the ark he was instructed to build.[24] The dimensions given for the length made it one and a half times the length of a football field. Its cargo capacity would hold more than one and a half million cubic feet. It had three levels, each with individual rooms or stalls or nests for the animals, to prevent the chaos that would erupt if the animals were not confined. The walls were finished almost to the roof, leaving a gap of eighteen inches to let in light and ventilation. It had only one door. And it was waterproofed with tar inside and out.

Noah built the ark! We know he had never seen rain, because at this time it had not rained on the earth.[25] He had never seen a flood. He probably wasn't an experienced carpenter or zookeeper. It must have taken him 120 years to build, which meant he began 20 years before his first son was born.[26] Assuming his sons did not begin seriously helping him until they were at least ten years old, it means he probably worked close to thirty-five years by himself. Or did he hire local labor to help him? Even after his boys were old enough to help, did Noah hire others to assist in the work? And where would he have gotten the money for wages and materials? Did he have to do his "regular work" during the day and come home and "moonlight" on the ark at night? Did he have to sell the family business? The money for laborers and materials must have come from his own pocket. In other words, Noah must have put his whole heart, mind, soul, strength, and all that belonged to him into the work of the Lord! Why? Because God said so!

What a solution for loneliness—to not only know that God shares your feelings of loneliness but to throw yourself wholeheartedly into God's work! Noah would have had no time to feel sorry for himself. He would have had no time to be depressed or discouraged over his isolated life in the midst of a wicked, willful, watched, and warned world. He was just too busy!

Are you lonely? Why?

Because you are single? Divorced? Widowed?

Because you are the only Christian in your family or place of business?

Because you are lying on a hospital bed?

Because you are forgotten in a home for the elderly?

Because you are bound in a home with small children?

Because you spoke the truth, and now no one speaks to you?

Because you refused to lie?

Because you are doing what's right when everyone else is doing what's wrong?

Because you have been falsely accused and people shy away from you?

Because you just don't "fit in" with those around you?

God understands. He comforts: "In all their distress, he too was distressed. . . . he lifted them up and carried them."[27] The writer to the Hebrews encourages us when he tells us we have a High Priest in heaven who, as He intercedes for us, understands the feelings of our infirmities.[28]

What long line of "army tanks" have you confronted all by yourself? Are you actually lonely because you are not walking with or working for God on a daily basis?

The solution to loneliness is not to give in or give up or do what everyone else does or go where everyone else goes or look like and speak like and think like and act like the world around you so you won't stand out so sharply from the crowd. The solution is not to withdraw into an uninvolved, inactive life. The solution is found when we discover meaning in the midst of loneliness as God Himself shares our loneliness while we walk with and work for Him.

Two thousand years ago another solitary figure stood out in history. He stood alone against all the visible and invisible forces of evil in the universe. The sin of all mankind was placed upon Him as He walked to the place of sacrifice, carrying His own means of execution. He was betrayed by one of His best friends and denied by another. Not one person stood with Him—not the blind man to whom He had given sight, not the deaf man to whom He had given hearing, not the lame man to whom He had given strength, not the leper to whom He had given cleansing, not the adulterous woman to whom He had given forgiveness, not the dead man to whom He had given new life. No one stood with Him. He was crucified on a Roman cross, alone, suspended between heaven and hell, God and man.

As He hung on the cross, cursed and jeered by the very ones He was giving His life for, He was so overwhelmed with loneliness, enduring judgment and separation from God as He became sin for us,[29] that He cried out, "My God, my God, why have you forsaken me?"[30] Then He gave His life to reconcile us in a right relationship with the Father. When we receive Him by faith, He will never leave us or forsake us, "so we say with confidence, 'The Lord is my helper; I will not be afraid. What can man do to me?'"[31] And we will never truly be lonely again, because He shares it with us.

✍♥

THE HIGH SCHOOL assembly was jammed with students who had gathered to hear a recruiting pitch from a representative of each of the armed forces. Each representative was given five minutes to tell those assembled why they should sign up for his branch of the service. Following the assembly, those interested could meet the recruiters in the gym. The first one to speak was a captain in the air force. He got so carried away with the description of his chosen military field that he took eighteen minutes. Not to be outdone, when the army sergeant followed, he took nineteen minutes. The navy lieutenant, still smarting from a football loss to the army earlier in the year, spoke for twenty minutes. By this time, the frustrated and frantic organizer leaned over and told the marine major he only had three minutes to speak.

The major stood up in front of the assembly and didn't say a word as he let his gaze go up one row and down another, carefully examining the audience of young people in front of him. Finally, he broke the silence with this brief challenge: "The marines are looking for a few good men and women, and I'm not sure I see any. If you think you are one, meet me in the gym."

Following the assembly, the major was swamped with volunteers.

God is also looking for a few good men and women.[32] Men and women who are willing

to go against the current of popular opinion,
to hold firm convictions in a world where "anything goes,"
to speak the truth when it is not politically correct,
to live their lives blamelessly when the world says character doesn't count,
to walk with God when everyone else is running away from Him.

God is looking for those who believe

that what He says is more important than what anyone else says,

that what He thinks is more important than what anyone else thinks,

that what He wants is more important than what anyone else wants,

that His will is more important than their own.

God is looking for another Noah. Another Meshach. Another Shadrach. Another Abednego. Are you what God is looking for? We'll know who you are, because you will stand out from the crowd.

Don't bend! Don't bow! Don't even slouch! Stand up! Speak out! One person with God is not alone but a majority!

# 7

## *I Overcome Your Helplessness*

GENESIS 7

In August 1990, the tiny oil kingdom of Kuwait was suddenly invaded by the massive, mobilized army of Iraq. In a matter of hours, Kuwait was overrun by her hostile northern neighbor. Her streets rumbled under Iraqi tanks, her oil fields were set on fire, her women were raped, her men were slaughtered, and her wealth was looted. With billions of dollars in oil revenue and one of the highest standards of living anywhere in the world, Kuwait was utterly helpless to defend herself against the ruthless aggression and lustful greed of Saddam Hussein.

When have you felt totally insecure and utterly helpless?

When your child ran away from home, leaving no trace?

When a spouse walked out into the arms of another?

When the doctor diagnosed a fast-spreading terminal disease?

When your income would not stretch to cover your expenses and the creditors would not extend another loan?

When you stood watching as flames devoured your home?

When the river overflowed its banks, flooding your community?

When the sea rose up and claimed your property?

When our whole world falls apart, we can overcome our helplessness through God, our Savior.

Noah went through the equivalent of a nuclear holocaust when the entire world of his day was destroyed in a worldwide flood that was the judgment of God on Cain's civilization. Not only did Noah survive this devastation; he overcame triumphantly as he and his family were secure emotionally, mentally, spiritually, and

146

physically throughout the living nightmare. His security and help rested in a moment-by-moment obedience and dependence upon God's Word.

## OVERCOMING THROUGH OBEDIENCE TO GOD'S WORD

I wonder how Noah reacted to God's announcement that He was "going to put an end to all people"? Did Noah's stomach turn over? Did he go weak in the knees? Did his mind temporarily go blank, then begin to race as he thought of the implications? Did he react as Daniel said he did when he was informed of God's judgment, testifying that he "had no strength left, my face turned deathly pale and I was helpless?"[1] While we don't know the answers to these questions, we do know that when Noah most surely felt utterly helpless, he turned to God's Word.

Whom or what do you turn to when you feel helpless? Do you turn to a friend? A lawyer? A banker? A doctor? A counselor? While you and I may need the help of such resources, our first reaction should be to turn to God and His Word. Noah turned to God and listened carefully to His instructions.

### *Follow God's Instructions*

Once Noah got over the news of impending judgment, his attention must have been seized by the knowledge that God was going to provide a means of salvation from that judgment for his family and for himself. Noah must then have realized with intense clarity that their very lives depended upon his obedience to every Word God said. So Noah listened intently to God's specific instructions about building the ark as well as housing the animals. "Take with you seven of every kind of clean animal, a male and its mate, and two of every kind of unclean animal, a male and its mate, and also seven of every kind of bird, male and female, to keep their various kinds alive throughout the earth. Seven days from now I will send rain on the earth for forty days and forty nights, and I will wipe from the face of the earth every living creature I have made" (Gen. 7:2–4).

Surely this announcement must have seemed preposterous to Noah! How could he get so many animals on one boat, even if the boat was almost the size of a modern-day ocean liner? Was he tempted to protest, "God, this is impossible! I can't do this!"

Just how big was his assignment? We know that there are more than eighteen thousand different species of mammals, birds, reptiles, and amphibians today. If the number is doubled to include two of every kind, with several thousand extras added to make up the five additional pairs of each "clean" species, then double all of that to include any that have become extinct, the total figure is about seventy-five thousand animals that Noah was required to stuff into that ark![2] That's a lot of animals! But when we consider the fact that the larger animals, such as elephants, dinosaurs, rhinoceroses, and giraffes, could have been represented by babies, the average animal would have been smaller than a sheep. And a lot of them would have been much smaller—like lizards, frogs, roaches, and chiggers—things I would definitely have left off the ark![3]

And surely Noah must have wondered just how he would go about finding all these pairs of animals. He may have pictured himself beating the bushes, scouring the desert, hiking up mountains, and combing the valleys to come up with the required list. Old Noah's mind must have been spinning toward the brink of sanity when God reassured him, "Two of every kind of bird, of every kind of animal and of every kind of creature that moves along the ground will come to you to be kept alive" (Gen. 6:20).

Perhaps God was saying He would put into the appropriate animals an instinctive knowledge of an approaching storm. Then, much like rats fleeing a sinking ship or cockroaches sensing seismic disturbances and being used to predict earthquakes or birds migrating when the seasons begin to change, that instinctive awareness may have led the animals to the safety of the ark. However it occurred, we know that "pairs of clean and unclean animals, of birds and of all creatures that move along the ground, male and female, came to Noah and entered the ark, as God had commanded Noah" (Gen. 7:8–9).

According to the dimensions given,[4] when Noah had all the animals assembled on the ark, only 60 percent of the available space would have been occupied. The remaining 40 percent would be available for food storage and living quarters of Noah and his family. In other words, there was room for seven of every clean kind of animal and two of every unclean kind of animal plus Noah and his family—and food for all. It all worked, as impossible as it had seemed!

God is our Helper.[5] When the task He assigns is beyond our ability and we are totally helpless to fulfill it, He steps in and takes over. He does what we can't. His strength is perfect in our weakness.[6]

On my first trip to India, I landed in Madras around midnight, then left my hotel at five o'clock the next morning to catch a plane to Kovalon. I was met in

Kovalon by several church leaders who transported me by car to a hotel where I rested for the night. The next day, riding in that same car that was led by a Jeep with armed guards, I traveled across the southern tip of India to Tinnevelly. On the way our little caravan stopped in a village where I was transferred to the Jeep. The Jeep then proceeded to climb over rocks, gullies, and trees through the jungle to a mountain clearing. As we bumped along the rugged trail, people began running through the jungle to welcome my arrival, clutching their Bibles, ringing their bells, and blowing their horns. When we finally stopped, I got out and made my way the last hundred yards or so to a newly constructed church, which I had the privilege of dedicating.

Following the brief ceremony, I climbed back into the Jeep, went back down the mountain, and was transferred back to the car for the continuing journey, with a stop next at Dohnavur, the lovely oasis Amy Carmichael had carved out of the desolate Indian landscape. Dohnavur was originally founded as a home for little Indian girls who had been rescued as babies from temple prostitution. The life expectancy of the girls in such a situation was twelve years of age.

Today Miss Carmichael lives in heaven, and Dohnavur is operated as a home for Indian boys and girls, who are raised in Christian love. The leaders and super-visors are adults who were themselves raised in the home. Being in Dohnavur was a deeply moving and emotional experience, especially since all my life I have been blessed by Miss Carmichael's testimony and writings.[7]

We stayed at Dohnavur only a few hours, then continued cross-country until we came to Tinnevelly, where I was warmly greeted at the bishop's house. As I was shown to my room, my host told me I would be picked up in an hour by a driver who would take me to a meeting of all the religious leaders from the area, and then I was to preach an evangelistic message in a soccer stadium! Having just ridden for eleven hours across roads that looked more like wide ruts, dedicated a jungle church, and toured Dohnavur, I couldn't imagine doing anything except falling across the narrow bed before me. No doubt sensing my exhaustion, my gracious host closed the door, and I collapsed on the floor, telling God over and over again, "This is impossible! I can't do this!"

For the entire one-hour period, I stayed on my knees, asking God for His help. When I heard the soft knock on my door, I felt like a prisoner whose guard had come to lead me to the guillotine. Within minutes, I found myself looking at sev-eral dozen brown, upturned faces with flashing smiles and warm eyes, waiting expectantly for me to say something. At that moment, God brought verses to my mind from Hebrews to encourage these faithful religious leaders not to lose confidence but to persevere in their faith and they would be richly rewarded.[8] They seemed genuinely appreciative as I left to go to the soccer stadium.

Several blocks from the stadium, I could hear the roar of the large crowd. I secretly prayed that I was actually hearing a soccer game going on and that I could get by in some small meeting. But when the car pulled through the gate, to my amazement and actual horror, I saw a sea of ten to fifteen thousand people crowded into a stadium, waiting for the "evangelist from America." After a brief ceremony of introduction to various leaders, I was led to the stage. I had been traveling since before dawn, and it was now after dark. The stage was lit with floodlights that attracted every flying insect in southern India. When I looked down at the light blue dress I was wearing, it was covered with creeping, crawling, and fluttering bugs! I looked to my right and left, and I was surrounded with Indian bishops in long white robes, ceremonial ribbons crisscrossing their chests, with bare feet out of their respect for what they considered to be holy ground. I looked straight ahead into a mass of faces silhouetted by the lanterns placed around the field. As the meeting began, I kept whispering to the Lord, "This is impossible! I can't do this!"

Within a short time I realized I was being introduced, and the master of ceremonies motioned me forward to the pulpit. A nice-looking Indian gentleman stepped up to the front of the stage with me, stopping on my left side and then looking expectantly at me. I realized he was the interpreter. For the last time, I prayed, "God, I can't do this." Then I opened my mouth in total obedience and dependence upon the God who had put me in that place, and in the simplest terms I knew explained who God is and how my listeners could know Him for themselves. When I gave the invitation to receive Jesus Christ as Lord and Savior, hundreds of Indians responded to give their hearts to Christ!

Like Noah, I know by experience that God is a God of the impossible. When we are utterly helpless, He is our Helper. But He requires the cooperation of our obedience.

What seemingly impossible task has God given you to do? Have you done it, or are you procrastinating? What if Noah had procrastinated and told God he would build the ark but at a time when he felt he was more rested, more capable, when he had had sufficient training, when his financial situation was more stable, when his family was more self-sufficient, when it was just more convenient? If he had had the attitude many of us do when God gives us an assignment that is beyond our ability, he would have been totally exposed in his helplessness and unprepared for the awesome devastation when it struck.

Instead of procrastination, we see unquestioning and unhesitating obedience. Four times in the next few verses we're told that Noah did everything just as God commanded him (see Genesis 6:22; 7:5, 9, 16).

*Accept God's Invitation*

God had been watching Noah's obedience. He knew all about Noah's hard work, his perseverance, the sacrifice of his time, his energy, his money, his family, his entire life, especially during the 120 years it took to build the ark! "The LORD then said to Noah, 'Go into the ark, you and your whole family, because I have found you righteous in this generation'" (Gen. 7:1). The King James Version of the Bible indicates this was more of an invitation than a command when it translates the same verse as, "And the LORD said unto Noah, 'Come thou and all thy house into the ark; for thee have I seen righteous before me in this generation.'" The invitation suggests that God was already in the ark, inviting Noah to join Him there.

The offer God extended to Noah was an invitation to be saved from the judgment that was coming. What if Noah had refused the invitation, saying, "No, I believe there are other ways to be saved from the judgment that lies ahead," or "I want to enjoy my life as it is a little longer. I'll come into the ark, but not yet. I'm having too much fun out here," or "I don't want to leave and lose my old friends," or "I don't believe judgment is really coming anyway. That's such an old-fashioned, negative concept"? If that had been Noah's attitude, he would have perished. Because judgment did come. On his own, Noah would have been totally helpless to survive the Flood that destroyed all living things outside the ark.

God has also told you and me that judgment is coming—physical death that ushers us into eternity, where our sin has condemned us to hell.[9] Hell is a place of intense, unending physical suffering, insecurity, instability, darkness, loneliness, dissatisfaction, and worst of all, separation from the One for whom we were created.[10] Because we are all sinners, hell is our inevitable eternal destination. On our own, we are absolutely, totally helpless to avoid it.

At the same time God warns us that judgment is coming, He issues an invitation to come into the Ark He has provided as the means of salvation from it. Jesus

Christ is the Ark in which we hide, our Savior from the storm of God's coming judgment. When did you accept His invitation to "come in"? If you haven't done so, what is your excuse?

God's judgment is like the rain. When the rain falls, it falls on everything. If I go outside, on my own I am helpless to stay dry. So I put up an umbrella. Then, instead of falling directly on me, the rain falls on the umbrella, and I stay dry underneath it. God's judgment falls on everyone because all of us have sinned.[11] On my own, I am helpless to avoid it. So I put up the "umbrella" of the blood of Jesus Christ shed at the cross. When judgment falls, it falls on Christ instead, and under His blood, I am saved.[12]

One morning before my Bible class began, I was standing in the narthex of the church, watching the women coming across the parking lot in the pouring rain. One woman caught my attention because she was running without an umbrella. By the time she stepped into the church, she was soaking wet. To my amazement, I noticed she was clutching an umbrella in her hand. When I asked her why she hadn't put up her umbrella to protect her from the rain, she laughingly replied, "Oh, it was just too much trouble."

Please, go to the trouble to put up the umbrella of the blood of Jesus Christ! Please, come into the Ark of salvation from God's judgment!

When Noah accepted God's invitation and entered the ark, it may have been that the sun was still shining, the sky was still blue, the birds were still singing—it was a day like every other day since the beginning of creation. As Noah surveyed the world around him, there was no obvious reason to believe that judgment was coming except that God said it was. There was no obvious reason to enter the ark, except God said, "Come. Now. Today."

Do you have a complacent attitude toward the Ark because you just don't feel you need to be saved? Do you feel you understand why some people accept God's invitation to come to Christ, because it's obvious with all the bad things happening in their lives that they need Him, but you don't? Are you sure you don't need the Ark? The sun may be shining and the sky may be blue in your life today, but what about next week? God has issued the invitation to come, saying now is the day of salvation.[13] He calls us to come into the Ark for our eternal protection, our eternal security, and our eternal salvation from His judgment. But ultimately, you and I respond for the same reason Noah did—because God said so. If you would like to accept God's invitation to come into the Ark, quietly bow your head and by faith pray this simple prayer:

*Dear God, I confess to You that I am a sinner and therefore am under con-*
*demnation and in danger of eternal judgment. I want to be saved. I believe Jesus*
*Christ is the Ark who provides salvation in Himself. I choose to leave my old life,*
*repent of my sins, and come into the Ark. I claim His blood shed at the cross to for-*
*give me of my sin, covering and protecting me from the wrath to come. I believe*
*Jesus Christ rose from the dead to give me eternal life. I ask You to give me eternal*
*life as I now invite Him to come live within me as my Lord and Savior. I will*
*seek to live my life for Him from this moment on. In Jesus' name, amen.*

If with all your heart, mind, and soul you have just prayed this prayer or one similar, then praise God! You are saved! The moment Noah entered the ark, he was saved. He didn't have to keep asking God to save him. He didn't doubt that he was really saved. He just trusted God's means of salvation to be sufficient. And it was.

When Noah entered the ark, his family followed his example: "And Noah and his sons and his wife and his sons' wives entered the ark to escape the waters of the flood" (Gen. 7:7). It seems safe to assume that if Noah had not led the way, his family would not have accepted God's invitation, and they would have perished in the Flood. Who in your family will escape God's coming judgment because you were the first to accept God's invitation to be saved? How thrilling to be the one who sets the example and leads others to salvation, especially when those others are members of your own family!

Although no details are given about Noah's wife, it's worth noting that she must have stood beside him throughout the building of the ark as well as subsequently following him inside. It is doubtful that she fully understood what her husband was doing, and it must have  required a lot of sacrifice on the part of the family, yet she submitted. And her submission to her husband led to the security and well-being of her and her children!

Surely no other principle in all the Bible arouses more intense hostility in the hearts of American women than the principle of submission to their husbands. It grates against our very nature and individualism and self-esteem. But there is no getting around it. Blessing comes to the home and to the marriage when we obey God's command to "submit to [our] husbands as to the Lord."[14]

What if Mrs. Noah had stood, hands on her hips, wagging her finger in Noah's face, and protested, "Noah, I've had about all I can take. First, you leave the good job you had and take up carpentry as a full-time hobby. Then you spend the family savings that was to go for the boys' future on more and more supplies for your endless woodworking. You have been so consumed with your work we haven't had a family vacation in 120 years! In fact, I can't remember when we really sat down to a nice family dinner. And now you're telling me that I have to go into that big boat with seventy-five thousand smelly, noisy, dirty animals, some of which creep and crawl? I don't think so. It's either that boat or me. Take it or leave it!"

Obviously, Mrs. Noah did not have an unsubmissive attitude like that, and one reason was surely that she recognized her husband was acting in submission to God. As a result of Noah's submission to God and his wife's submission to him, their family was saved.

What blessing is God withholding from your family because, as the husband and father, you refuse to submit to God or because, as the wife and mother, you refuse to submit to your husband?

Noah, along with his wife, family, and all the animals, entered the ark. But nothing happened. They spent the night and the next day there, but nothing happened. They spent the next night and the next day there, but still nothing happened. For seven days in a row the sky was blue and the sun was shining and nothing unusual happened at all (see Genesis 7:10). It must have seemed as though judgment was not going to come, that salvation was unnecessary.

Why did God wait seven days after Noah entered the ark before sending the Flood?[15] Possibly the delay was to give Noah time to get his family settled and all of the animals arranged in their stalls. Or maybe God was giving the world one last chance to repent.

During the process of building the ark, as it took size and shape, I wonder if Noah's neighbors came to watch. Perhaps word got out about what he was doing, and people came from miles around to see. The New Testament tells us that Noah was "a preacher of righteousness."[16] Did Noah stand in the door of the ark—an old man with a long, flowing gray beard—urgently, desperately pleading with those who had gathered outside the door: "Repent! Judgment is coming! The only way to be saved is to come into this ark. Please come in. Please accept God's provision of salvation. Anyone who refuses God's invitation will perish. There is no other way to be saved. Repent! Judgment is coming!"?

Imagine how the people of Noah's day must have responded to his message of salvation. Did they laugh? Did they ridicule him? Did they consider him a fool? Or a dangerous fanatic? Did they criticize him for being divisive,

  intolerant,

    narrow-minded,

      unloving,

        negative,

          or exclusive?

Maybe they just shrugged their shoulders and ignored him. The world was beautiful, life was as it always had been, and they just didn't see a need for salvation from a judgment they didn't think was coming anyway.

Who is mocking your decision to accept God's offer of salvation from judgment? Perhaps you're feeling a little unsure about your decision yourself because nothing seems to have changed since you made it. You have no special feelings or emotions. Your life seems to be the same as it has always been. Circumstances remain unchanged. In this situation you may begin to doubt your decision because nothing has happened to confirm it was right.

Other than the animals coming to him, Noah waited in the ark for seven days with no confirmation he had made the right decision. But his acceptance of God's invitation was based not on other people's opinions, not on his own feelings, and not on the circumstances of his life, but on sheer obedience to God's Word alone.

Finally, after seven days had passed and the animals were all in place and Noah and his family were settled in their space; "then the LORD shut him in" (Gen. 7:16). One of the kindest, most merciful and gracious acts of God was shutting the door of the ark with His own hands. Hundreds and thousands of people were still outside, including Noah's brothers and sisters, cousins and in-laws, nieces and nephews, aunts and uncles, as well as friends and neighbors. Can you imagine what would have happened if Noah had shut the door? All his life he would have wondered, *Did I shut it too soon? If I had waited five minutes longer, would someone else have come in?*

God, in His sovereignty, knew that not one more person in the whole world was going to repent and come in, so He shut the door.

Whom do you know who thinks a loving God would never "shut the door" and leave him or her to judgment? The world of Noah's day would say from hard experience to that person, "Think again." Because God did shut the door of the ark on a world filled with people and allowed them, by their own choice, to come under His judgment. Outside the ark, they were utterly, hopelessly, eternally helpless to withstand it.

Our helplessness is overcome through obedience to God's Word as we follow His instructions and accept His invitation. In doing so, we come to depend on Him, and Him alone.

## OVERCOMING THROUGH DEPENDENCE UPON GOD'S WORD

The storm that no one thought was coming came "in the six hundredth year of Noah's life, on the seventeenth day of the second month—on that day all the springs of the great deep burst forth, and the floodgates of the heavens were opened" (Gen. 7:11). The date given for the Flood is so specific it emphasizes that this was a literal, historic day in human history. Noah and the precious cargo of life within the ark were completely helpless. They had to depend upon God alone in the midst of the most devastating and destructive storm that has ever occurred in human history on planet Earth.

### During the Storm

The Flood came suddenly, all at once. It did not start to drizzle then begin to rain harder and harder until the waters rose and flooded the earth. Instead, "the springs of the great deep burst forth, and the floodgates of the heavens were opened" (Gen. 7:11).

On the second day of Creation, God separated the waters below from the waters above (Gen. 1:7). Apparently, at that time, God buried water below in underground reservoirs, oceans, lakes, and rivers. The water above must have been gathered into a type of vapor canopy that trapped billions of tons of water, giving the earth a greenhouse effect. When God sent the Flood, the earth's crust ruptured so that all the underground fountains burst forth like thousands of geysers, or uncapped "water wells." And the vapor canopy must have split, dropping an avalanche of billions of tons of water on the earth. The resulting atmospheric change would then have caused it to rain "on the earth forty days and forty nights" (Gen. 7:12).

What would it have been like to be inside the ark and suddenly hear the water crash on the roof and feel the thrust of the water erupting underneath and to hear the screams of the people and animals outside the ark who came under judgment? It would have been terrifying to feel the gigantic barge jerked from side to side as though it were a leaf in the wind! And when the crashing and thrusting and jerking ceased, it must have sounded like forty days and forty nights of living under Niagara Falls as the torrential rains pounded the roof.

What did Noah think? Was he wondering, *Did I put enough pitch over there? Did I make that rafter as strong as God said?* During judgment, it was vital for his peace of mind to know that he had been totally obedient to God's Word. And since he had done "everything just as God had commanded him," he just had to depend upon God's power to save him during the storm.

Are you afraid of the storm of God's judgment? If you are inside the Ark because you have deliberately accepted God's invitation extended to you at the cross of Jesus Christ, there is no need to fear. God's power to save is sufficient for you and me, even as it was for Noah.[17]

Like Noah, is your whole world falling apart? Other than the fear of judgment, what storm is rocking your boat? A storm of

    public criticism?

        physical suffering?

          financial loss?

            emotional abuse?

               social rejection?

                  racial prejudice?

                     relational tension?

                        personal doubt?

In the midst of your storm, place your trust in God alone. Get down on your knees, tell Him what you are going through, and then open your Bible and ask Him to give you a command or promise that will strengthen your faith. Plead for His mercy and grace to keep you secure and give you peace of mind.

Following the thrilling experience of seeing Jesus feed more than five thousand people with only five loaves and two fish, the disciples were commanded by Jesus to get into a boat and cross the Sea of Galilee while He went up into the mountain to pray. They obeyed His command, certain of His will, but during the night a storm arose, and they were in danger of capsizing.

As they strained to keep the boat afloat, they were unaware Jesus was watching them. Although they had not seen Him, He had never let them out of His sight. As the storm raged around the disciples, He went to them, walking on the water. When they saw Him, their storm suddenly got worse because they thought He was a ghost! They screamed in terror, but He immediately spoke to them, giving them peace through His Word. Then He climbed into the boat, and the storm ceased.

If you are in the midst of a storm that has suddenly taken a turn for the worse, look up! Your Savior sees you where you are and will come to you. He will give you peace through His Word in the midst of the storm. Open your Bible and read what He has to say. And if you pray and invite Him into the "boat" of your life, giving Him control and authority over the winds and the waves, He will come in and still the storm.

The circumstances in your life may not change—or they may change completely. Regardless of your circumstances, the storm raging inside you will cease, and you will have peace.

Years ago I felt engulfed in a storm of fear when financial difficulties were swamping my "boat." As I wept and prayed and pleaded for God's help, He seemed to speak to me through a passage of Scripture from the life of the apostle Paul, who had been caught up in a storm at sea under circumstances that were beyond his control.[18] As I took to heart what Paul said to his shipmates, God not only gave me direction as to how to ride out the storm but also a promise that He would see me through it. And the storm within ceased as I had peace. Within a few months, the storm without settled down as I obeyed what I believed God had said to me, and I was able to reach the "land" of financial stability in safety.

Noah's storm raged until the entire world was submerged under water. Job says that the waters "overturned" the earth, possibly indicating this was when the earth tilted on its axis.[19] Peter confirms that the world, "being overflowed with water, perished."[20]

The Bible describes the Flood as a worldwide deluge, not a localized storm.[21] "The waters rose and increased greatly on the earth, and the ark floated on the surface of the water. They rose greatly on the earth, and all the high mountains under the entire heavens were covered. The waters rose and covered the mountains to a depth of more than twenty feet. Every living thing that moved on the earth perished. . . . Everything on dry land that had the breath of life in its nostrils died. Every living thing on the face of the earth was wiped out. . . . Only Noah was left, and those with him in the ark" (Gen. 7:18–23).

The Flood was God's judgment on the wicked, willful world of Cain's civilization; it serves as a warning to our world today. God destroyed the world once, and the Bible says He will do it again—not by water but by fire.[22] Judgment is coming on our world, possibly in our lifetime. Mankind will be helpless in the face of it unless each person individually follows God's instructions, accepts His invitation, and then trusts Him—not only in the storms of life but also in the silences that follow.

*During the Silence*

God's invitation to come into the ark was the last recorded time He spoke to Noah until after the Flood had receded 371 days later. Think of the deafening silence! After the initial forty days and forty nights of rain, there would have been no sound at all. Perhaps the gentle lapping of the water on the sides of the ark and probably the noisy confusion of the animals within the boat, but that was it. As far as the eye could see, the vast horizon was just one watery wasteland. The only visible object in the entire world was the ark, rocking in the cradle of the deep.

There was not one thing Noah could do to relieve or change his situation. He could not steer the ark, and if he could, what would he aim for? He could not paddle to increase the speed, and if he could, where would he be going? He could not build a lifeboat and bail out. He could not lobby for government assistance. He was absolutely, completely helpless.

But the silence in the world would not have been as disturbing as the silence from God. Is God silent in your life? Are your prayers unanswered and your Bible reading lifeless? Have you accepted God's invitation to come into the Ark by committing your life to Jesus Christ, only to feel as though God has withdrawn from you? Instead of feeling His love and joy and peace and presence in your life, is there just His silence? Why? Could it be God is teaching you to live by faith, not by your feelings? Could it be that He is teaching you, after you have been obedient, that you must be dependent as well?

When God is silent, the first thing we can do is to go back to the last time God seemed to give us instructions and make sure we have followed them in obedience. If we have been obedient to the best of our understanding, then we must simply depend upon Him to see us through. God had told Noah He was going to send judgment on the earth, and He had. God had told Noah to build an ark, and Noah had. God had invited Noah and his family to come into the ark to escape the judgment, and Noah had. Noah then had to rest in God's Word and wait for deliverance from the storm until "God *remembered* Noah" (Gen. 8:1, italics added).

$\mathscr{L}$❤

FOLLOWING the death of Jesus of Nazareth, Joseph of Arimathea went to Pilate and requested the body. Normally, the bodies of executed victims were either dumped in a mass grave or left for the dogs and vultures. In this case, Joseph, a member of the ruling religious body of Israel, boldly asked for the body of Christ so he could bury Him in his own new, unused tomb. Pilate granted Joseph's request.

So Joseph, who had been a secret believer in Jesus, went to the cross to remove the dead body before the Sabbath began at sundown. He was joined by Nicodemus, another religious ruler who previously had come to speak with Jesus at night. Together they tenderly extracted the nails from Jesus' hands and feet, gently lifted His lifeless body from the cross, then carried it to Joseph's tomb, where the body was washed, anointed with a fortune of spices, then wrapped for burial. They lovingly laid the body in the tomb, then rolled the heavy stone across the entrance to seal it from marauding animals or thieves.[23] It was Friday, and Jesus was crucified and buried.

At that point, Jesus of Nazareth was humanly helpless. He was dead, buried, cold, motionless, lifeless. His disciples were shocked by the sudden turn of events, grieving over their loss, and terrified of the Romans. They were paralyzed into a suspended state of numbness.

To make matters worse, the devil, that old Serpent who had bruised the heel of the Seed of the woman, was panicked that his head was going to be crushed! So he cleverly arranged for a Roman guard to seal the tomb and keep watch over it while he massed all of his invisible forces of evil over the tomb to make sure Jesus stayed buried![24] It was Saturday, and Jesus was in the tomb.

But Sunday was coming!

And God *remembered* Jesus . . .

# 8

I AM THE GOD OF SALVATION

## *I Calm Your Fearfulness*

GENESIS 8

Several years ago, the border of Thailand was jammed with more than one hundred thousand terrified refugees from Burma who were packed into overflowing camps. They lived in constant turmoil and fear that the government troops would cross the border into their camps and massacre them.

On another continent, the Hutu tribe in Rwanda had just turned on the ruling Tutsi tribe—slaughtering more than one million men, women, and children. While the stories of panic and horror tumbled out of the country, the streets of Rwandan villages ran with rivers of blood. On one occasion in the capital city of Kigali, hundreds of women were herded onto a bridge. Then their menacing captors began swinging machetes, forcing the women to jump off the bridge onto the concrete pavement one hundred feet below. In spite of such bloodletting, one tribe was able to hold on to its power, and the other tribe fled the country in fear of retaliation, becoming refugees in neighboring nations. The refugee camps became increasing targets for terrorists, prompting hundreds of thousands of Hutus to abandon the camps and march back to their country in unending lines of misery. New refugee camps were established just to care for the children who were lost to their parents in the constant shuffling back and forth—children whose haunted eyes and vacant stares reflect the horror of what they had seen and what they feared they would see again.

Fear. It strikes young and old, rich and poor, great and small, of every nation, of every culture, of every generation, on every continent. When have you been struck by it? Are you living in fear even now?

Following the robbery of our home, I found myself terrified by strange noises and sudden interruptions. A phone call with just the sound of breathing but no voice on the other end of the line, a car sitting idly at the mailbox, or a salesman who appeared from nowhere at my front door would send me into a terrified panic. My heart would race, my breathing would get shallow, my stomach would knot, and my knees would feel so weak I would have to sit down whenever I even thought of the possibility of going through another similar experience. Fear was, and is, paralyzing.

Have you ever been a victim of crime? If statistics are accurate, more than half of the American population will be victimized at some time during their lives. Ann Landers once said that out of the ten thousand letters she got each month, one problem surfaced more than any other, and it was fear.[1]

Fear of the future,
     fear of the unknown,
fear of consequences,
     fear of violence,
fear of exposure,
     fear of poverty,
fear of old age,
     fear of loneliness,
fear of rejection,
     fear of death,
fear of God . . .

And right on the heels of fear is worry. What are you afraid of that has you literally sick with worry? Medical studies have proven that worry attacks the central nervous system, the circulatory system, and the digestive system of our bodies. Charles Mayo, of the Mayo Clinic, said, "You can worry yourself to death, but you cannot worry yourself to a longer life."[2] The word *worry* comes from a root word in Old English that means "to choke or to strangle," and it can strangle our good health as well as choke our emotions until we are not able to adequately function.

As I concluded the writing of this very chapter, my husband received a call late one Sunday evening from a passing motorist who had seen flames leaping over Danny's office building. Not wanting to worry me, Danny took the call, then slipped out of the house to investigate. Two hours later he returned with the shocking news that his office had been destroyed. The second floor of his building was just a charred ruin while his own office on the first floor had such extensive smoke and water damage that it had been condemned. Within a few hours, my husband, who had missed very few days of work in thirty-five years as a dentist, was out of work! Not only was he unable to care for his hundreds of patients and his staff members whose livelihood depends on his practice, but our income was immediately cut off—in a year when we not only had routine bills to pay but also two weddings to put on! The twin companions of fear and worry immediately knocked at our door. What a personal blessing to know how to answer that knock! It was an answer I had been reminded of in a fresh way during the previous days as I had meditated on Noah's experience.

Noah was exposed to such frightening experiences he could have worried himself to death; after all, he survived the equivalent of a nuclear holocaust. While Sunday school stories conjure up in our minds the picture of Noah as a quaint, folksy, old zookeeper with a plump, rosy-cheeked wife, he was in fact a very strong, courageous man of character and faith who could have been tremendously traumatized by the most violent catastrophe in history.

Having heard the crash of the water on the roof of the ark as the skies rolled back, dropping billions of tons of water on the earth; having felt the thrust of the water underneath when the earth's crust ruptured and the fountains of the deep sprang forth like the exhaust from huge jet engines; having heard the screams of those outside as they were caught in the deluge—how did Noah feel the next time he saw a storm brewing on the horizon? Or the next time he heard thunder? Or felt a raindrop?

Surely Noah knew the paralysis of fear and the total paranoia of worry. But he also knew by experience that the God of the storm is also the God of all comfort, able to calm his fears as he kept his faith in God and his focus on God.[3]

## CALMED BY KEEPING YOUR FAITH IN GOD

Noah was totally helpless to change his situation. There was nothing he could do except to stay on the ark and tend to the needs of his family and those of the animals until God in some way brought deliverance. He had to keep his faith in God while simply waiting out the silence that followed the storm.

### Waiting in the Silence

Although He had been silent, God had not forgotten Noah. In fact, since Noah and his family were the only living persons on the face of the earth, we can be sure they had God's total, undivided attention every moment.

Did you think God's silence in your life meant He had forgotten you? Oh, no! God says He has engraved your name on the palms of His hands.[4] He says that a mother could forget her nursing baby at mealtime before He could forget you![5] You are in God's heart and on His mind every moment. He is fully informed of your circumstances and will bring about change when He knows the time is right. God has not forgotten you, nor did He forget Noah.

In His own time and way, God began to change Noah's circumstances. "But God remembered Noah and all the wild animals and the livestock that were with him in the ark, and he sent a wind over the earth, and the waters receded" (Gen. 8:1). When the text says God "remembered," it simply means the time had come for God to act. On His own initiative, which required nothing of Noah except patient waiting, God sent a wind to evaporate the waters and dry up the earth. Not only did God send the wind, but "the springs of the deep and the floodgates of the heavens had been closed, and the rain had stopped falling from the sky" (Gen. 8:2). Apparently the fountains that had erupted from the underground reservoirs, gushing through the earth's crust, were somehow stopped.

After the underground reservoirs had emptied, did they collapse into gigantic sinkholes, which formed the basins for our oceans as we know them today? Certainly as the earth's crust sank, it would force the rest of the earth up so that "the water receded steadily from the earth" (Gen. 8:3). As the water receded into the newly formed basins, it would push the sediment up, creating continents and new mountain ranges that scientists tell us are relatively young in the history of our planet. And as the "floodgates of the heavens" closed, the vapor canopy must have spent itself, giving way to clear days and bright sunshine.

I wonder if Noah was just going about the chores he had been doing every day for weeks and months, feeding the animals, cleaning the stalls, separating the cats and dogs, foxes and hens, snakes and mice, when he was startled by a shaft of light coming through the open space just below the roofline. Did he drop his broom and stumble over the feed bucket as he yelled for his wife and family while scurrying toward the upper deck and the window he had put into the side of the ark? With trembling hands did he remove the crossbar and throw back the shutters, gasping as the brilliant sunshine stung his eyes and the icy wind blew across his face? With his eyes watering and his voice choked with emotion, did he embrace his wife while he shouted his praise to the God who had sent the storm, but who also sent the sunshine? Noah knew God had remembered him and was moving to change his circumstances in answer to his silent prayers.

What shaft of light has God sent into your life to let you know He remembers you? Perhaps it's just a small change in your circumstances that has encouraged you to patiently persevere in your waiting, knowing God is at work.

After five months of floating on an endless sea, Noah must have felt a tremendous jolt as the gigantic barge shifted back and forth, with the big timbers groaning under the strain as it settled on firm ground. "At the end of the hundred and fifty days the water had gone down, and on the seventeenth day of the seventh month the ark came to rest on the mountains of Ararat" (Gen. 8:3–4). Then there was absolute stillness—no gentle rocking on the water, no movement underneath the boat, just an unfamiliar, almost-forgotten stillness broken only by the frightening sound of the gale-force wind whistling around the eaves of the ark, wailing mournfully as it whipped over the bare mountain ridges. Noah knew the ark was no longer floating but had landed on solid ground.

Noah's experience comes to mind when from time to time I must take very long airplane flights. Some of the longest without a break have been from Los Angeles to Fiji, from Seattle to Hong Kong, from Amsterdam to Johannesburg, and from Tokyo to Chicago. Such flights can seem endless when, after eating meals, watching more than one movie, reading books, writing papers, talking with passengers, and sleeping fitfully, there are still eight hours left on the flight! After being in the air fourteen to seventeen hours, even though the flight itself is smooth with little turbulence, there is no way to adequately describe the deep sense of relief when the big jet touches down on the runway, and I know I am once again on the ground.

Surely my sense of relief in being back on the ground after a one-day flight is just a shadow of Noah's feelings when he realized the ark had touched down after being afloat for months! Relief, joy, and excitement must have competed for the most dominant emotion, but I wonder if there was also just a tinge of fear . . . the kind of fear I experience when the long flight is over and the big jet touches down—on foreign soil. It is the fear of the unknown and the unfamiliar.

The ark touched down in what would have been an entire world of unfamiliar territory. "And on the seventeenth day of the seventh month the ark came to rest on the mountains of Ararat. The waters continued to recede until the tenth month, and on the first day of the tenth month the tops of the mountains became visible" (Gen.

8:4–5). The fact that it took an additional three months to see the tops of the other mountains indicates that the ark had come to rest on the highest mountain. Today the highest mountain in the Ararat range is seventeen thousand feet.[6] That's a long way up! And a long way to look down from the window of the ark!

At first, when Noah gazed out of the window, drinking in the warmth of the sunshine and breathing the clean, fresh air, it must have looked like he was on an island in the midst of a vast lake with the tops of the mountains looking like other islands in the sea. But as the water continued to recede, what did he think when he realized he was on top of a mountain range seventeen thousand feet high? Surely he felt another sharp pang of fear as his eyes searched the landscape and found nothing he recognized.

What situation are you in that God is changing, but now you are becoming apprehensive about just what those changes will mean? Is He working out much needed changes in your job, but now you realize you are going to be working under new managers who may not give you the freedom you've had in the past? Is He working out much needed changes in your marriage, but now you realize you're going to have to make some unselfish, major adjustments? Is He working out much needed changes in your character, but now you realize you've got to get serious about prayer and Bible reading? Are you beginning to wonder if it's more change than you had bargained for?

As Noah became aware of the gradual yet drastic changes taking place in his circumstances, he must have feared what they would mean to his everyday life. Did he think that it was almost more change than he could cope with? He was an old man to be starting out in a new job requiring a new home and a totally new environment. But like the psalmist, Noah knew he should "wait for the Lord and keep his way. He will exalt you to inherit the land; when the wicked are cut off you will see it."[7] As Noah waited on God, he had to keep his faith, trusting that the same God who had saved him from the storm of judgment that had "cut off" the wicked would enable him to inherit the "land" of his new life. As he waited for the answer to his prayers, he watched in hope that God would answer and deliver him.

*Watching in Hope*

Forty days after the water had receded so that the tops of the other mountains had been spotted, Noah decided to test the livability of life outside the ark. It may have been very tempting to fling open the door and jump into the new world after months of being cooped up on the ark. But some things take time. If he had rushed prematurely into the world outside the ark, he would have endangered himself and his fellow passengers because of the precarious condition of the earth. Mudslides, avalanches, and falling rocks would have been just some of the hazards he would have encountered as the earth continued to settle.

So instead of flinging open the door and charging down the gangplank, "Noah opened the window he had made in the ark and sent out a raven, and it kept flying back and forth until the water had dried up from the earth" (Gen. 8:6–7). Since ravens feed on dead things, the bird Noah sent out could land on a floating carcass, pick at it, then come back to the ark to rest.

After a week's time, Noah "sent out a dove to see if the water had receded from the surface of the ground. But the dove could find no place to set its feet because there was water over all the surface of the earth; so it returned to Noah in the ark. He reached out his hand and took the dove and brought it back to himself in the ark" (Gen. 8:8–9).

What was Noah doing when he sent the raven and the dove out of the ark? The most obvious meaning is that Noah needed enlightenment. The one window in the ark was probably placed high up, almost under the eaves of the roof to keep it away from the turbulent swells and crashing waves of the water during the storm. Because of the angle created by the height of the window and his own lower position inside the ark, as Noah looked out, it is doubtful he could have seen below the ark to the surface of the water. Most probably, he could only see the sky and perhaps the farthest horizon, which in time included a view of the topmost peaks of other mountains in the Ararat range. It may be that God's mercy protected Noah from seeing the initial details of devastation—floating human bodies and animal carcasses. So Noah used the birds as a way of getting information about the condition of his surroundings.

Noah's need for enlightenment as he sought to begin a new life would be similar to our need to have detailed, practical information if we were moving into a new neighborhood or beginning a new business or a new ministry or in some other way beginning a new life. We wouldn't send out birds; we would seek out zoning laws, marketing polls, school districts, transportation patterns, church availability, and other information that would help enlighten us in practical ways before we took the first real step.

Another view of what Noah was doing is not so obvious but is perhaps more meaningful. It is easy to imagine that Noah not only needed enlightenment about the conditions of his surroundings outside of the ark but also needed encouragement because of the conditions inside the ark. He almost seemed to be like the captain of a riverboat who knows the channel is growing shallow and constantly takes depth soundings to reassure himself the boat is safe. When God had told Noah He was "going to bring the floodwaters on the earth to destroy all life under the heavens," He had also said He would establish a covenant with Noah and his family to keep them alive along with all the animals who would come to him (Gen. 6:17–18, 20). Noah had God's promise that God would bring him through the judgment, through the storm, through the Flood to new life on the other side. Noah sent out the birds as a way to watch for signs of encouragement that God was fulfilling His promise.

Have you been in a situation that has proven to be extremely stressful? It may not have been as stressful as a nuclear holocaust or a devastating flood, but has the pressure been great enough so that consuming fear and worry have been your constant companions? When you find yourself drowning in overwhelming circumstances, ask God to give you a promise to which you can cling—a promise on which you can base your hope. Hope that is based simply on what you want or what you feel is not a genuine expression of faith. What people really mean when they say they have lost their faith or no longer have any hope is that they no longer feel things are going to work out the way they want. Instead our hope must be based on God's Word. If you haven't done so already, ask God to give you a specific promise regarding your situation to establish a genuine basis for your hope.

Noah's hope of deliverance was based on God's promise to him; therefore it was valid. However, even genuine hope and faith can reach the point of needing encouragement and confirmation—especially after a long time of waiting in silence and inactivity.

When God gives you His Word, you may have to wait in silence for a long time, just helplessly trusting Him to deliver you in His own time and in His own way. But then, out of the darkness, He may send a shaft of light that suddenly lets you know the situation is changing. At that time, you may send out the "birds"—prayers for encouragement and enlightenment that will strengthen your faith and increase your hope in Him.

At one time in Israel's history, the Midianites invaded her land, destroyed her crops and livestock, and ravaged the countryside. So Israel cried out for God to save her. He answered her prayer by raising up Gideon to lead her to victory in battle over the Midianites. But when Gideon was handed the leadership assignment, he balked, protesting, "But Lord, . . . how can I save Israel? My clan is the weakest in Manasseh, and I am the least in my family."⁸ When God assured Gideon He would be with him and would empower him to defeat the enemy, Gideon accepted. Shortly thereafter he was challenged in his leadership position, so he prayed, "'If you will save Israel by my hand as you have promised—look, I will place a wool fleece on the threshing floor. If there is dew only on the fleece and all the ground is dry, then I will know that you will save Israel by my hand, as you said.' And that is what happened. Gideon rose early the next day; he squeezed the fleece and wrung out the dew—a bowlful of water. Then Gideon said to God, 'Do not be angry with me. Let me make just one more request. Allow me one more test with the fleece. This time make the fleece dry and the ground covered with dew.' That night God did so. Only the fleece was dry; all the ground was covered with dew."⁹

Gideon's prayer is referred to as "putting out a fleece," a test similar to sending out the raven and dove. A "fleece" is a practical circumstance or situation that could conceivably happen but probably would not without divine intervention. It is used not to discern God's will as much as it is used to confirm God's will.

Recently, when I was in Alaska, the chairman of the committee managing the conference in which I participated told me of a "fleece" she had put before the Lord several years ago. She said she had felt led in 1990 to ask Elisabeth Elliott to speak to her conference in 1992, only to be turned down. The chairman responded by asking Elisabeth to keep the invitation on file for the future. The committee secured another speaker, but a year and a half later, several months before the 1992 conference was to take place, the person canceled. As the chairman began praying earnestly, not for just a speaker but for the specific one of God's choice, she put out her "fleece." She prayed, "Lord, we want the speaker of Your choice. And in order for us to be assured that the person is Your choice and not ours, would You have whomever You have chosen to contact us."

Within one week, the chairman received a letter from Elisabeth Elliott asking if the committee would still be interested in having her, as she was available to come! The entire committee rejoiced in the confirmation of God's choice by way of the "fleece"! When Elisabeth Elliott arrived for the conference and compared notes with the committee chairman, her decision to go to Alaska had coincided in time with the chairman's prayer.

The raven may have been Noah's "fleece," revealing Noah's need for enlighten-ment and encouragement as well as confirmation to his faith that the Flood was over and deliverance was near. It could also be that Noah's sending forth the raven and the dove indicated his eagerness to receive all that God had for him. He knew God had promised to bring him through the Flood to a new beginning. There was no real need for him to send out the birds since God's Word, not his knowledge of the condition of the surrounding land, would determine the timing of his exit from the ark. His sending out the birds may have been evidence of his unwillingness to complacently settle for life inside the ark when God had promised him a new life on the outside.

At first glance, this seems like an obviously natural frame of mind. However, faced with the endless devastation of the surrounding expanse, Noah may have been tempted not even to look outside much less think of actually going outside. All of his responsibilities on the ark were probably manageable and well under control by this time. And the ark was safe and familiar while the rest of the world was not. Of course, you and I might think that after being on the ark for nine months with seventy-five thousand animals, anyone would want to get out. But that may not have been the case.

When Jesus confronted a man beside the pool of Bethesda who had been para-lyzed for thirty-eight years, He asked, "Do you want to get well?"[10]

At first, it must have sounded like a thoughtless question. Surely anyone who had been lying down for so long would want to get up. But Jesus knew it can be easier to lie on a cot, letting people carry you around, waiting on you hand and foot, than to pick up all the responsibilities of life that are required when you can walk. The man answered that he did indeed want to get well, and immediately Jesus told him to get up, pick up his pallet, and walk. And the man did.

God can change our circumstances, but sometimes He waits for us to show real desire for change as well as our faith in Him. As Noah once again climbed up the three flights of steps inside the ark to release the dove through the window, he was eagerly and persistently seeking the change in his life God had promised.

How do you and I show our eagerness to receive all that God has promised us? One way is through persistent prayer as we ask God for change and seek His Word about the change, then persistently and respectfully pray until He brings it about.[11] If you have asked God to change your circumstances in some way, claiming His prom-ise for yourself or for a loved one, what are you doing to demonstrate your faith?

The Korean church is known around the world for being a praying church. Korean Christians pray and fast on specially designated mountains for days, weeks, and even months. Literally hundreds and thousands of Christians attend daily prayer sessions at 4:30 a.m. One old Korean lady who attended the early-morning prayer meeting every day always put her husband's empty shoes on the front pew of the church, saying, "Here are my husband's shoes, Lord. I believe one day my husband will be here to fill them." One year after she began demonstrating this confident hope by bringing her husband's shoes to the prayer service, the shoes were filled! Her husband came with her and placed his faith in Jesus Christ as his Lord and Savior.

What "shoes" do you have to put before the Lord? What "raven" or "dove" do you have to send out in prayer? Biblical hope is not a "hope so" attitude. It is confidence that although you have not received what God has promised yet, you know you will.

As Noah threw open the shutters, did he offer a silent prayer as he flung the dove up into the air? Since doves don't eat dead things or like high altitudes, if the dove remained gone, Noah would know the waters had receded to lower areas. He would know God was about to fulfill His promise to deliver him and the others on the ark. Was he holding his breath as the dove flew off, watching the flash of its white wings against the blue sky and the swooping pattern of its flight? Surely it was with a sinking sensation that he realized the dove was returning to the ark, unable to find a place to rest. Noah "waited seven more days and again sent out the dove from the ark. When the dove returned to him in the evening, there in its beak was a freshly plucked olive leaf! Then Noah knew that the water had receded from the earth" (Gen. 8:10–11).

As Noah used the dove to continue to test the change in his surroundings, his faith must have been encouraged and his hope must have been increased. After releasing the dove in the morning, imagine the tension of waiting all day for the dove to return. I wonder, did he wait by the window, or did he just go about his affairs with frequent glances to the open window to see if the dove had returned? All day long his thoughts must have continually returned to the little dove, wondering if it was safe, wondering what it had found, wondering if it would return. And every time he thought of the dove, did he offer a silent prayer so that he was "praying without ceasing"?[12] When he finally did see the bird perched on the window ledge, he must have sprung for the window. As he once again took the dove in his hand, he gently extracted a twig from its beak. An olive twig! Olive trees can survive underwater, and apparently this one was not only still living but beginning to sprout into new life! Things were beginning to grow! In spite of the weeks and months of being submerged underwater, the earth was still alive! God was answering his prayer! God was at work to fulfill His promise! The time for deliverance was near!

Noah knew the earth was drying off and it wouldn't be long before it would be inhabitable again. "He waited seven more days and sent the dove out again, but this time it did not return to him" (Gen. 8:12). The dove obviously had found land in which it could nest, feed, and live. One month later, "Noah then removed the covering from the ark and saw that the surface of the ground was dry" (Gen. 8:13). The covering was probably part of the roof that, when removed, would enable Noah to take a 180-degree survey of the surrounding landscape.

As Noah surveyed his surroundings 314 days after the Flood had begun, what did he see? Stretching as far as the eye could see would have been mountain peak after mountain peak rippling into the distance like the giant waves of a sea, with deep valleys in between. Although the earth had been preserved, it would have been obvious that it had also been devastated. The lush fields had given way to barren wilderness; the cascading flowers had given way to rocks; the velvet grass had given way to mud. Instead of moist, warm air, there was an icy bite to the mountain wind in Noah's face as it whistled around the eaves of the ark at seventeen thousand feet. Instead of endless days of blue sky, there were now dark, scudding clouds. Instead of forests teeming with wildlife, there were sheer slopes of nothing. No life, no beauty, no movement, but also no wickedness. The extreme corruption and crime, godlessness and unrighteousness of Cain's civilization had been washed away. The entire world was clean and fresh, waiting for the human race to begin again. What an awesome responsibility for Noah! What a time to not only keep his faith in God but to keep his focus on God.

## CALMED BY KEEPING YOUR FOCUS ON GOD

Three hundred and seventy-one days after the Flood began, "God said to Noah, 'Come out of the ark, you and your wife and your sons and their wives. Bring out every kind of living creature that is with you—the birds, the animals, and all the creatures that move along the ground—so they can multiply on the earth and be fruitful and increase in number upon it'" (Gen. 8:15–17). We can almost hear the "Hallelujah Chorus" playing in the background! What a day of rejoicing that must have been! God had been faithful to see him through!

*The Faithfulness of God*

Like Jeremiah, who would serve God years later during another troubled time of judgment, Noah could say, "I remember my affliction and my wandering, the bitterness and the gall. I well remember them, and my soul is downcast within me. Yet this I call to mind and therefore I have hope: Because of the LORD's great love we are not consumed, for his compassions never fail. They are new every morning; great is your faithfulness."[13]

Jeremiah's God was Noah's God, and He is your God. He has not changed. If He was faithful to watch over Noah and all those within the ark, bringing them safely through the storm, He will do the same for you. Just as He was faithful to preserve Joseph through thirteen years of slavery in Potiphar's house and Pharaoh's prison, just as He was faithful to preserve the little baby Moses floating on the Nile in another much smaller ark, just as He was faithful to preserve the three Hebrew boys in Nebuchadnezzar's fiery furnace, and just as He was faithful to preserve Daniel in the lion's den, God will be faithful to you. Why? Because God is faithful! He cannot be less than Himself! Keep your focus on God's faithfulness and on God's greatness!

*The Greatness of God*

Did God speak to Noah in his early-morning quiet time in a still, small voice that impressed his mind? Did it take a moment for what God had said to sink in? That the year of

floating and drifting,
of waiting and watching,
of looking and longing,
of praying and working was over?

Did tears spring to his eyes?
Did a grin spread across his face?
Did excitement fill his heart?
Did thoughts and plans tumble in wild abandon across his mind?
Did he shout for joy, calling his family to tell them the waiting was over and they could enter the new world?

Was it Noah himself who opened the great door? Then did the entire family go stall by stall, deck by deck, to loose the animals in an orderly progression for the grand exit? Did they have to coax the deer and prod the elephants and drag the bears and lead the oxen and get out of the way of the hippos? Were the pigs squealing and the lions roaring and the hyenas laughing and the cattle lowing and the sheep bleating and the ducks quacking? Was it just a noisy bedlam of excitement as "all the animals and all the creatures that move along the ground and all the birds—everything that moves on the earth—came out of the ark, one kind after another" (Gen. 8:19)?

Before the Flood, God had said, "Come into the ark" (Gen. 7:1 KJV). The clear implication was that God was already inside, inviting Noah to join Him there. After the Flood, when God said, "Come out of the ark" (Gen. 8:16), the implication is that He had left and was asking Noah to follow. The great God of the Exodus, who led His people out of bondage to slavery in Egypt, parting the Red Sea to allow them to pass on dry ground and so escape the armies of Pharaoh, the great God of the Exodus from Persia, who led His people out of captivity to rebuild the temple in Jerusalem, the great God of the Exodus from Nazi Germany, who led His people to reestablish their homeland in Palestine—that same great God led Noah, his wife, his sons, his sons' wives, and all the animals out of the ark, into a new world!

God's greatness has not been diluted or depleted in any way over the years of time. He is just as great today as He has been in the past. So why do you think He cannot lead you out of trouble? Why would you think He is incapable of leading your entire life so that you find peace and joy and love and fulfillment? Why do you think He is unable to lead your children in the right direction that will be pleasing to Him and good for them? Why do you think He cannot lead your loved one out of the darkness of sin into the light of salvation and love? God is great!

As "Noah came out, together with his sons and his wife and his sons' wives" (Gen. 8:18), he knew the life that had been preserved on that ark was all the animal and human life there was on planet Earth. I wonder if the first step he took out of the ark and onto the surface of the new world felt a little like Neil Armstrong taking the first step out of the lunar landing vehicle onto the surface of the moon, when he said, "One small step for man. One giant leap for mankind."

Surely Noah felt a stab of fear as he gazed on the unfamiliarity of the landscape all around him. Surely he was overwhelmed with the awesome task assigned to him of starting the human race all over again. Surely he was apprehensive about the future his family would face. But immediately, we see him claiming calmness for any fears he might have by keeping his focus not only on God's faithfulness and greatness but on His graciousness as well.

*The Graciousness of God*

The very first thing Noah did in the new world was to worship God through sacrifice as had been proscribed to Adam and Eve when God killed the animals in order to clothe them with skins after they had sinned. And for the first time in the Bible an altar is mentioned as the place of sacrifice. "Then Noah built an altar to the LORD and, taking some of all the clean animals and clean birds, he sacrificed burnt offerings on it" (Gen. 8:20).

The clean animals and birds that Noah sacrificed would probably have been the domesticable ones. Therefore, they would have been the ones Noah would need the most in rebuilding his life—animals and birds that perhaps he had even developed an attachment to during the year's voyage in the ark. But he took one-seventh of all of his flocks and herds and offered them in an extravagant sacrifice to the God of his salvation! Surely the sacrifice was one

> of praise to God for His faithfulness and greatness,
>
> of thanksgiving to God for His grace to save himself and his family,
>
> of confession of his own sin and unworthiness of such grace,
>
> of repentance from anything that would not be pleasing to God,
>
> of rededication of his life to the One who had saved it.

Noah must have been totally overwhelmed by the awareness that out of all the people who had been living on planet Earth, God had saved him. Why? It was just God's grace! Noah had been righteous and blameless as he had walked with God, but he knew that did not make him worthy of salvation. His heart must have felt ready to burst with the intensity of his gratitude. There could be no other way to express what was in his heart than to give back to God the life that He alone had saved.

Years later, there was another extravagant sacrifice of praise offered by a grateful woman to a gracious God. Shortly before His crucifixion, Jesus was the honored guest at a feast held in one of His favorite homes, presumably to celebrate the new life of His friend Lazarus. While Jesus, along with Lazarus and other guests, was reclining at the dinner table, Lazarus's sister, Mary, entered the room with an alabaster box. The box contained very expensive perfume—equal to a year's wages—that would have been her dowry. Mary took the box of perfume that represented her future hopes and dreams, broke it, and poured it on the head of Jesus. When she was criticized by those in the room as being exceedingly wasteful, Jesus sharply rebuked them while gently praising her for a beautiful act of sacrificial worship that filled the house with the fragrance of the perfume.[14]

"The LORD smelled the pleasing aroma" (Gen. 8:21), and the fragrance of Noah's sacrifice, like Mary's, was a blessing to His heart. God accepted Noah's sacrifice just as He had accepted Abel's.

How extravagant is your sacrifice to God? Do you give God as little as you think you can get by with?

A little bit of energy and effort when you're not too tired?

A little bit of time you have no use for?

A little bit of money you don't really need yourself? A little bit of love left over from others?

A sacrifice is not a sacrifice until it's a sacrifice! Is your sacrifice a real sacrifice? We give to God

if we can afford it,

if we feel like it,

if we want to,

if we have nothing better to do,

if it's comfortable,

if it's not too inconvenient,

if it's not too hard,

if we get some credit . . .

How can you and I think such stingy sacrifices are pleasing to God?! At the least, such sacrifices reveal an ingratitude in our hearts and an ignorance in our understanding of what God has done for us. At the worst, He will not accept such sacrifices, just as He rejected Cain's.

Noah could have rationalized his selfishness by saying he needed every single animal available to begin repopulating the planet or in reworking the fields or in rebuilding a home. And in the view of many today, he would have been commended for his pragmatism and his good business decisions. But Noah knew you can't outgive God. Instead of being afraid he wouldn't have enough of what he needed for himself and his family, instead of laying up treasures on earth, instead of trying to secure his future by hoarding everything for himself, Noah knew that a God who is faithful, great, and gracious deserved nothing less than an extravagant sacrifice! As he kept his focus on who God is, Noah poured out his heart in worship. And God responded by reassuring Noah of His goodness.

### The Goodness of God

Noah's fears of living in the new world were greatly eased as God reassured him, "Never again will I curse the ground because of man, even though every inclination of his heart is evil from childhood. And never again will I destroy all living creatures, as I have done. As long as the earth endures, seedtime and harvest, cold and heat, summer and winter, day and night will never cease" (Gen. 8:21–22).

God confirmed that although the Flood had washed the earth clean, erasing it of any remnant of sin or any shred of Cain's civilization, the heart of man was still evil. Since Adam had chosen to disobey God, sin had entered the human race and was now so deeply embedded in man's nature that man was born "bad." Yet in spite of the sin and rebellion that God knew lurked in the very next generation of Noah's sons and would increase with every subsequent generation, God committed Himself to spare the earth His previous judgments. While He did not remove the curse He had placed on planet Earth following Adam and Eve's sin in the garden, He vowed He would not increase the curse. And He promised that never again would He destroy all life on the planet as He had done during the Flood.

As evidence that He was good and would keep His promise, God pointed to the very cycles in nature. As you and I see the winter snows give way to spring flowers and the summer's heat give way to autumn's briskness, we are reminded that in back of the changes is the God who never changes. The sun that always rises every morning and always sets every evening, the stars that always come out in the night sky, and the moon that always goes through its monthly phases—all reveal the glory of God, who is good!

God, as the Judge of all the earth, determined the wickedness of Cain's civilization could no longer be tolerated, and He sent the Flood to wash it away. God, who judged the world, is the same God who saved the world from His own judgment by providing the ark as a means of escape. Praise God! That's His goodness!

Like pouring oil on troubled waters, our knowledge of who God is calms our fears. So . . . keep your faith, and keep your focus!

177

God is faithful
    and great
        and gracious
           and good
               and kind
                   and loving
                       and patient
                           and holy
                               and righteous
                                   and just
                                       and merciful.

As His creation, we belong to God. He holds us accountable for our actions, our attitudes, and our activities. He has measured us against the perfect standard of His glory and rendered the verdict—we have fallen short. We do not measure up, and the sentence is death, judgment, and eternal hell. The flood of His wrath against our sin is inevitable.[15]

But God is not only our Creator and Judge, He is our Savior. He has provided the Ark as our escape from His judgment. The provision of our means of escape required the most extravagant sacrifice that has ever been or will ever be. Because the Ark is Himself.

God left His throne at the center of the universe. He set aside His glory, and He humbled Himself as He took on human flesh. He confined Himself to a woman's womb for nine months.

He submitted to the human birth process.

He lived inside the small body of a toddler.

He grew into an adolescent.

And He became a Man.

He came to His own—those whom He had created for Himself—but they didn't receive Him.

They contradicted His Word.

They challenged His authority.

They denied His claims.

They questioned His motives.

They mocked His power.

They rejected His person.

And God in Christ submitted Himself to their slapping, spitting, mocking, taunting, flogging, and stripping, then allowed them to nail Him to a cross where He gave His own life as a sacrifice for their sin. And mine. And yours. His own death satisfied His own judgment for sin, and we are saved. Hallelujah! What a Savior! He has provided the Ark as a means of escape from His own wrath against your sin. Won't you come in?

Three days after the burial of the lifeless human body of the Lord of life, the Creator of the universe who became our Savior, God raised Him from the dead!

It was early Sunday morning before dawn. An elite, handpicked Roman guard was watching the tomb in which Jesus of Nazareth had been laid. Knowing their very lives depended upon their vigilance, the eyes of the soldiers never dimmed, their ears never dulled, their minds never strayed, their bodies never relaxed as they carried out their assignment to keep any and all away from the tomb. No one was to get in. Certainly no one was to get out!

Suddenly, in the darkness, the ground began to rumble and shake as though a mighty rocket was being launched, and a violent earthquake erupted. Then, before the horror-filled gaze of the guards, against the inky blackness of night, an angel clothed in light as dazzling as new snow under a noonday sun descended from heaven, walked over to the tomb, rolled away the stone, and sat down on it! The guards became violently ill, then passed out in terrified unconsciousness because they had seen past the angel and the rolled-away stone into the tomb! And the tomb was empty! It was empty! JESUS OF NAZARETH HAD RISEN FROM THE DEAD! HE'S ALIVE!

And He who has invited you and me to come into the Ark of salvation from His judgment for our sin through the Cross now invites us to follow Him out of the tomb into abundant, new, eternal life!

Won't you come out?

# 9

## I Understand Your Weakness

GENESIS 9

He was a strongly built man with graying hair swept back from his face, sparkling black eyes, and a smooth, round face that, for all its sweetness, revealed nobility and strength of character. He sat in a circle that included members of my family, relating his story with poise and dignity. His name was Wang.[1] Wang was born into a country that was one of the most repressive in the world of its day. He said he never felt the stress of repression, because he never knew freedom. Before Wang's brother was killed in the national revolution, he taught four-year-old Wang the Lord's Prayer. His mother was a deeply committed Christian who loved the Lord Jesus Christ yet never had the opportunity to know the Scriptures well. She was unsuccessful in her attempts to transmit her faith to Wang.

One day Wang came home and announced he was going to join the national army. As he left with his small bag stuffed with all his worldly goods, his mother kissed his cheek and said, "Son, I will pray for you every day and every night."

Wang joined the army of his very repressive and also very impoverished nation. In order to make the meager rations stretch to supply all the troops, the army watered down the food, so Wang was always hungry. He noticed that military athletes were well fed, so he tried out for the wrestling team. Not only did he make the team, but for the next four years he was the wrestling champion of his nation.

One night after a wrestling match, he was walking back to the barracks when he remembered that his mother had said, "Son, I will pray for you every day and every night." Suddenly he was overcome with an intense longing for God. He didn't know what to do. He looked furtively around him, saw no one, and right there in the darkness, he dropped to his knees and recited the Lord's Prayer. From then on, before every match, he prayed that prayer along with one of his own, "God, if You are real, keep my mother safe until I can see her again."

When his tour of duty in the army was up, he was discharged and sent home. He arrived in his mountain village late one night. As he looked through the moon-lit streets, he could see a light in the window of his mother's apartment—and the silhouette of his mother's figure, watching for him. He ran home the last few yards, the door swung wide, and he was welcomed into his mother's warm embrace. That night, after he had gone to bed, he heard the sound of his mother weeping. He got up and slipped into the kitchen to find his mother distraught. The only reply she would give to his concerned inquiry was, "Son, go to church with me tomorrow." He was unable to tell his mother of his prayers and agreed to go with her to church.

The next day in church, the pastor asked those who wanted to establish a per-sonal relationship with God to raise their hands. Without hesitation, Wang fearlessly raised his hand for all to see. The pastor took him aside, answered his questions, and led him in a prayer of confession, repentance, invitation, surrender, and conversion!

As Wang related to us the details of that morning, he grasped his knees with both hands, rolled forward in his chair, and let out a great, warm, hearty laugh of joy as he recalled the thrill of those moments when he first knew his sins were for-given, that he was saved from God's judgment, that he had received eternal life, that he was right with God!

Wang went on to become a mechanical engineer, making a small fortune in a very dangerous job. After eleven years he felt God calling him to be a pastor. He gave up his lucrative job and helped to lead a small congregation of courageous believers who worshiped God in a nation ruled by a government that was hostile to any religion.

As I listened to Wang tell his story and felt his passion for Christ expressed in a life surrendered to Him at great cost to himself, I felt I was in the presence of real greatness. What a blessing his testimony was to all those gathered to hear him that evening.

Several years later, Wang received permission from the authorities in his coun-try to come to America. We were delighted to have such an outstanding man of God in our vicinity. Along with others who had been blessed and moved by his story, we had him in our home for meals, introduced him to friends, took him to conferences, secured a car for him, and just generally sought to make him feel welcome and at home. I will never forget when he asked us to also loan him a television. My husband and I exchanged glances, then gladly gave our own TV to him for his use as long as he wanted it. As he took it, he looked at us and said, "Don't you have anything larger?"

It seemed to either be a turning point in Wang's attitude or perhaps just an opening of our eyes to what was happening in his life. Wang began to wheedle sympathy from friends as he asked for a newer model car than the one he had been given, the latest set of *Encyclopedia Britannica*, designer clothing, and other items he wanted. We watched in sorrow as a truly great man yielded to the temptations of freedom, worshiped at the altar of materialism, and became consumed with greed and resentment of those who had what he wanted but couldn't get. While it was difficult to find fault because of the deprivation we knew he faced back home, we also knew that what we observed was the exposure of human weakness that resides in all of us. Even in the best of us.

There is not a more outstanding man of God in all of the Old Testament Scriptures than Noah. Because he was righteous before God and blameless before men, he had found such favor in God's eyes that God had used him to save the entire world of his day. As he stepped off the ark, he stepped into a brand-new life. And the human race, represented by Noah and his family, could begin all over again.

How thrilling to experience a brand-new beginning! But the Flood that had washed away the wickedness of Cain's civilization had not washed away the sinfulness in the human heart. It lurked like a dark shadow in the brilliant sunshine of the new day.

But God understands our weakness and has made provision for it. We experience His provision first when we heed His principles.

## OVERCOMING WEAKNESS BY HEEDING GOD'S PRINCIPLES

The first seventeen verses of Genesis 9 are a direct quotation in God's own words giving principles for you and me and the entire human race to live by. God has certain Creation principles that He stated before there was ever a Jew or Muslim or Buddhist or Hindu or Christian on the planet. These principles apply to the entire human race without exception. If we want to live a life that works, overcoming the weakness that resides in all of us, we must heed these principles. If we do not want to heed these principles, we have that freedom, but our weakness will be our downfall, and we will never live a life that works as it was created to work in the beginning. It would be similar to having a new computer with a Pentium processor but using it only as a typewriter. It would do the job, but it wouldn't even come close to fulfilling its potential. If we do not heed God's principles for our lives, you and I can exist on this planet yet not even come close to fulfilling our potential or experiencing the abundant life God intended us to possess when He created us.

As we observe the disintegration of the society all around us, it becomes increasingly clear that one primary reason for the collapse is because, due to our ignorance of God's principles, our indifference to God's principles, or our outright rejection of God's principles, our human weaknesses have become dominant, and life just does not work. What are some of these Creation principles? While many have been given in the previous chapters of Genesis, several very important ones regarding government, nourishment, and punishment are given to Noah as he takes the first steps of a fresh start for the human race.

## Principles for Government

When Noah came off the ark, he was faced with an entirely empty planet. Where would he go? Where should he live? God did not leave it up to Noah to guess but gave him clear directions: "Then God blessed Noah and his sons, saying to them, 'Be fruitful and increase in number and fill the earth. The fear and dread of you will fall upon all the beasts of the earth and all the birds of the air, upon every creature that moves along the ground, and upon all the fish of the sea; they are given into your hands'" (Gen. 9:1–2). God was commanding Noah, as He had commanded Adam and Eve years before, to scatter throughout the globe and fill the earth. This wise command was given so that man could gain control over the earth making it suitable for human habitation.

When God gave dominion over the earth to Adam and Eve, it was a dominion of love and understanding. Noah was again given dominion over the earth, but this time God said the entire government of the world, including the supremacy of man over every living thing on the planet, would be rooted in fear and dread. This fear may have been partially for the protection of the human race since the animals would multiply at a more rapid rate and could have exterminated man. God was enabling man to take charge of his earthly home.

183

It is our God-given responsibility as descendants of Noah to exercise rulership over our environment in such a way that it will continue to be suitable for human habitation. Strip mining, industrial pollution and waste, indiscriminate logging, the careless invasion of forests, rivers, wetlands, and coastal areas, and the unregulated hunting of wild animals and harvesting of the seas as well as many other thoughtless and selfish actions all are offensive to the Creator as we abuse the planet He has entrusted to us.

What are you doing to exercise your God-given rulership of the environment? What do you need to do to be a good steward of the sacred trust of the planet God has given each of us? As our earth runs out of clean air, clean water, and other natural resources necessary for human habitation, we should be reminded that the deteriorating condition of our planet is directly related in part to our refusal to heed God's Creation principle of government. Planet Earth would last longer and be a much more pleasant place to live if each of us would take God's command concerning the government of the earth more seriously.

*Principles for Nourishment*

God had given Adam and Eve fruit, vegetables, and grain to eat as their dietary nourishment.[2] Perhaps it was the perfect environment before the Flood that made meat unnecessary for the health of the human body since man was not given permission to eat it. However, that restriction changed after the Flood as God instructed Noah, "Everything that lives and moves will be food for you. Just as I gave you the green plants, I now give you everything" (Gen. 9:3). As he stepped into the new world, Noah was given all the major food groups for his use: fruit, vegetables, grain, meat, and, we assume, the milk products associated with the meat.

A professor of pediatrics at the University of Colorado, Dr. Jim Hill, has warned that "we have a whole generation of kids who are going to be obese adults." Obesity is directly linked to heart disease, diabetes, and hypertension, among other health risks. While researchers define being overweight as 20 percent heavier than the standard recommendation, a recent poll reports that 35 percent of adults and 14 percent of children age six to eleven in America are overweight enough to be unhealthy.[3]

Many of our dietary problems today, as well as other major diseases, can be traced to the abuse of the balanced nutrition God gave Noah and his descendants. Chemicals such as food preservatives, growth stimulants, artificial sweeteners, and insecticides were never given to us by God as food. Although many of us do not have the resources nor the capability to obtain totally natural foods, we can be careful to make sure our diets are as balanced and as healthy as possible. Next time your children insist on a diet of candy, soda, french fries, ice cream, fast food, and junk food, take the time to explain that healthy eating is one of God's principles and that we heed His principles for our own benefit and to enjoy a life that works.

God gave one prohibition concerning Noah's diet when He instructed him, "But you must not eat meat that has its lifeblood still in it" (Gen. 9:4). This principle was given partially for safety and sanitation in food preparation. In the days when there was no refrigeration, meat drained of the blood of the animal would not spoil as quickly as meat with the blood in it. But it was also the first in a lengthier list of laws that were later given to Moses to impress people with the uniqueness of the blood of an animal. God required a blood sacrifice as a means for man to get right with Him because He said that "without the shedding of blood there is no forgiveness."[4] Therefore, when Jesus Christ, God's Lamb, shed His blood on the cross, the people who knew not only this Creation principle but also the Mosaic Law knew His life was in the blood, and His blood had been shed for forgiveness of sin.[5] While the prohibition against eating blood in the meat was lifted at the cross when the symbolism was fulfilled in the death of Christ,[6] the principle of sanitation in food preparation is one we still need to adhere to today.

Think about your eating habits. Do you eat too much? Too little? Is your diet heavy on fat? Sugar? Sodium? Chemicals? What adjustments do you need to make for your own benefit in order to heed God's Creation principles regarding nourishment?

As I visit other countries, I enjoy asking those who have visited America to give me their greatest impressions. To my amazement, again and again, from Africa to India to Australia, I have been told that one of the greatest impressions foreign visitors have of our great nation is

> not the skyscrapers,
> not the network of super highways,
> not the quality of the telephone service,
> not the variety of foods in the grocery stores,
> not the bulging racks in the clothing stores,
> not even the beauty of our mountains and shores and forests and parks.

The greatest impression is the obesity of the American people! As I have reflected on my travels on every continent in the world, I realize that although I have seen large, overweight individuals everywhere, only in America have I seen the excessively obese people my foreign friends have described.

Because Americans seem to have difficulty doing things in moderation, we not only have the excessively obese, but we also have an increasing number of eating disorders, such as bulimia and anorexia nervosa. While much has been said about the danger of projecting waiflike women as symbols of beauty because it can pressure young girls to starve themselves, what are you and I doing to counter that pressure by teaching our children God's principles for nourishment? Overflowing doctors' offices, hospitals, and other health care facilities all give witness to our ignorance of God's principles or our indifference to God's principles or our outright rejection of God's principles that involve our diet.

While the principles of government and nourishment are unheeded in many instances, the principle of punishment is often followed, but not in a way that is compatible with what God said in the beginning. The principle is the one we associate with capital punishment.

### Principles for Punishment

What could be more repulsive to a civilized society than the official taking of human life? Yet God, Who created man, knew that the heart of man "is deceitful above all things, and desperately wicked: who can know it?"[7] And because out of the heart come "the issues of life,"[8] God knew it was only a matter of time before the wickedness that was in man's heart would give outward expression in all manner of sin: anger, fighting, stealing, raping, lying, wars, and killing, to name just some of the violence that was to come. Later, the law He gave to Moses that serves as a foundation for all the laws we abide by today would address the consequences society must apply to these sins. But there was one sin of primary importance that God gave special attention to as Noah established human life on planet Earth after the Flood. It was the sin of first degree murder, the sin of one human being willfully taking the life of another human being. "And for your lifeblood I will surely demand an accounting. I will demand an accounting from every animal. And from each man, too, I will demand an accounting for the life of his fellow man. 'Whoever sheds the blood of man, by man shall his blood be shed; for in the image of God has God made man'" (Gen. 9:5–6).

The principle of capital punishment was not given primarily as a deterrent to crime but out of God's demand for reverence of Him and respect for man, because human life is made "in the image of God."

In eighteenth-century England, it was a felony to deface a coin bearing the king's image. Defacing the coin was considered to be so disrespectful and dishonoring to the king it cost the life of the person who did it. If it was a felony to deface the coin with the king's image, how could it be considered less serious to deface the image of God by willfully taking another person's life?

In our enlightened, progressive, sophisticated society, we would ask, "How can you show respect for human life by taking it in an execution?" The answer is very simple. Because God says so. It is His Creation principle.

The centuries-old discussion of the validity of capital punishment was pushed to the forefront of modern debate by the trial of Timothy McVeigh, the man accused of bombing the Oklahoma City Federal Building in April 1995. One thousand people were notified to prepare for jury duty in McVeigh's trial. Each of the 352 jurors who were actually called were subjected to rigorous questioning, revealing a wide range of opinions on many issues.[9]

Invariably, each potential juror was questioned as to his or her views on the death penalty. The defense lawyers were looking for jurors who had convictions against imposing the death sentence on anyone while the prosecution was looking for jurors who were equally convicted that it is a valid punishment for certain crimes.

How would you have answered the lawyers' questions concerning capital punishment? Thirteen years ago I was confronted by a situation that caused me to carefully examine the biblical basis for my views on the death penalty. In the early-morning hours of November 2, 1984, I stood in a darkened room adjacent to the death chamber of North Carolina's Central Prison, the maximum-security facility for men located in my city. Surrounding me were the law officers who had worked to see justice done to Velma Barfield, who had been convicted of several murders, including that of her own mother.

Beside me was Jimmie Little, the state-appointed attorney who had diligently sought mercy instead of justice for Velma. In front of me was a solid glass wall that allowed a clear view of the execution chamber. The little room was hot, stuffy, crowded, and dark, with an undercurrent of whispers and the rustling of clothing as everyone strained for the best view of the window.

Within a few moments, Velma was wheeled into the chamber on the other side of the glass wall; she was strapped to a hospital gurney. An attendant checked her pulse and her blood pressure, then an IV was attached to her arm. Her graying curls were like a little cap around her quiet face, her lips moving in what I knew to be private conversation with her Lord. Then the attendant left the room, and Velma was alone, a small woman draped in green surgical sheets, lying on a hospital gurney, waiting to see face-to-face the One who had forgiven her sin and saved her from His judgment. I leaned over and whispered to Jimmie Little that it didn't look like the pearly gates to us, but for Velma it was.

I saw the fluid begin to drip into her IV and knew the sodium pentothal given first would soon put her to sleep. I don't know when the sodium pentothal gave way to Pavulon, the lethal drug that took her life. I just know that within what seemed like hours, but was probably no longer than ten or fifteen minutes, a doctor stepped out from behind the green curtain, checked Velma's pulse again, and pronounced her dead.

Several days later a newspaper reporter called and asked if I was angry and bitter toward the state for what it had carried out on that dark night. I replied that anger toward the state had never entered my mind. I was angry toward sin! Sin that would pervert and destroy what life is about. Sin that would cause such suffering and death. In my estimation, and in Velma's also, because of her sin she deserved to die based on God's Creation principle of punishment. Her death didn't ease the pain she had caused; it just heightened the anger against all sin that carries with it the sentence of death.[10]

Before the execution, I had appealed to the governor of our state on Velma's behalf. When Cain murdered Abel, God did not take his life but instead exercised another Creation principle, that of mercy. God preserved Cain's life but marked him in such a way that he was an example to all of society of what life was not meant to be. My appeal was an appeal for mercy. I was not asking the governor to free Velma but to preserve her life and use her within the women's prison as an example to others. The governor denied the appeal. While I believe my appeal was valid, I believe the governor's decision was also valid. And it may be that the consequences of God's mercy in allowing Cain to live, which produced the wicked civilization that provoked the Flood, give silent witness to the necessity of the Creation principle of punishment.[11]

The principle is clear, that a person who willfully takes the life of another human being forfeits his or her own life. The application of the principle is where we run into trouble. This difficulty in applying the principle is one of many reasons why it is critically important to have men and women of integrity and courage in leadership positions in our law-enforcement agencies and courts of law as well as in our lawmaking bodies. It is questionable whether any human government will ever be able to apply the principle of punishment with absolute justice. We can only work to elect those leaders we believe will carry it out most fairly and then abide by their judgments.

And we can also redouble our efforts to teach our children God's principles, talking "about them when you sit at home and when you walk along the road, when you lie down and when you get up."[12] Because life lived according to the Creator's principles works.

As we read our newspapers and watch the evening news, the serious and violent crime sweeping our nation makes us ever more mindful of the necessity to operate according to God's principles. Our society is falling apart because, in our arrogance and pride, we think we have found a better way to live than the Creator has ordained from the beginning.

In what area of your life are you not heeding God's principles? The principles are not given to us

> to hinder,
> to frustrate,
> to limit,
> to deny,
> to lessen,

or to block our enjoyment or possession of a wonderful life. Instead, they were given to guard you and me against the weakness God knows is in each of us—a weakness that will keep us from living life the way it was meant to be lived. These principles were given to strengthen us where God knows we are weak. We heed God's commands for our own benefit.

Because God understood human weakness and knew that man would fail in spite of having His principles to live by, He gave Noah a covenant, a binding contract of commitment from God to the entire human race.

## OVERCOMING WEAKNESS BY RECEIVING GOD'S COVENANT

God's covenants were commitments He initiated and guaranteed with His own Word. The fulfillment of God's covenant is unlike a human contract that depends on the commitment of two or more parties who enter into it; the fulfillment of God's covenant depends solely on Himself. Those who enter into the covenant with Him do nothing to earn or maintain it; they simply receive it for themselves.

*The Significance of the Covenant*

The first of five covenants[13] God made in the Bible was to Noah: "Then God said to Noah and to his sons with him: 'I now establish my covenant with you and with your descendants after you and with every living creature that was with you—the birds, the livestock and all the wild animals, all those that came out of the ark with you—every living creature on earth. I establish my covenant with you: Never again will all life be cut off by the waters of a flood; never again will there be a flood to destroy the earth'" (Gen. 9:8–11).

A minister in our city recently explained this passage by telling her congregation that up until the Flood, God had not been involved in the human race. When He finally did notice the people on earth, He became so angry He wiped them out. But as God spoke to Noah following the deluge, she said, He was horrified by His fit of temper and resolved to change by making this covenant, which said He would get involved with His creation from that point on. Is that really what God was saying? Hardly!

God understood Noah's weakness. God knew that every time Noah or one of his sons sinned and every time Noah heard of someone else's sin, he would be terrified that God's judgment was going to fall. He would live in constant fear, analyzing the sin in his own life and the sin in the world, trying to determine how much was too much—because Noah was weak, and he would constantly fail and he would constantly sin.

As a solution to human weakness, God reassured Noah that His commitment to the preservation of the human race did not depend on man's goodness or sinlessness but on His own Word. While Peter prophesies that "by the same word the present heavens and earth are reserved for fire, being kept for the day of judgment and destruction of ungodly men,"[14] God clearly promised Noah He would never again destroy the earth by water. And even in the judgment by fire yet to come, God will preserve the human race through those who have placed their faith in Jesus Christ.

Perhaps just then, with the little group huddled on the bleak and barren peak beside the looming hulk of the monstrous, dry-docked ark, with the smoke still ascending from the burnt offerings on the altar, Noah heard a distant rumble of thunder. Looking up, perhaps he saw huge, dark clouds piling up over the mountains, with sheets of rain already descending into the valleys. As he felt his heart begin to beat wildly and his knees get weak and his breath come in shallow gasps, did lightning suddenly crack and pop, filling the air with electricity and an eerie glow? Was he terrified, wondering, *Lord, is it going to happen again? Are You going to send another flood? Is judgment coming? After being saved from Your judgment, am I going to lose my salvation?*

*The Sign of the Covenant*

God, with great love and tenderness, understood Noah's weakness. So He gave Noah a sign that would be more than just an encouragement; it would be the symbol of His covenant. "And God said, 'This is the sign of the covenant I am making between me and you and every living creature with you, a covenant for all generations to come: I have set my rainbow in the clouds, and it will be the sign of the covenant between me and the earth. Whenever I bring clouds over the earth and the rainbow appears in the clouds, I will remember my covenant between me and you and all living creatures of every kind. Never again will the waters become a flood to destroy all life. Whenever the rainbow appears in the clouds, I will see it and remember the everlasting covenant between God and all living creatures of every kind on the earth'" (Gen. 9:12–16).

Even as God spoke, the sunlight may have broken through the boiling clouds and pounding rain, producing a breathtakingly beautiful arch of colors stretching from one peak to another. As God explained to Noah the meaning of the rainbow, surely peace and gratitude flooded his heart as he knew, based on God's Word alone, that he was safe and secure.

My husband promised my daughter Morrow that on her sixteenth birthday he would take her to New York City. For months that was all Morrow talked about. She pasted little notes all over his office, she reminded him at mealtimes, and she constantly dreamed of what they would do on their special trip. There was no doubt that Morrow was not going to forget her father's promise to her! Her remembering her father's promise was not the critical factor. The critical factor was that she remembered that her father remembered his promise to her, since he would be the one to pay for the trip and actually take her to the city.

God gave Noah the sign of a rainbow to symbolize His covenant. When the thunder clouds rolled and the lightning zigzagged across the sky and the rain began to fall and Noah was consciously aware of sin in his life and the lives of others, he was to look up and see the rainbow. The purpose was not for him to remember God's covenant but to remember that God remembered His commitment to the human race. What a difference!

God has kept His Word to Noah and his descendants. While planet Earth has seen some disastrous floods, none has been so great as to overflow the entire earth. Every time I see a rainbow, I remember that God remembers the first covenant He made with man.

Thousands of years after Noah, God made the fifth and last covenant with man when He promised He would "make a new covenant. . . . I will put my laws in their minds and write them on their hearts. I will be their God, and they will be my people. No longer will a man teach his neighbor, or a man his brother, saying, 'Know the Lord,' because they will all know me, from the least of them to the greatest. For I will forgive their wickedness and will remember their sins no more."[15] God committed all that He is to forgive man of his sin, offer him eternal life, and reconcile him in the personal relationship with his Creator that he lost in the garden of Eden. The contract was signed in the blood of Jesus Christ.[16]

When you and I enter into this covenant, we are permanently, eternally saved from judgment for a new beginning in a new life. But God knew that after our salvation experience, as we sought to live a new life, we would sin again. And because of the continuing struggle with sin and failure in our lives, we would be tempted to doubt our salvation. So God gave us a sign of the new covenant. Jesus said it was the sign of His broken body and His poured-out blood.[17] It was the sign of the cross.

Have you become so overwhelmed with your own weakness and failure and sin and inability to live a life that is pleasing to God that you have begun to doubt your salvation? Then look up! Take a good, long look at the cross and remember that God remembers He loves you, He has forgiven you, He is eternally committed to you, and you are saved! Forever! Praise God! His covenant is unconditional! All you and I need to do is receive it for ourselves.

God is so good! But man is not. Therefore, as we live, conscious of our own weaknesses, we overcome by heeding God's commands and receiving God's covenant, then when all is said and done, just trusting in His compassion and mercy.

## Overcoming Weakness by Trusting in God's Compassion

At no time is human weakness any more exposed than when the mighty fall. Our newspapers have recorded from time to time the sin and failure of public, popular, and seemingly powerful religious figures. The higher the position of leadership, the longer and harder the fall from it. All who love God and seek to honor His name are sickened and saddened each time such a story comes to light. Those of us who are not as visible in life or ministry echo my father's vow before God, asking that his life be taken before he would ever bring shame to God through anything he would say or do. Yet human failure and weakness is so prevalent we could think it must be inevitable.

*God's Compassion for Our Failures*

I was once sitting in an audience when the speaker asked, "What do you think God expects of you?" I mentally ticked off a list of things I thought God expected of me: obedience, faithfulness, holiness, love, service. To my astonishment, the speaker went on to say, "All God ever expects of you is failure!" I wanted to raise my hand and say, "I can do that! I can live up to the expectations of God! I know I can fail!" But then the speaker added, "However, He has given you the Holy Spirit so that you need never fail." Right! Without Christ I can do nothing, but in Him I can do all things![18] The difference between strength and weakness, righteousness and wickedness, success and failure, is Jesus—the Holy Spirit—in us.

Noah did not have the Holy Spirit within him since he lived before Pentecost.[19] His actions after the Flood simply reveal that Noah needed Him, because "Noah was a righteous man, blameless among the people of his time, and he walked with God" (Gen. 6:9). And he had worked for God more than 120 years! And he had worshiped God with an extravagant sacrifice! And his whole life had borne witness of God! Yet "Noah, a man of the soil, proceeded to plant a vineyard. When he drank some of its wine, he became drunk and lay uncovered inside his tent" (Gen. 9:20–21). How could a man of Noah's character and faith be found in such a position? The text implies Noah deliberately lay uncovered in his tent in a sinful way. How could he? How could he have consistently resisted the wickedness of Cain's civilization for hundreds of years, how could he have remained so steadfast in the face of such overwhelming opposition and discouragement, how could he have experienced the power of God to bring him safely through the Flood—and then end up in a drunken stupor? Because Noah, like the rest of us, was a son of Adam and Eve with an inherited sinful nature lurking within him! Watch out! If it could happen to Noah, it could happen to any one of us!

I wonder if Noah was the sort of person who could handle pressure and crisis but not the everyday temptations of life. Or perhaps he was riding on the victory of having survived the Flood, feeling so invincible in his faith he thought he was immune to temptation. Had he ceased to worship and witness and walk and work for the Lord on a daily basis because he was old and tired and had grown complacent? Could it be that he knew what his weaknesses were and was on guard in those areas of his life, but he just wasn't prepared for this new temptation? And of course, Satan was and is no gentleman. He did not respect Noah's past victory; nor did he respect Noah's level of maturity or his relationship with the Lord. And Satan won't respect you or me either.

In what way has your human, sinful weakness been revealed? Was it because of one of the same reasons suggested for Noah's failure? Was it for the exact reason Noah failed—because you were drunk?

It is doubtful that Noah deliberately intended to get drunk.[20] He probably drank one glass of wine, enjoyed the taste, drank another glass of wine, enjoyed the taste, drank another glass of wine, enjoyed the feeling coming over him . . . and then enjoyed still another glass of wine.

Surely he never intended to get drunk. And if he had not been drunk, he would not have uncovered himself. And if he had not uncovered himself, he would not have exposed his children to temptation. And if he had not exposed his children to temptation, the impact on his grandchildren—the entire human race—might have been very different.

One of the insidious tragedies of drinking is that a person may be unaware of when drunkenness begins. And while drunk, things never even considered when sober are done with abandon. Today many others can testify to this truth along with Noah:

> battered wives,
>> abused children,
>>> divorced couples,
>>>> pregnant teenagers,
>>> car-crash victims,
>> bankrupt businessmen,
> raped women and girls.

Drinking can lead to very serious sin because it robs us of our self-control and weakens our will to resist temptation. That old Serpent the devil, who had been unable to corrupt Noah and his family for more than six hundred years as he applied every wicked device of Cain's civilization, succeeded with the help of alcohol. What success has alcohol given the devil in your life?

There is no record that Noah confessed or corrected his sin, but it seems to be implied by his attitude and actions following his failure. Certainly you and I are given the promise that "if we confess our sins, he is faithful and just and will forgive us our sins and purify us from all unrighteousness,"[21] because God is compassionate in our failures—just as He is compassionate in our families.

*God's Compassion for Our Families*

Noah's sin had shameful repercussions in his family. One of the most awesome realities of being a parent is that our children watch us—even when we are unaware they are watching. Noah's son, "Ham, the father of Canaan, saw his father's nakedness and told his two brothers outside" (Gen. 9:22). The Hebrew text implies that Ham saw his naked father lying in a drunken stupor and gloated over the sight.

Maybe for years Ham's heart had been more intertwined in the activities and attitude of Cain's civilization than anyone knew. Although he must have been glad to have escaped judgment, had he secretly yearned for some of the pleasures of sin? Did he resent his father for the righteousness of his life that denied his sons those very things? Maybe he just resented his father for having pressured him into carpentry and zoology when he had wanted to go into real estate. Was he basically lazy and therefore resentful of the hard work his father had always demanded of him? Whatever the reason, when Ham caught his father in a moment of weakness, those years of silent resentment must have boiled to the surface as he not only gazed on his father's figure but ran to gleefully tell his brothers what he had seen.

What sin have you committed in the privacy of your own home when you thought no one was watching? Have you gotten drunk? Have you taken too many prescription drugs? Have you indulged in pornography on video or the Internet? Has your sin given opportunity for your children to gloat so that they are also involved in sin? Or perhaps you are the child who has observed your parents' private sins. Who have you told? Have you rationalized your taletelling by calling it a prayer request or therapy or healing of memories, when in fact it's a form of revenge on a parent you have secretly resented? King Solomon wisely admonished, "He who covers over an offense promotes love, but whoever repeats the matter separates close friends."[22] One of the definitions for love given in the New Testament is that "love does not delight in evil. . . . It always protects."[23]

One of the greatest failures in the Bible was the apostle Peter. His most notorious moment of sin was when, after vowing that he would die for Jesus, he actually denied ever having known Him. And he denied Him not just once but three times. Yet God, in His mercy and grace, restored Peter so completely that he was given a prominent leadership position within the early church, opening the door of opportunity for the Gentiles to receive the gospel. And Peter, who understood the shame of failure and the humiliation of sin, encouraged Christians to "love each other deeply, because love covers over a multitude of sins."[24] What sin are you discussing that you ought to be covering?

Noah's other two sons, Shem and Japheth, reacted very differently than did their brother, Ham. They "took a garment and laid it across their shoulders; then they walked in backward and covered their father's nakedness. Their faces were turned the other way so that they would not see their father's nakedness" (Gen. 9:23). Their every action conveyed their love and respect and honor for their godly father. In their gentle tenderness and loving consideration we can see a reflection of the heavenly Father. God Himself must have seen the worn-out old warrior who had succumbed to sin in one moment of weakness after hundreds of years of resistance and covered him with His love. Thank God! He has compassion on us in our failure and in our families . . . and in our future.

### God's Compassion for Our Future

How did Noah feel when he awoke from his stupor and realized what he had done? Did he sit on the edge of his bed, head in his hands, retching with nausea and guilt? As his mind raced back over the last few hours and how he could have gotten into such a condition, did the Words of God's covenant come back to his mind: "I now establish my covenant with you and with your descendants after you"? What else could he do but just trust in the compassion of a gracious, merciful God? "When Noah awoke from his wine and found out what his youngest son had done to him, he said, 'Cursed be Canaan! The lowest of slaves will he be to his brothers.' He also said, 'Blessed be the LORD, the God of Shem!

May Canaan be the slave of Shem. May God extend the territory of Japheth; may Japheth live in the tents of Shem, and may Canaan be his slave'" (Gen. 9:24–27).

As did many of the patriarchs in the Old Testament, before he died Noah prophesied concerning his children. The prophecies are amazing for their accuracy that is borne out in subsequent history. In this case, Noah gave his attention first to Ham's son, Canaan, who turned out to be rebellious and wicked and whose descendants, the Canaanites, dragged Israel into idolatry. In time, they did become Israel's slaves.

In contrast, Noah told Shem that his future would be tied up in a wonderful way with God. His descendants became the Shemites, or the Semitic tribes. Abraham and his family, the nation of Israel, were Semites, as was the Lord Jesus Christ when He came to earth. The sixty-six books of the Bible were written almost exclusively by descendants of Shem. The Lord was indeed his God.

Japheth was told he would become a large nation that would come to "the tents of Shem" for a relationship with God. Japheth's descendants are the Gentiles who, in a very real sense, have to go to the "tents" of Shem—to the Bible and to Jesus Christ—in order to know God.

As Noah uttered his predictions, he must have been amazed himself at what was being foretold. He must have been conscious of deep conviction and extreme clarity of thought as he looked at his sons and grandson standing before him and knew what they would become. When he opened his mouth to speak, he knew also it was not something he was saying on his own but something God was saying through him.[25] As he listened to himself, he must have been enormously comforted that, in spite of his weakness and failure, God would keep His covenant to future generations. Because God understands our human weakness.

❧

THE WEEK before Velma Barfield was executed, I visited her in the prison where she was incarcerated. After signing in and passing through secured fences, the guard ushered me across the manicured lawn and through a double set of doors into a building where I signed in again with another officer inside what resembled a metal cage. As I entered a room off to the side, I was warmly greeted by Velma, who was seated at a table. I sat in a chair that had been placed at a right angle to hers. When I tried to adjust the placement, I discovered that the chairs and table were solidly bolted to the concrete floor.

As we began to converse, it soon became apparent that Velma needed reassurance of her salvation. Because the state of North Carolina had refused to extend mercy to her and would execute her within the week for her crimes, she was beginning to question God's forgiveness and grace in her life. So I drew a word picture for Velma by asking her, "Velma, have you ever walked along the beach?"

"Yes," she said, nodding her head up and down.

"Have you seen the small holes in the sand that the ghost crabs make?"

"Yes."

"Have you walked farther down the beach and seen a medium-size hole in the sand like children make when they're digging a moat for a sand castle?"

"Yes, I've seen holes like that."

"Have you ever seen really gigantic holes on the beach, where perhaps a dredger was digging out a waterway?"

With a somewhat puzzled expression that showed she thought I had gotten off track from her initial concern, she simply nodded affirmatively.

Then I asked, "Velma, what happens to all those holes when the tide comes in?"

Her brow wrinkled as she thought for a moment. Before she could respond, I leaned over and looked lovingly in her eyes. "Velma, the water covers all those holes equally, doesn't it? Big, medium, small, they are all covered by the tidewater."

As she began to comprehend the meaning of what I was saying, Velma's face softened and her eyes moistened with tears. "Velma," I continued, "the blood of Jesus is like the tide. When you claim it as a covering for your sin, it covers all your sin. Past, present, future sins as well as small sins like gossip and little white lies, medium-size sins like losing your temper, and great big sins like murdering your own mother, are all covered equally under the blood of Jesus. You're forgiven, Velma."

And you are, too, if your sin is under the blood of Jesus Christ. When you receive the new covenant extended to you by God at the cross, He commits all He is to you. His forgiveness of your sin,

> your salvation from His judgment,
>> your reconciliation with your Creator,
>>> your acceptance into His heavenly home,
>>>> your eternal life,

all are unconditionally guaranteed by the signature on the contract. Do you doubt this? Then heed God's commands, trust His compassion, and take a good, long look at the cross and remember that God remembers His covenant with you.

# 10

## I Reject Your Religiousness

### GENESIS 10

One of America's favorite pastimes is baseball. When a player takes his turn in the game, he steps up to home plate, gripping his bat firmly in hand. The pitcher throws the ball toward him, and he swings at the ball. If he misses, that's strike one. The pitcher then throws the ball again, and the batter takes another swing. If he misses the second time, that's strike two. When the ball is thrown the third time, and the batter swings and misses, that's strike three, and he's out of the game. He has lost the opportunity to score for his team.

In some ways, the first eleven chapters of Genesis are like a baseball game. The world of humanity, represented by Adam and Eve, is the batter who stepped up to home plate for the first time in the garden of Eden. The ball—the opportunity to live forever in a right, loving relationship with the Creator and so possess the fullness of His blessing—was thrown. But through man's choice to disobey God, the world of humanity missed, and that was strike one.

In Noah's day, humanity was back up to bat. The same ball—the opportunity to live in a right relationship with the Creator and receive His full, personal blessing—was thrown. This time the world chose to disregard God, and that was strike two.

Chapter 11 of Genesis describes the third time the world of humanity came up to bat. The same ball was thrown as the world had the choice to live in a right relationship with God and so receive His blessings. But instead the world chose to defy God, and that was strike three. Generally speaking, the world from that point forward was out of the ball game, having lost the opportunity for a personal relationship with God along with the blessings He gives. This time, instead of the

200

world of humanity being driven from paradise or washed away in a flood, it was kicked "out of the game"—scattered all over the planet where it still lives today in disobedience, disregard, and defiance of God.

The world of humanity that was allowed to live on planet Earth while separated from a personal, right relationship with the Creator became very religious. One of the first things the human race did was to establish a means of worshiping God, all the while harboring disobedience, disregard, and defiance of Him in the heart.

As we look around at our world today, we can easily name the major religions of Buddhism, Mormonism, Hinduism, Islam, Taoism, Confucianism, Judaism, and Christianity, as well as hundreds of minor religions, such as tribal and regional religions, animism, and spiritism. Our world, while rebellious, is also very religious.

I recently spoke with a professor of religion at one of the most prestigious and intellectual universities in our country. She said that although she considered herself to be a Christian, she was confused by all the other religions in the world. She had recently written an article for the university newspaper, describing a trip she had taken to India. She related that when she arrived in Calcutta, she was deeply impressed with how good the Hindu people seemed to be. And she remembered that her godly grandmother had prayed for their salvation for years—prayers that to this professor seemed to be totally unnecessary. Why did the Hindus need to be "saved" when they were so "nice"?

Why do we pray for the salvation of people in other countries, cultures, and religions? Why does the Christian church send out missionaries? Why can't you believe what you want and I believe what I want and everyone in the world believe whatever they want as long as we don't hurt each other?

The answers are to be found in Genesis, where we see that the root of every religion in our world today outside of Judaism and Christianity can be traced back to the Tower of Babel.

## HE REJECTS THE REBELLION

When Noah and his wife, his sons, and their wives stepped into the new world, we can imagine the difficulty they may have experienced in leaving the vicinity of the ark. It had been their safe haven, their refuge during the violence of the storm. It offered shelter and comfort and familiar surroundings as well as a tie to their past life. But the mountain peak on which the ark rested was cold, barren, wind-swept, and susceptible to sudden storms. There was no possibility of planting crops or digging wells at that altitude. So the little band of survivors began to wind their way down the steep mountainside to the valleys and plains below. They must have settled in a lush valley, where Noah planted the vineyard that produced the wine that gave opportunity for temptation.

Then, months or years later, the growing family once again began to drift eastward. Perhaps the migration was precipitated by Noah's confrontation with his son Ham and his grandson Canaan. Although there had been sharp rebuke as well as blessing following the confrontation, the descendants of Noah, the sole inhabitants of the earth, must have found comfort and strength in each other as they faced the challenge of establishing a civilization in the new world. They continued to drift until they came to the wide, open, fertile plains of what would be modern-day Iran and Iraq. Yet as they drifted, they did not disperse but instead clung together, in contradiction of God's command issued when He gave His covenant to Noah. God's will was clearly expressed in His command to "fill the earth," which implied a migration that would scatter the survivors through-out the world.

Recently, my two daughters and I stayed in a hotel where an alarm went off in the middle of the night. In my sleepiness I kept hitting the clock beside my bed, thinking the previous occupant had left the alarm set to ring at an early hour. I even wondered at the flashing light, thinking the hotel had put in alarm clocks that were guaranteed to waken even the soundest sleeper. It finally registered with me that the alarm and lights were not coming from the clock beside my bed but from a round disk on the wall—the fire alarm! It was screeching too loudly to go back to sleep, and the front desk did not answer when I called; as I looked out my sixth-floor window, I saw fire engines in the drive below! I yelled for my girls, threw on some clothes, grabbed my pocketbook, and ran down the hall to the stairwell. When I opened the door, I smelled an acrid odor. Then, two floors down, the stair-well turned into a waterfall as water poured from underneath the doors leading to the first through the fourth floors. Despite the odor and the water, we made it safely down the stairs to the outside lawn, where we waited to see what would hap-pen next. As I looked around at the other guests, I was amused by each one's appearance and attitude, as I'm sure they were by mine. Pajamas, nightgowns, sweatshirts, boxer shorts, and hair curlers adorned bodies that looked wrinkled, worn, angry, and scared. Since my girls thought this was a great, fun adventure, we livened things up for everybody.

One by one we drifted to the front of the hotel and made our way into the lobby that was jammed with guests. In a couple of hours, the coffee shop opened and we were served a complimentary buffet breakfast. Guests were now more relaxed, talking across the tables to each other. Strangers had become friends, and we all felt somewhat bonded by our experience.

By 8:00 a.m. we were told we could return to our rooms on the sixth floor. Apparently the difficulty had been caused by someone who had set off the fire alarms and activated the sprinkler system as his or her idea of a joke. But no one thought it was funny, especially those who had been staying on the first four floors and had all their belongings drenched in water.

As minor as this trauma was in my life, I could still feel the immediate bond it gave between others and myself who shared the same crisis. The same bond can be felt when an entire planeload of people experiences mechanical failure on their aircraft and they go through an emergency evacuation. It's the same bond people in a city or town experience when a tornado or hurricane passes through and leaves everyone's life in shambles. When faced with a common problem, often people come together and stay together, drawing comfort from each other.

Following the Flood, it's not surprising that Noah and his family wanted to stay together. But as they continued to live, move, and stay together, their collective migration was in defiance of God's will. God had given them the same command twice to make sure there was no misunderstanding of what His will was for them. As He made His covenant with Noah and his descendants, He had instructed, "Be fruitful and increase in number and fill the earth. . . . As for you, be fruitful and increase in number; multiply on the earth and increase upon it" (Gen. 9:1, 7). It was God's will that Noah and his descendants scatter out over all the earth. They were to fill the earth. Instead, they clung together.

*Rebellion against God's Will*

It is possible that by the time the Tower of Babel was begun, there were thousands of people on the earth. Genesis says, "Now the whole world had one language and a common speech. As men moved eastward, they found a plain in Shinar and settled there" (Gen. 11:1–2). Like nomads or Bedouins today, Noah's descendants drifted together, gradually migrating back to the region that was close to where the garden of Eden had been. Their migration stopped in the plain of Shinar, where they planned to settle together permanently, in direct defiance of God's stated command.

As you look around at the people in our world today, what evidence of defiance toward God's will do you see?

God has said it is His will that all men should repent.[1] Are the majority of people today obeying God's will or openly defying it?

God has also said it is His will that we be thankful in all things.[2]

Are the majority of people today obeying God's will or openly defying it?

God has said it is His will that all men receive Christ, believe in Him, and be born again.[3] Are the majority of people today obeying God's will or openly defying it?

God has said it is His will that we serve others sacrificially.[4] Are the majority of people today obeying God's will or openly defying it?

God has said it is His will that all people abstain from sexual immorality.[5] Are the majority of people today obeying God's will or openly defying it?

We don't even have to look around in the world today. We can look around in our own families and churches to find that the vast majority of people right across the board are living in open defiance of the will of God. In fact, many people today don't even know what God's will is, even though He has stated it clearly again and again and has written it down in black and white so there can be no misunderstanding.

As Noah's descendants entered the plain of Shinar, they saw a vast, fertile region that would support their crops and livestock. It wasn't long before one of their own saw the opportunity to seize the moment for personal advancement. As the settlers considered ending their migration and making a permanent home, Nimrod stepped into the picture as their leader.

*Rebellion against God's Way*

Rather than trust God to lead them, Noah's descendants looked to one of their own for leadership. Years later, the wisest man who ever lived (outside of Jesus Christ), mused, "A man's steps are directed by the LORD. How then can anyone understand his own way?"[6] Noah's descendants rejected God's direction and placed themselves under a man named Nimrod. His very name means "rebel." He "grew to be a mighty warrior on the earth. He was a mighty hunter before the LORD; that is why it is said, 'Like Nimrod, a mighty hunter before the LORD.' The first centers of his kingdom were Babylon, Erech, Akkad and Calneh, in Shinar. From that land he went to Assyria, where he built Nineveh" (Gen. 10:8–11).

Nimrod was the Lethal Weapon, the Terminator, and the Rambo of his day. He lived by violence as a "mighty warrior," making his living off of killing people. He was a "mighty hunter," killing animals not just for food but for sport. And he did all this "before the Lord," that is, he did it right in God's face. He believed in God, and he knew God was watching; he just didn't care. He had no fear, no respect, no reverence for God at all. He lived by his own strength as a self-made man who was totally self-sufficient and self-reliant.

Nimrod must have had such a strong sense of self-confidence that he inspired confidence in others. He was so sure of himself, others put their trust in him. They must have admired his macho manners, his power plays, his physical strength, and his mental intelligence. He could point to all the cities he had plans for as evidence he was a man of great vision. But he was also a man of decisive action. He had no moral character, yet the people followed his leadership. And he led them in rebellion against God that was cleverly masked under the cloak of religious expression.

Who are our leaders today? Who are the role models for our children? Who is the modern-day Nimrod who is leading us in rebellion against God? While we can point to specific athletes, entertainers, corporate executives, and politicians who have no moral character yet have great influence on our culture, I wonder if one of the real Nimrods of our day is the materialistic, humanistic system itself.

Surely a people, city, or nation that defies God's way and His leadership in their lives is ripe to defy His will. Under Nimrod's leadership, Noah's descendants became the Babylonians, whose very name is synonymous with rebellion against God. They not only defied God's will and God's way; they defied God's work.

*Rebellion against God's Work*

When a person is outside of God's will, nothing that person does is God's work.[7] Noah's descendants were busy, busy, busy, but everything they did was wasted because the work had no eternal value in God's sight. Under Nimrod's leadership they began to make plans to build a city. But out on the vast plain of Shinar, there were no trees for wood and no rocks of any size with which to build. So as they pondered the lack of raw materials, they came up with the clever idea of making their own. "They said to each other, 'Come, let's make bricks and bake them thoroughly.' They used brick instead of stone, and tar for mortar" (Gen. 11:3). Even the materials they used in their work were imitations of the real thing. The buildings made out of such materials did not last except as symbols of defiance toward God.[8]

What is the work of God? It is the exertion of time, energy, heart, mind, body, and strength that you and I make to do His will. Jesus stated clearly that "the work of God is this: to believe in the one he has sent."[9] Instead of believing in the One God has sent, the majority of people today believe in evolution, which leads them to put a lot of time, energy, and effort into believing in themselves,

their science,

their technology,

their philosophy,

their policy,

their psychology—

as the sum total of reality.

This humanism leads to

self-centered,

self-promoting,

self-gratifying,

self-righteous,

self-indulgent,

and self-made work.

The lives and jobs and businesses and education and families and societies of the world are just an imitation of the real thing. All that we see about us is just a shadow, just a poor reflection of what God intended.

But the people living in the shadows of reality thought it was the real thing. They said to each other, "Come, let us build ourselves a city, with a tower that reaches to the heavens, so that we may make a name for ourselves and not be scattered over the face of the whole earth" (Gen. 11:4). Their work was not haphazard. It was carefully planned, organized, and thought out. The stated purpose was to make a name for themselves—to elevate man and his accomplishments above everything else.

The means of accomplishing this goal would be to deliberately defy God by banding together. They refused to scatter out over the face of the earth as God had commanded. And their rallying point would be a tower that would reach into heaven. The tower would symbolize a world religion that would serve as the "opiate of the people," giving them a deeper sense of meaning and purpose that would

206

satisfy their craving for the spiritual dimension of life—a satisfaction that was also false and would so preoccupy and distract them it would keep them from the truth.

Did the Babylonians reason that since God had promised He would never again destroy all living things that there would be safety in numbers if everyone defied Him? Assuming God would not be pleased, they had found a solution. They decided to work their own way back into heaven without Him by building a tower that would assist them. They arrogantly assumed that if they worked hard enough and long enough, if they were sincere in their efforts and could accomplish their goal, that God would owe it to them to let them into heaven. They assumed God would just have to accept them on their own merit and on their own terms. At that moment in human history, world religions were born. Karl Barth, one of the twentieth century's premier theologians, said that all religion is man reaching up to God in his own way, according to his own terms, on his own merit, in his own strength. Christianity alone is God reaching down to man.

All non-Judeo-Christian religions are an expression of man's defiance of God, including His way, His will, and His work. If you ask most people today why they think God will let them into heaven, they will say something like, "I try to be good. I go to church. I'm not perfect, but I believe God will weigh my good deeds against my bad deeds, and I hope the good outweighs the bad. If it does, He will let me into heaven." It is man's pride that believes God somehow owes him a heavenly home or eternal life as a reward for

> good deeds or
>> extra effort or
>>> religious activity or
>>>> personal morality or
>>>>> earnest sincerity.

In their pride, the builders of Babel assumed they could work their way into God's presence and He would accept them on the basis of what they had done. They were wrong then, and they are still wrong today.

God has said that "all our righteous acts are like filthy rags,"[10] and "there is no one righteous, not even one,"[11] and "without holiness no one will see the Lord."[12] So how does one get into heaven? Jesus gave clear instructions, "Not everyone who says to me, 'Lord, Lord' will enter the kingdom of heaven, but only he who does the will of my Father who is in heaven,"[13] and "I am the way and the truth and the life. No one comes to the Father except through me."[14] Who do you know who is trying to get to heaven some other way than by God's will, which is to place your faith in Jesus Christ and in God's accomplished work at the cross? All religions are man's organized attempt to get around God's stated will and way and work and Word.

Holy Week of 1997 will long be remembered for the tragic and ironic event that was flashed from California to the front and center of our nation's attention. The very week that Christians worldwide celebrated the cross and the resurrection of Jesus Christ as God's provision for man's salvation and eternal life, thirty-nine men and women were found dead in a mass suicide that took place on a multi-million-dollar estate in the exclusive area of Rancho Santa Fe in San Diego County.

Investigators found the bodies lying in a very orderly fashion. Each body was stretched out on a bed, clothed in black, draped with a purple shroud, a plastic bag over the head, with a neatly placed suitcase at the feet. Bit by bit, it was discovered that the thirty-nine bodies belonged to members of a small cult called Heaven's Gate that believed, among other things, that they could enter paradise by leaving their bodies and catching a ride on a UFO that was hidden in the tail of the Hale-Bopp Comet.

While we want to scream, "That's crazy!" "That's mad!" "That's tragic!" "That's sad!", Margaret Signer, the University of California at Berkeley psychology professor who is also an internationally recognized expert on cults, responded, "Cults don't recruit crazy people or dumb people. They want normal to intelligent people, people who can be obedient to ideas."[15] In this case, the idea perpetrated by the leader, Marshall Applewhite, seemed to be that heaven's gate could be entered if a person denied all sexual appetites and identity and caught a ride on a UFO.

Wayne Cooke, a cult member who committed suicide later and separately from the other thirty-nine, explained in his suicide note, "I'd rather gamble on missing the bus this time than staying on this planet and risk losing my soul."[16] While we want to weep at such deception, the confusion can be traced back to the Tower of Babel and man's defiance of God's Word.

*Rebellion against God's Word*

Once again, the world that was in rebellion against God was being watched by Him; it had His undivided attention. "But the LORD came down to see the city and the tower that the men were building" (Gen. 11:5). The world that thought it was getting by with defiance and rebellion wasn't getting by with a thing. Did the

Babylonians think that because they did not hear God or see God, God really was-n't there? Or if He was there, He was incapable of doing anything about their rebellion? Or if He was capable, He didn't really care what they did? How did they rationalize their defiance? How could they sleep at night knowing they were shaking their little dust fists in God's face, pridefully insisting on their own will and their own work as being sufficient to secure God's grace and blessing?

God graciously spoke to the world. He would not have done so had the Babylonian situation been beyond redemption. God warned the world when He said, "If as one people speaking the same language they have begun to do this, then nothing they plan to do will be impossible for them" (Gen. 11:6).

What does God have to say about the "one language" in our world today? We don't all speak the same language, but communication is almost unimpeded. Through the Internet, cyberspace, the worldwide information highway, satellite hookups, and other means, the world once again is showing signs of uniting. While this unity is trumpeted as a sign of a progressive new world order and unlimited opportunity for mankind, it is opposed by God. God opposes all unity that is outside of Jesus Christ. Why? Because it is a unity against God, whether realized or not.

There are some lengths of rebellion to which man cannot go as an isolated individual. His defiance is limited by his own boundaries. But when man cooperates and unites in rebellion, "then nothing they plan to do will be impossible for them." Nothing.

Not even weapons of mass destruction.

Not even the cloning of a sheep that may eventually lead to the cloning of a human being.

Not even partial-birth abortion.

Not even the enslavement of an entire race of people.

Not even the genocide of an entire race of people.

Separated from God, humanity's skill, science, and technology outstrip its wisdom to use and apply what it knows, and man becomes exceedingly dangerous and wicked. The only hope is that God will intervene and put a stop to man's rebellion—which is what God did at the Tower of Babel.

Once again, God warned the world of impending judgment. "Come, let us go down and confuse their language, so they will not understand each other" (Gen. 11:7). As He spoke, it was as though He was offering the world a chance to see its religion for the rebellion it was and then to repent. The rebellious builders still had time to avert His judgment of worldwide confusion if they would turn away from their wicked ways and seek Him. But it was as though God spoke to thin air. No one was listening. There was not one righteous man before God. Not one man who was blameless among the people of his day. Not one man who was walking with God. Not one!

If judgment is on the mind of God today, who will know? If He warns of catastrophe, confusion, and crisis to come, who is listening? Who will even deliver the message?

Several years ago, I received an engraved invitation to the White House to have breakfast with the president and his wife. When I called to respond to the invitation, I inquired as to the reason for the occasion and was informed it was an ecumenical prayer breakfast. On the designated day at the designated hour, I arrived at the White House and was ushered through security. After waiting briefly in a room where I was surrounded by the portraits of the former first ladies, I was led upstairs to a large room where religious leaders from all over the country were gathering around tables serving juice and coffee. We then proceeded through a receiving line where the president and his wife and the vice president and his wife graciously greeted each guest. As I entered the East Room, which had been set with round tables for approximately two to three hundred people, I made my way to the table I had been assigned. To my astonishment I discovered it was the president's table! In a few moments he joined the eight others at the table that included myself, a well-known Jewish rabbi, two pastors of prestigious congregations, one of the president's former pastors, a professor of sociology who is also an activist, and the head of a large church denomination. After a prayer offered by a Greek Orthodox archbishop, we had breakfast. During the meal, the president talked of sports, politics, and then problems. Some of the problems he mentioned were his own; some were on a national scale. I just listened to what he and the others at my table were saying but did not have the opportunity, nor the inclination, to interject any thought of my own.

Following breakfast, the vice president introduced the president, who then spoke for about twenty minutes to the room filled with religious leaders on two subjects that he said were particularly on his heart that day: immigration and welfare reform. He quoted a Catholic priest who had recently died who had said he didn't want to spend one minute of his limited time on earth in acrimony and division. Then he opened the floor for discussion from those present.

One by one the religious leaders raised their hands then rose to their feet when recognized by the president. They spoke with articulation, poise, and warmth as they affirmed the president's policies as well as his person. My heart began to beat fiercely as I listened to what was being said. Not one religious leader addressed the real problem in our nation. I found myself praying silently, asking God to give me the president's attention. He did. When I was recognized, I rose to my feet, then as clearly as I could I said that while I could not give him counsel on welfare reform and immigration, I could pinpoint the basic problem in our nation. I continued by saying that the basic problem is a spiritual one, and it is sin. All of our ethnic, cultural, and religious differences find common ground when we acknowledge that there is a God, He is our Creator, and one day each of us will give an account to Him for the way we have lived our lives. Our problems in this country would be solved if we would get right with God.

When I finished my remarks, I sat down, grateful for the opportunity to have spoken the truth in such a gathering. The president did not respond publicly to my remarks but later thanked me for them privately. While I know there were godly men and women present at that breakfast, what I still find appalling is that not one of the religious leaders who spoke was identifying the basic problem in our nation for the president. They were suggesting political solutions for what is really a spiritual problem of sin and rebellion against God. While our nation is on the verge of moral and spiritual bankruptcy, the religious leaders were discussing welfare reform and immigration! God help us all!

God warned the Babylonians, but they didn't seem to hear His Word. Was it because they were trying so hard to impress each other no one was willing to speak the truth? Was it because He had no messenger who could deliver the message with relevance? Was it because they were too busy to listen? Was it because they just didn't believe a loving God would judge them?

God speaks today, but our excuses are much the same as those the Babylonians may have given; plus we read the newspaper and the newsmagazines, we listen to the talk shows and television commentary, we read the opinion polls and the best sellers, and we are just so busy listening to each other, we can't hear God. The rebellion in our world today that is characterized by defiance of God's way, God's will, God's work, and God's Word leads to nothing but confusion.

## HE REJECTS THE REBELLIOUS

Whether a person is rebelling against God in only one area of his life or his whole life is lived in rebellion against God, rebellion always leads to confusion. Several years ago, the leadership of a major denomination in our state rejected an amendment to the denomination's constitution that would have required ministers, elders, and deacons to be faithful in marriage or chaste in singleness.[17] The resolution allows ministers to live with same-sex partners, saying that the denomination was not so concerned with the letter of the law as it was with the need to be loving and tolerant of those who are different. As a result, confusion has gripped the rank-and-file church members, who in essence have been told that what God has said in His Word is not so. It will not be long before the confusion begins to scatter the people, a trend already evident in that the denomination has lost more than 1.5 million members in the last few years. Genesis says, "So the LORD scattered them from there over all the earth, and they stopped building the city. That is why it was called Babel—because there the LORD confused the language of the whole world. From there the LORD scattered them over the face of the whole earth" (Gen. 11:8–9).

What would it have been like to show up for work on the day that judgment fell? Did a workman on the twentieth tier shout out for someone to bring him some mortar, but he was given water instead? Did another craftsman ask for more bricks, but he was given a brush? Did someone ask for a donkey, and he was given dirt? After a while, did the workmen get frustrated, thinking everyone else was having fun and mocking them at their expense, so they just quit? And what did they think when they went home and asked their neighbor if they could borrow the lawn mower but were given a cup of sugar instead? When did they realize they could no longer understand each other's language? Can you imagine the yelling, the screaming, and the wild gestures until finally everyone was worn out?

There was no solution. Those within a particular family could understand other family members but couldn't understand anyone outside the family circle. There was nothing left to do but pack up and leave to escape the confusion. And so the proud, rebellious Babylonians scattered all over the world.

How did God confuse their language? Did He change the thought patterns in their minds so they thought differently? Did He change something in their ears so they heard differently? Did He change the actual words as they came out of their mouths? It's interesting that the confusion which was God's judgment on the rebellion was a breakdown in communication. The evidence of the thoroughness of God's judgment is very apparent today in the more than three thousand languages and dialects in our world at the present time.

The confusion of languages is very obvious when the United Nations General Assembly meets. Each nation's delegate has a set of earphones so he or she can hear what is being said and understand the business that is being transacted in his or her own language. Even when the delegate understands, there is often a disagreement that leads to a delegation's walking out of the proceedings in protest of the decisions being made. One of the most famous incidents was when the former leader of the Soviet Union, Nikita Khrushchev, became so frustrated during a session at the United Nations that he took off his shoe and banged it on the table! Even when we speak the same language, sometimes communication is difficult.

As the Babylonian families, clans, and tribes began to scatter throughout the earth, how harmful was the confusion? God's judgment on the Tower of Babel doesn't seem nearly as severe as it was in the day of Adam and Eve's expulsion from the garden or in the day of Noah when the world was flooded. We tend to think of God's judgment as being expressed as fire falling from heaven or the earth opening up and swallowing the wicked or lightning striking someone. But God's wrath was revealed at the Tower of Babel when God simply removed Himself from the world's affairs and gave man over to wallow in his own rebellion and confusion.[18]

The tragedy of this particular judgment was that the people who were scattered all over the world were separated from God. If they had dispersed in obedience to His command, He would have gone with them. They would have known His presence and blessing and guidance and protection. Instead, although He was still in control of their world, He was removed from them on a personal level. He let them go into a terrible freedom that would lead them further and further away from Him, deeper and deeper into sin and rebellion. It was as though mankind yelled, "God, we don't want to know You. We don't want You telling us what to do and how to run our lives. Leave us alone. Get out of our lives." And so God did. Generally speaking, He let man go all over the world without Him.

Chuck Templeton was a gifted preacher and well-known church leader who turned his back on God while in the ministry. He became an agnostic who took opportunity to publicly attack God's people. He had just finished writing a book entitled *Farewell to God* when he was diagnosed with Alzheimer's. Then, when my father called to ask him once again to read the New Testment gospel before he could no longer seriously consider his eternal destiny, Mr. Templeton refused, saying he had been there, done that. I wonder . . . as Mr. Templeton abandoned God publicly and privately, is God now abandoning him?

When you insist on leaving God, He will let you go and leave you to yourself. The most frightening form of judgment is not necessarily fire falling from heaven or the earth opening up to swallow you but God removing Himself from your life. One of the most solemn thoughts about our national condition as we see

record-breaking floods and

fires and

earthquakes and

hurricanes and

tornadoes and

droughts and

hailstorms

as well as seemingly unsolvable problems of race, immorality, and drugs, and our insistence on separation of church and state to the extreme is . . . is God now abandoning us? These social problems—and it may very well be our environmental problems—are a direct result of our saying we don't want God in our schools and we don't want His name said in public. When we remove Him from our official, national life, He removes Himself from us.

The descendants of Noah's three sons left Babel and the presence of God. They went out around the world like a plague of "Cains," spreading the epidemic of a rebellious, godless, sinful, wicked, defiant civilization wherever they went.

### The Rebellious in the North and West

The descendants of Japheth were the first to leave. Their names indicate the places they eventually settled. "The sons of Japheth: Gomer, Magog, Madai, Javan, Tubal, Meshech and Tiras. The sons of Gomer: Ashkenaz, Riphath and Togarmah. The sons of Javan: Elishah, Tarshish, the Kittim and Rodanim. (From these the maritime peoples spread out into their territories by their clans within their nations, each with its own language)" (Gen. 10:2–5).

Gomer scattered and settled in Germany, Turkey, and Armenia.

Tubal and Magog scattered and settled the Black Sea area, including the territory occupied by the former Soviet Union. The ancient Scythians can also be traced to Magog.

Madai became the Medes and the Persians, who stayed in the Iran-Iraq area. His descendants also can be traced to the Aryans in India.

Javan was the father of the Greeks and Romans.

Meshech's name is the root word for "Moskva," from which we get the name of Russia's capital city, Moscow.

Tarshish scattered out and settled in Spain, but Tarshish would also include the farthest points west of Shinar.

*The Rebellious in the South*

The descendants of Ham were the next to pull out. They basically went in the opposite direction from Japheth's family. "The sons of Ham: Cush, Mizraim, Put and Canaan. The sons of Cush: Seba, Havilah, Sabtah, Raamah and Sabteca. The sons of Raamah: Sheba and Dedan. Cush was the father of Nimrod. . . . The first centers of his kingdom were Babylon . . . in Shinar. From that land he went to Assyria, where he built Nineveh. . . . Mizraim was the father . . . (from whom the Philistines came). . . . Canaan was the father of Sidon his firstborn, and of the Hittites, Jebusites, Amorites, Girgashites, Hivites, Arkites, Sinites. . . . Later the Canaanite clans scattered and the borders of Canaan reached from Sidon toward Gerar as far as Gaza, and then toward Sodom, Gomorrah. . . . These are the sons of Ham by their clans and languages, in their territories and nations" (10:6–20).

Put scattered and settled in Libya and northern Africa.

Mizraim became the father of the powerful and sophisticated Egyptians.

Cush settled in Ethiopia.

Canaan's name was given to the territory he settled, which we now think of as Palestine, an area that includes the Gaza Strip and the land of the Philistines. It was also the promised land God gave to Abraham.[19]

Sidon's descendants were the ancient Phoenicians, world renowned for their seafaring skills.

The Jebusites' holdings were seized by Israel's King David and became the city of Jerusalem.[20]

The Sinites are thought to be the progenitors of China and Japan, countries whose people have always been associated with the prefix *sino*, as in Sino-Japanese war, or Sinology, the study of Chinese history.

215

In Ham's descendants, we read a who's who of the enemies of God's people in the Old Testament. Names like Pharaoh of Egypt, who enslaved the children of Israel, releasing them only under the great duress of God's judgment;[21] Goliath, the giant of Philistia, who defied the living God and those who served Him;[22] the city of Nineveh, capital of Assyria, which was exceedingly wicked but was spared judgment initially when it responded to the preaching of Jonah,[23] yet in the end enslaved the Northern Kingdom of Israel; the city of Babylon, which symbolized the enemy of God during the reign of Nebuchadnezzar, who destroyed the temple of God, the city of God, and the people of God;[24] the Hittites, Amorites, and Hivites, along with others who became so wicked God told the Israelites to drive them from the land;[25] and the Canaanites, who infected Israel with their wickedness, leading her into judgment,[26] all represent those who have set themselves against God and His people.

Ham's sinful, rebellious nature, which was evident in his reaction to his father's drunkenness, exploded into expression and dominated his descendants for years to come.

Why do we think that our lives are our own and we can live them as we choose without hurting anyone else? If left unchecked, sin not only is passed down to the next generation; it increases with each passing generation. The wickedness and rebellion of Noah's descendants spread like a cancer throughout successive generations, all over the world as they went north, west, south, and east.

*The Rebellious in the East*

The Shemites were the last to leave, and they didn't travel far. Their descendants settled the area described as the Middle East. "Sons were also born to Shem, whose older brother was Japheth; Shem was the ancestor of all the sons of Eber. The sons of Shem: Elam, Asshur, Arphaxad, Lud and Aram. The sons of Aram: Uz, Hul, Gether and Meschech. Arphaxad was the father of Shelah, and Shelah the father of Eber. Two sons were born to Eber: One was named Peleg, because in his time the earth was divided; his brother was named Joktan. [Joktan was the father of thirteen sons, including Ophir, Havilah and Jobab.] The region where they lived stretched from Mesha toward Sephar, in the eastern hill country. These are the sons of Shem by their clans, languages, in their territories and nations" (Gen. 10:21–30).

Aram was the father of the Aramaeans, whose language, Aramaic, was adopted as the world's "first language" and was commonly spoken in the day of Jesus Christ.

Uz settled northern Arabia, which was apparently the homeland of Job, a man whose classic struggle with why bad things happen to good people has become a source of strength, comfort, and hope to millions of people since.[27]

Peleg's name means "division," and he was named because when he was born, the earth was divided. This either refers to a continental drift of the physical planet or the division of peoples as a result of God's judgment at Babel.

Ophir and Havilah settled the area of Saudi Arabia.

Eber's name is the root word for "Hebrew," from whom descended Abraham and the Jews.

These names comprise the Table of Nations, the record of Noah's descendants through his three sons, which has been described as being "absolutely alone in ancient literature, without a remote parallel, even among the Greeks. . . . The Table of Nations remains an astonishingly accurate document."[28] While the genealogy of Noah's sons is amazing for the accurate description of the placement of people all over the world, it is heart wrenching as we read, "These are the clans of Noah's sons, according to their lines of descent, within their nations. From these the nations spread out over the earth after the flood. . . . From there the LORD scattered them over the face of the whole earth" (Gen. 10:32, 11:9). It's as though we can feel the wind of God's Spirit sweeping over the plain, scattering the people of the world as they exercised their freedom of choice and separated themselves from the very One by whom and for whom they were created. It's as though we can hear the thunderlike rumble of God's voice crying in the wind a loving farewell, "I love you! I love you! I love you! I created you because I intensely wanted you to know Me and wanted you to be known by Me. But I am not going to force you to have a relationship with Me you don't want. So I will let you go. But I will never for one moment forget you. You will always be on My mind. You will always be in My heart."

God scattered Shem, Ham, and Japheth's descendants all over the world as judgment for their sin of rebellion against Him. The descendants never collectively repented. They still fill the world of our day:

the slavelike masses in North Korea,
the starving masses in India,
the silent masses in China,
the spoiled masses in America,
the sophisticated masses in Europe,

the secular masses in Australia,

the sickly masses in Africa . . .

are masses of people living in rebellion against God, a rebellion that has been passed down through the generations from their fathers before them, a rebellion that is at times cleverly cloaked in organized religious expression.

But the various religions of the world, which are in themselves mini Towers of Babel, do not diminish the truth—the truth that there is:

One God who has revealed His glory as the Creator, who brought us into existence that we might know Him and be known by Him.

One God who as our Father holds us accountable for the sin and rebellion in our lives.

One God who has provided an Ark as a means of escaping His own judgment for our sin.

One God who cannot be approached on our own terms or on our own merits or by our own efforts.

One God who is the same yesterday, today, and forever, unchanging in His love for the masses in the world He sees one by one as individuals whom He created

to know joy

and love

and peace

and goodness

and kindness

and gentleness

and mercy

and strength

and hope

and fullness of life

through knowing Himself in a personal, permanent, love relationship. While God rejects our religiousness, He does not reject us.

Did the almighty Elohim, glorious in His eternity, deity, activity, and identity, shed celestial tears as with a broken heart He watched the jewels of His creation willfully turn their backs on the very reason for their existence? "I love you! I LOVE YOU! I LOVE YOU! I love the world so much, I will give My one and only Son, that whoever believes in Him will not perish in a life of

emptiness
brokenness
sinfulness
bitterness
wastedness
loneliness
fearfulness
weakness
religiousness
hopelessness
. . . but will have eternal life."[29]

Jesus Christ announced He is the Way back to God, He is the Truth about God, and He is the Life we were meant to have in the beginning. Regardless of how high or elaborate or intricate or noble or impressive the religious towers of our day are, no one on this entire rebellious planet of any generation or age will ever get into heaven unless they enter through Jesus Christ.[30]

ELIZABETH CARTER was a young American woman who taught English in mainland China. On a weekend outing with friends, she hiked up Tai Shan, a holy mountain, not too far from the city where she worked. At the base of the mountain, as she began her ascent, she saw an old beggar sitting beside the path. She felt very impressed to speak with him and tell him about God. Because her friends hurried on up the path, Elizabeth suppressed the urge to stop and speak, and so she passed him by.

During the afternoon of exploration on the mountain, her thoughts kept returning to the old beggar. She began to deeply regret having not spoken to him, knowing he would most likely have left before she returned. As she descended the summit in the early evening, she resolved to make the time to speak to him if he was still there.

When Elizabeth reached the base of the mountain, to her eager surprise, the old beggar was still sitting exactly where he had been before. This time she went over to him and gently began to speak to him. She told him that there is a God who created all things, that the great Creator God had created him because He loved him and wanted to be known by him. She told the old man that God had

219

sent His Son to earth to die on a cross as a sacrifice for the man's sin, and that if he placed his faith in God's Son, Jesus, he would be forgiven and would receive eternal life.

As Elizabeth continued telling the old man about God, tears began to slip down his weather-beaten face, moistening his few wispy, white whiskers. Thinking she had offended him in some way, Elizabeth asked what was wrong. The old man smiled through his tears and said softly, "I have worshiped Him all my life. I just didn't know His name."

Whether a beggar in mainland China,

a tribesman in New Guinea,

a businessman on Wall Street,

a Bedouin chieftain in the desert,

or a soccer mom in the United States,

every single person ever born has an instinctive knowledge of the God for whom we each were created.[31] But most people living on planet Earth do not know really His name.

His name is Jesus.

# 11

## *I Banish Your Hopelessness*

GENESIS 11:10–12:24

During World War II, a German prisoner of war was being held in a Russian prison camp. His food was the bare minimum for survival substance; his housing was wretched, his clothing tattered and worn. He was mistreated, isolated, and miserable. He was able to make it from one day to the next for four years only by clinging to the hope that one day he would be released and would go home to become a great artist. Finally, the war ended, and he was released to go home.

The former prisoner arrived in Vienna, Austria, filled with anticipation of seeing his family and beginning the fulfillment of the dream that had kept him alive through his living nightmare. In spite of his malnutrition and ill health, there was a spring in his step and a gleam in his eye as he disembarked from the train that had transported him from Russia. He was greeted by his wife whom he had not seen since before the war. On the way home from the train station, he confided to her his dream of being a great artist. His wife gave him a look of withering disparagement as she chided, "Now that you are free, you must give up those foolish dreams." The German POW did not respond but continued the journey home in quietness. When he arrived home, the spring was no longer in his step, and the gleam was gone from his eye. Within two weeks he died.

What the German POW's wife did not understand was that "hope deferred makes the heart sick."[1] In the case of the POW, hope denied was fatal, because hope keeps the human spirit alive in even the most miserable of circumstances.

Following the rebellion at the Tower of Babel, the human race, which was separated from God, was scattered all over the world in absolute, utter, total, complete, endless, eternal hopelessness.

221

There was no chance in a lifetime that the people could ever fulfill their potential
    or experience lasting satisfaction
        or enjoy deep peace
            or find real joy
                or be unconditionally loved
                    or live forever!

They would never know the Creator for whom they were created. They would never know the very reason for their existence. They would never be free of
    emptiness,
        brokenness,
            sinfulness,
                bitterness,
                    wastedness,
                        loneliness,
                            helplessness,
                              fearfulness,
                                weakness,
                                  or religiousness.

They were utterly hopeless in themselves. And their descendants who fill our world today are still utterly, absolutely, completely, finally hopeless! Yet there is hope in God!

## HOPE IN GOD'S PLAN

Almost from the moment that God let the world go at the Tower of Babel, He began unfolding His plan to reconcile it to Himself. He did this by reaching down into the world of humanity that was in rebellion against Him—down into one nation, one tribe, one family from which He chose one man through whom He would begin making preparations for sending the Redeemer. Genesis says, "Sons were also born to Shem, . . . the ancestor of all the sons of Eber. . . . When Eber had lived 34 years, he became the father of Peleg. . . . When Peleg had lived 30 years, he became the father of Reu. . . . When Reu had lived 32 years, he became the father of Serug. . . . When Serug had lived 30 years, he became the father of Nahor. . . . When Nahor had lived 29 years, he became the father of Terah. . . . After Terah had lived 70 years, he became the father of Abram" (Gen. 10:21, 11:16–26).

Abram, Terah's son, Eber's great-great-great-grandson, a descendant of Shem, a descendant of Noah, was just one man among tens of thousands of people on Planet Earth. He lived in the most civilized, progressive, magnificent city of his day, Ur of the Chaldees,[2] when the entire world was separated from God and living in rebellion against Him.

Ur was a seaport located on the Persian Gulf, considered the most magnificent city in the world, eclipsed later only by Babylon. It was an exciting, highly sophisticated, bustling world center that revolved around several universities offering the best education in the world of that day, international banking and shipping, and religious worship of a moon god and moon goddess.

Abram, living in Ur, was raised in a well-to-do, idolatrous family.[3] Increasingly, his spirit must have become restless and uneasy. Perhaps he noticed the way the sun came up every morning and wondered at its faithful, clocklike precision. Perhaps he observed the birth of a baby and marveled at the miracle of the tiny new life. Perhaps in closing a business contract he had an opportunity to cheat and so get the advantage but refused because he knew it was wrong, then questioned afterward how he knew what was right and wrong. Maybe he went to the temple with his father to worship the moon god and was struck by the futility of bowing down to a stone carved by human hands.

Abram must have begun to think that there had to be more to life than buying and selling and making money and worshiping a stone. His mind and heart must have been drawn to search for a deeper meaning to life and for the very reason for his existence, because the glorious, living God of the universe, who had created the heavens and the earth, the great Lord God who had planted a garden, then formed man from the dust of the earth to live in it and be His companion, the mighty Creator who had breathed His own life into Adam, leaned out of heaven and spoke to Abram!

### God's Personal Plan

Not since He had spoken to Noah, committing Himself to the human race, and not since He had spoken as though to Himself at the Tower of Babel, warning Nimrod and his followers that their rebellion would lead to confusion and judgment, had God's voice been heard on planet Earth. Whether Abram heard an audible voice or felt a distinct impression on his mind or in his spirit, he knew he was being addressed by a living God. As Abram heard God's voice, he must have been deeply convicted that this was the One for whom he had been searching all of his life. As he listened carefully, God unveiled His plan to Abram as He spoke to him personally.

Abram became aware that out of all the people living on planet Earth, the living God was speaking to him. "The LORD had said to Abram . . ." (Gen. 12:1), and Abram must have trembled in awe, scarcely allowing himself to breathe as he hung on every syllable of every word of God. He knew the plan God began to unfold for him was very personal; no one else in the entire world was included at that point. But there was a "catch."

*God's Conditional Plan*

God promised to bless Abram, but Abram would not receive all God had for him unless he claimed it by leaving everything—his familiar surroundings, his comfortable lifestyle, his old friends, his values, his job, his home, and even his family—and set out on a life of faith. God told him, "Leave your country, your people and your father's household and go to the land I will show you" (Gen. 12:1). Abram did not know where God would lead, just that he was to follow. God's command was clear. He was to put God first in his life if he wanted to receive God's blessing.

As Abram looked around at the beautiful city in which he lived, with its vast estates and swaying palm trees;

as the bustling noise of the traffic of caravans from India, China, Egypt, and Europe passed outside his door;

as the shrill cry of the vendors in the market overflowing with every fruit, meat, and grain to satisfy even the most discerning palate pierced the air;

as he gazed at the stately ships with the tall sails coming and going in the busy harbor;

as he smelled the fragrance of the spices and perfumes that were bought and sold for international trade;

as he heard the laughter of his friends making plans for a weekend outing;

as he listened to the chatter of his family around the table during the evening meal;

as he climbed into his soft bed or dressed in his clean linen robes or bathed in the perfumed fountain—

did Abram flinch? Did his stomach turn over? Did he question what he had heard or doubt for even a moment that it might not be worth his time—all of his time—or his life—all of his life—to follow God by faith? How could he leave everything to ride on a camel and live in a goat's-hair tent and be isolated from family and friends and walk down dusty roads to who knows where?

*God's Radical Plan*

If Abram obeyed God by putting Him first and following His leading by faith for the rest of his life, his life would be dramatically different. He must have known that God was not just adding a weekend hobby or an additional commitment to an already busy life but describing a radical change:

"I will make you into a great nation": He would change Abram's position from a childless man to a great patriarch.

"I will bless you": He would give Abram personal, permanent satisfaction.

"I will make your name great": He would increase his reputation until he was world renowned—forever.

"And you will be a blessing": He would change his ambition in life to one of making great impact on others.

"I will bless those who bless you, and whoever curses you I will curse": He would give Abram a unique identification with God Himself.

"And all peoples on earth will be blessed through you" (Gen. 12:2–3).

The ultimate blessing God was promising to give Abram was the Seed, the Offspring He had promised to Adam and Eve who would be the One to reconcile God and man, bridging the great gulf between them that sin and rebellion had created. The Seed would not be given in the next generation but in one of the succeeding generations of Abram's descendants. As a result of Abram's faith and obedience to God, the entire world that was created by God yet separated from Him would be given the opportunity to come back into a right relationship with Him and so be blessed.

The plan God revealed to Abram was so radical, Abram would never be the same again if he agreed to it. Even his name would change from Abram to Abraham. God's plan for Abram's life would be the beginning of the solution to all the problems that had swarmed out of the Pandora's box of sin afflicting the human race since the garden of Eden. The world would never be the same.

*God's Obtainable Plan*

Living in the midst of a rebellious world, Abram took God at His Word. "So Abram left, as the LORD had told him; . . . Abram was seventy-five years old when he set out" (Gen. 12:4). There is no record of any hesitation, doubts, questions, fears, or even tears! It was as though Abram had been waiting all his life for the call from God, and when he received it, he responded immediately with steadfast eagerness, faith, and hope: "By faith Abraham, when called to go to a place he would later receive as his inheritance, obeyed and went, even though he did not know where he was going. By faith he made his home in the Promised Land like a stranger in a foreign country; he lived in tents. . . . For he was looking *forward*."[4] Abraham left his comfortable, convenient, yet wasted life in Ur and set out on a pilgrimage of faith that took him to a land God promised to give him and his descendants forever.[5]

## HOPE IN GOD'S PROVISION

Through Abraham, God began the long process of unfolding and accomplishing His plan to provide the Redeemer who would take away man's sin and bring him back into a right relationship with his Creator. Abraham's family became the chosen nation of Israel that provided the audiovisual aid of the sacrifices and ceremonies that pictured for the world God's terms for man to have a right relationship with Him. It was also Abraham's descendants who recorded the revelation of God through the written prophecy, history, biography, and poetry that we call the Bible.[6] And it was Abraham's descendants who provided the human lineage for Jesus Christ.

*God's Provision through the Jews*

Abraham's twelve great-grandsons became the fathers of the tribes of Israel who were driven to Egypt by famine, then enslaved there. With a powerful display of His glory, God brought them out of Egypt with a mighty hand, overthrowing Pharaoh and leading them safely through the wilderness under the direction of Moses. God revealed His glory to Moses and gave him the law Abraham's descendants were to live by if they wanted to please Him and receive His blessing. He prescribed the sacrifices and ceremonies necessary if the people who were sinners were to approach Him in His holiness and righteousness. And He promised

Moses He would raise up a prophet like himself—a prophet who would lead God's people not out of bondage to slavery but out of bondage to sin.[7] When Moses died, God raised up a military general named Joshua to lead Israel into the land of Canaan so the people actually possessed the land God had promised to Abraham.

For years the nation of Israel was ruled by prophets who gave them God's Word and judges who presided over her affairs until the people cried out to be ruled by a king as were the nations around them. God let them have their way, and they chose Saul to be their first king. He was a handsome, charming, personable, skillful leader who had no real character. His actions revealed that he had turned away from God even though he professed to know and serve Him. So God raised up His own king, a shepherd boy who became a man after God's own heart and the greatest king of Israel, the one by whom every subsequent king was measured.[8] David's throne would endure forever, because the promised Seed of Abraham, the Redeemer of the world, would be One of his descendants.[9]

When David died, his son Solomon reigned with wisdom and power, expanding Israel's borders until she occupied almost all of the land God had sworn to give to Abraham. But Solomon forsook complete obedience to the Lord as he grew older, and the kingdom he left behind was divided between his son Rehoboam, who ruled the Southern Kingdom, and Jeroboam, who ruled the Northern Kingdom of Israel. Although God sent outstanding prophets like Elijah and Elisha to give guidance to the Northern Kingdom, it quickly fell into idolatry and was eventually carried off into captivity by Assyria.

Under the influence of some of the greatest of the Old Testament prophets, such as Isaiah and Jeremiah, the southern kingdom seemed more inclined to follow God. But in the end, it too succumbed to the idolatry of the world that had permeated national life. God had warned of impending judgment, but His people had turned a deaf ear to Him. So He raised up the Babylonians as His instrument, judging Israel severely as her land was obliterated, her villages razed, Jerusalem leveled, the temple destroyed, and the people carried off into captivity where they languished for seventy years. Through prophets like Ezekiel and Daniel, God kept a remnant of faithful believers, even in captivity.

Finally, the Persian empire overtook the Babylonians. Cyrus, king of Persia, issued a decree that all the captives from Israel were free to return home if they so chose.[10] A small remnant returned to rebuild the temple and the city walls of Jerusalem. Inspired by Nehemiah and Ezra, Zechariah and Malachi, Israel reestablished her national life and identity. After God's final promise to Israel to "send my messenger, who will prepare the way before me. . . . The Lord you are seeking will come to his temple; the messenger of the covenant, whom you desire, will come,"[11] He became silent. He had promised a Redeemer to Adam and Eve. He had made a covenant with Noah, Abraham, Moses, and David, pledging all of His divine nature in commitment to fulfilling His promise of sending the Seed through whom He would redeem the world to Himself. Then, after working in Israel and through Israel and speaking to Israel through His prophets, for the next 450 years God did not say a word. The Greeks invaded and oppressed Israel and were repelled by the Maccabees. Then the Romans invaded and oppressed Israel. Still there was silence. Had God forgotten His promise? Had God broken His covenant? Had God's plan in some way been thwarted by the accumulation of man's sin or by man's archenemy, that old Serpent the devil? Was there indeed no hope for the descendants of Abraham or for the entire fallen race of Adam?

### God's Provision of Jesus

The years went by one after another. Each generation of believers hoped against hope the promise would be fulfilled in their time. Each woman who bore a son looked into the tiny infant face and wondered if he would be the One God would raise up to redeem the world to Himself. Under the tyranny of Roman occupation,
        with the sound of marching soldiers' feet on the streets and
            the burden of Roman taxes to pay and
                the addition of Roman laws to keep and
                    the sight of Roman cruelty to endure,
the flame of hope in God's promised Seed flickered but did not go out.

The days and weeks and months and years passed as they had before with no word from God—until one night that had seemed to be no different from any other. The Roman governor had issued a decree for a new tax system that would require a more accurate census of the population; the decree ordered every Jew living in Israel to go back to the town or village of his origin in order to register. The entire population was in upheaval as people shifted from town to town in compliance with the Roman ordinance.

One such little town was teeming with an influx of those coming in to register for the census. It was crowded to overflowing with people short of necessary housing and also short of temper! Beyond the outskirts of the little village, in the rocky pastureland that surrounded it, on this particular night things seemed a little more serene. The black, velvety sky was clear and studded with sparkling stars that had looked down on Earth since the beginning of time. Shepherds appeared to be sitting idly by their flocks but in fact were keeping a sharp lookout for anything or anyone who might harm the sheep entrusted to their care. In the distance, the lights from the town could be seen and the noisy commotion could be heard as more people were coming into the town than the town could hold. On the clear night air, sound traveled easily, and somewhere from the direction of the village inn someone slammed a door.

And a baby cried.

Suddenly, the night seemed to split in two! Without warning, the shepherds were confronted by an angel, who must have seemed as tall as a great tree, dressed in clothing like lightning, with wings that stretched from earth to heaven! The glory of God that permeated and pulsated around the angel enveloped the shepherds in white, golden light, and they were terrified! They heard a voice that rang with authoritative intensity yet thrilling clarity as the angel announced, "Do not be afraid. I bring you good news of great joy that will be for all the people. Today in the town of David a Savior has been born to you; he is Christ the Lord. This will be a sign to you: You will find a baby wrapped in cloths and lying in a manger."[12]

The cowering shepherds' petrified terror turned to astonished wonder as "suddenly a great company of the heavenly host appeared with the angel, praising God and saying, 'Glory to God in the highest, and on earth peace to men on whom his favor rests.'"[13]

As the angelic choir returned to its heavenly home, the night resumed its normal appearance. The star-studded velvety sky still stretched like a giant canopy over the sheep, which were huddled together sleeping quietly; the lights and sounds from the little town once again could be heard on the night air. But something was very different. An electrified excitement—the climax of generations of hope—permeated the stillness of the night. The shepherds took one look at each other and knew they could not remain where they were. They were compelled by the revelation of God's glory to investigate what the Lord had said to them through the angel's message.

They must have run at breakneck speed across the field, stumbling over rocks and bushes in the darkness, reaching the outskirts of the little town, out of breath, with hearts pounding in excited rhythm. Did they fan out through the streets, shouting to each other, "You take that street; I'll take this one! Check every stable! Check every manger! If you find one with a baby in it, give the signal, and the rest of us will come. Quickly!"? As they searched the village, how long did it take them to find the little stable behind the inn where there was indeed a baby wrapped in swaddling clothes lying in a manger, just as the angel had said? Did their sudden entrance startle the man standing guard over a young woman who had obviously just given birth? Before he could step forward to defend his charges, did the shepherds excitedly explain, "Sir, we don't mean to intrude. But sir, you won't believe what we just saw! We were just minding our business, keeping our flocks out in the pasture beyond the town, when an angel appeared to us and told us a baby had been born. Not just any baby, but *the* Baby, the Savior, the Promised Seed—the angel said the babe was wrapped in swaddling clothes and lying in a manger in this town. And sir, we've been up and down this whole village, and your baby is the only baby we can find in a manger. Sir, we don't want to bother you. We just want to see the baby. Could we please?"

The man must have motioned for the shepherds to come forward. The shepherds, in rough homespun clothes, smelling of sheep and campfire smoke, stepped up to the manger. They looked down at the tiny form lying on the hay. The Baby's hair was still damp from birth; His dark little eyelashes curled against His chubby cheeks as He slept peacefully, His little rosebud mouth moving silently from time to time as though He had much to say, but not yet. When did the shepherds realize they were gazing into the face of God?

How could the shepherds have torn themselves away from such a sight? When they did leave the little family to return to their responsibilities, they "returned, glorifying and praising God for all the things they had heard and seen, which were just as they had been told."[14] The Seed of the woman,

who would destroy the power of that old Serpent the devil; the Seed of the woman,

who would take away man's sin and bring him back into a right relationship with the God for whom he had been created; the Seed of the woman,

who would open heaven's gate and welcome any and all who place their faith in Him; the Seed of the woman had been given!

Praise God! The world of humanity that had been separated from God and unable to approach Him except indirectly through the Jewish sacrifices and ceremonies was now invited to draw near and be reconciled directly to Him through this Baby who had invaded time and space to be born! The world was back in the game it had been forced out of at the Tower of Babel.

Man's praise and worship of God for the revelation of His glory that night has not ceased.

The skeptic's doubt,
            the mocker's scorn,
                    the professor's criticism,
                        the public's apathy,
                            the crowd's jeers,
                                the pagan's blasphemy,
                                    the authorities' threats,
                                        the executioner's sword,
                                            the devil's lies,

have not diminished the Hope that was born that night nor dimmed the glorious dawn of His story that continues to radiate down through the years until it envelops your heart and mine. Because "in the beginning was the Word, and the Word was with God, and the Word was God. . . . The Word became flesh and lived for a while among us. We have seen his glory, the glory of the one and only Son, who came from the Father, full of grace and truth."[15]

Real meaning to your life is found in the glorious dawn of God's story, which breaks into full revelation in the person of Jesus Christ.[16] What an astounding truth! What a life-changing message!

Because He emptied Himself of all but love, you can be filled.

Because His body was broken, your life can be whole.

Because His blood was shed, your sin can be forgiven.

Because He submitted to injustice, you can forgive.

Because He finished His Father's work, your life has worth.

Because He was forsaken, you will never be alone.

Because He was buried, you can be raised.

Because He lives, you don't have to be afraid.

Because He was raised, you can be strong.

Because He reached down to you, you don't have to work your way up to Him.

Because His promises are always true, you can have hope!

The Creator has become your Redeemer!

# GOD'S STORY

A LITTLE BOY spent weeks carving a toy boat out of a block of wood. He fitted it with tall masts and cut linen squares for sails. The day came when everything was ready, but before taking it out for a test on the river, he lovingly carved his initials on the bottom of the boat. Then, with the boat tucked under his arm and excited anticipation in his heart, he made his way to the riverbank. He carefully tied a string to the toy so that as he placed it on the water he could hold the string, pulling the boat to himself if it drifted too far away.

The boy watched with fascination and pride as his little boat floated on the river, bobbing up and down with the ripples of the water. He was thrilled with the way it maneuvered the waves and current when the wind caught the sails and moved it swiftly to the center of the river. But in the excitement of seeing his handiwork perform as he had intended when he made it, he loosened his grip on the string, and it slipped out of his hand. The boat was swept away in the current of the river, floating farther and farther away from him. The little boy ran along the riverbank, calling to his boat, trying to snag it with a stick, but it was quickly carried downstream and lost to him.

The boy was devastated! He had spent hours planning and making the little boat and had grown to love it as though it were a living thing.

Several weeks later he was walking down the main street of his town when he passed the toy store. To his amazement, he saw his little boat displayed in the window! He rushed into the shop, reached for the boat, and carefully picked it up with both hands. He turned it over, and sure enough, his initials were clearly visible. He ran to the proprietor and exclaimed, "Mister, this is my boat! I made it!" Then he told the man all about it. The clerk looked at him rather indifferently as he took the toy from the little boy and replied, "I can see your initials and believe that this boat was yours. But it's mine now. If you want it, you are going to have to buy it back."

The little boy could hardly believe his ears. It was his boat. He had designed it. He had made it. But he couldn't have it unless he paid for it. So he left the store determined to do just that. He hired himself out to his mother and neighbors, mowing lawns, washing windows, weeding flower beds, doing anything anyone would pay him for. After several weeks, he had saved the amount needed to buy his boat.

His feet just didn't seem to move fast enough as he ran back to the toy store. With flushed face and trembling fingers, he counted out his nickels, dimes, and quarters to an exasperated clerk. He had exactly enough for the purchase price of the boat, so the proprietor went to the window, retrieved the boat from the display, and handed it to the little boy. With a look of triumphant joy, the boy clutched the boat to his chest as he hugged it to himself and said to no one in particular, "Oh, boy! You're twice mine! I made you, and I bought you!"

Like the little boy and his boat, God designed and created you because He loves you. He carved the initials of His own image in your life. But you drifted in the currents of sin and were swept from Him into the world. He worked for years, making the necessary arrangements to buy you back. Finally everything was ready. The purchase price He counted out was not nickels and dimes and quarters; it was the blood of His own dear Son. As He strode victoriously out of the tomb on Easter morning, you could almost feel Him hugging you to Himself, whispering triumphantly, "Oh, boy! You're twice Mine! I made you at Creation; now I've bought you at Calvary!"

"For God so loved *the world* that he gave his one and only Son, that whoever believes in him shall not perish but have eternal life."[17]

And so God's story, which began in the glorious dawn of Creation, is *continued . . .*

# NOTES

*Introduction: Genesis: The Memoirs of an Eyewitness*
1. Ecc. 1:14.
2. Read 1 Corinthians 1:30 (KJV) then read Proverbs 8:22–31.
3. 1 John 1:5.
4. Burton L. Visotzky, *The Genesis of Ethics* (New York: Crown Publishers, 1996).

*Prologue: The God You Can Know*
1. 2 Peter 3:8.
2. The Hebrew word for "day" is *yom* and can mean a twenty-four-hour period or an unspecified space of time.
3. John 3:16.
4. Eph. 1:4.
5. Compare Mark 15:25 with Mark 15:34.
6. John 1:1–3, 14, 5:19–27, 8:54–58.
7. John 1:29.
8. Heb. 13:5–6.
9. John 14:2.
10. Phil. 2:7–8.
11. Luke 1:26–38, 2:1–7.
12. Luke 2:7.
13. Luke 2:40, 52.
14. John 4:6, 8.
15. John 18:12.
16. John 19:17–18.
17. John 19:38–42.
18. John 1:3.
19. 1 John 4:4, 5:4.
20. Carl Sagan, *Parade* magazine, 19 September 1993, 4.
21. John D. Fix, *Astronomy: Journey to the Cosmic Frontier* (Rosewood, CA: William C. Brown Publishers, 1995), 570 and Appendix A, 12.
22. While every expert uses different figures to describe the size of the universe and no one can know for sure the exact numbers, we can all agree that the universe is big!
23. Ps. 147:4.
24. Ronald M. Atlas, *Microbiology: Fundamentals and Applications* (New York: Macmillan, 1987), 805.
25. Lawrence O. Richards, *It Couldn't Just Happen* (Dallas: Word, 1989), 103, 106, 139, 143–44.
26. John 11.
27. John 6:1–14.

28. Mark 4:35–41.
29. Mark 12:41–44.
30. Matt. 18:1–6.
31. Matt. 8:2–3.
32. John 12:1–8.
33. John 3:15–16, 36.
34. Heb. 11:1.
35. Luke 24:15, 30–31.
36. John 20:19–29.
37. John 21:1–7.
38. Isa. 40:13.
39. John 3:16 KJV.
40. John 6:44.
41. Eph. 1:20–22.
42. Acts 2:17–18.
43. Gen. 1:1–3.
44. Clear examples are found in Rev. 1:4–5, which says, "Grace and peace to you from him who is, and who was, and who is to come [God the Father], and from the seven spirits before his throne [God the Spirit], and from Jesus Christ [God the Son] . . ." as well as in Rom. 1:1–4, and 1 Pet. 1:1–2.
45. 1 John 4:16.
46. Eph. 1:4.
47. Rom. 5:8.
48. Matt. 6:6, 9; 1 John 4:16.
49. Rom. 8:15.
50. John 1:1–3, 14.
51. Col. 1:15–17.
52. Heb. 1:3.
53. John 1:18.
54. John 14:9.
55. John 3:34.
56. Rev. 1:5.
57. John 14:17.
58. 2 Pet. 1:21–22; 2 Tim. 3:16.
59. John 14:16.
60. John 14:26.
61. John 14:17.
62. Eph. 1:13.
63. 2 Cor. 5:5.
64. Eph. 1:14.
65. Rom. 8:35–39.
66. John 14:17, italics added.
67. Acts 2:4.
68. Ex. 13:21.

69. Ex. 40:34–35.
70. Ex. 33:18–23.
71. Ex. 34:29–35.
72. Eph. 2:21–22.
73. 2 Cor. 3:18.

*Chapter 1: I Fill Your Emptiness*
1. Paul Lee Tan, *Encyclopedia of 7700 Illustrations: Signs of the Times* (Chicago: R. R. Donnelly and Sons, 1979).
2. The Hebrew word for "hover" is *rachaph*, which means "to shake, flutter, pulsate, or energize." It may have been at this point that the Spirit of God formed the energy fields necessary as a basis for our environment and as a preparation for change.
3. Gen. 1:3, 6, 9, 11, 14, 20, 24, 26, 28, 29.
4. 1 Kings 19:11–13.
5. John 12:29.
6. Rev. 14:2.
7. John 1:1–3.
8. Through the centuries there has been much discussion as to whether the days of Genesis 1 are literal, twenty-four-hour days or longer periods of time. If you believe that each day of Creation represents a longer period of time, such as a geological age, consider the following: On the third day, fruit trees were made. On the fifth day the insects necessary to pollinate the fruit trees were made. If each day was longer than a twenty-four-hour period, perhaps even millions of years, how did the fruit trees survive without the necessary insects?

   On the other hand, if you believe the days were literal twenty-four-hour periods, consider this: Genesis 1 says that both Adam and Eve were created on the sixth day. Yet Genesis 2 describes God's creation of Adam as being followed by a longer period of time during which He gave Adam the desire for a wife. Then He created Eve.

   My personal conclusion is that the days of Creation represent one of the mysteries of God! The God whom we have considered so far, as revealed through what He says about Himself, certainly could have created the world in six twenty-four-hour days if He chose to do so. We just don't know if He did. What we do know is that God created everything!
9. A workbook designed as a companion to this volume is available from AnGeL Ministries. The workbook helps you read and apply God's Word, that you might experience the abundant life the Creator intended you to live. For more information, write: AnGeL Ministries, P.O. Box 31167, Raleigh, North Carolina 27622.
10. 2 Cor. 3:18.
11. There are two primary theories concerning how the earth came to be in a formless, void, dark, and fluid condition. The first is called the "gap" theory and is based on the Hebrew phrase for "formless and empty," which is *tohu wa bohu*, meaning "rendered a desolate, barren wilderness." Every time *tohu wa bohu* occurs in Scripture, it is associated with God's judgment. It implies that God intervened, and some catastrophe took place on planet Earth as a result of God's displeasure. By this interpretation, verses 1

and 2 would read, "In the beginning God created the heavens and the earth. Now the earth became *tohu wa bohu* because of divine judgment." Isaiah 45:18 says, "For this is what the Lord says—he who created the heavens, he is God; . . . he did not create it to be [*tohu wa bohu*], but formed it to be inhabited." The gap theory states that God did not originally create the earth in the condition described in verse 2 but that it deteriorated into that condition. Those who hold to this theory link the process of deterioration to the rebellion of Satan described in Isaiah 14. They conclude that the tremendous war that took place in heaven at that time resulted in a divine judgment that caused the earth to be in the condition we find in verse 2. Those who accept this theory also like to include geological ages at this point, since the gap in time could have been millions of years. There are two main problems with the gap theory: (1) Romans 5:12–14 and 1 Corinthians 15:21–22 both state that death came through Adam. In other words, there was no death in the universe until Adam, meaning there could have been no geological ages preceding his creation since geological ages include fossils, which are dead things, and (2) at the end of Genesis 1, God looks at everything He has made and says it is all very good. If Satan had been at work in the universe at that point, how could God have said it was all good? The other theory of how the earth came to be in the condition described in verse 2 is the "original chaos" theory. Those who accept this theory read verse 1 and 2 this way, "In the beginning God created the heavens and the earth. The earth was at first formless and empty. . . ." In other words, God did not intend it to remain that way, and verse 1 and 2 just describe the initial stage of His creative process without a gap.

Regardless of which theory you adopt, both have meaningful application for life. Many people today live formless lives—they have no shape or purpose or goal to live for. Their lives are empty, lacking in satisfaction and fulfillment. Darkness reigns in their lives through ignorance of the truth, emotional depression, or spiritual oppression. This kind of life can be "deep"—overwhelmed with a fluid condition that makes it unstable, inconsistent, rocking back and forth like the waves of the sea. In other words, life today can parallel the condition of our environment in the beginning. The two theories also can be two reasons why people's lives get into such a meaningless, empty condition. For some, the condition is the result of a "gap"—a catastrophe such as death, divorce, illness, bankruptcy, violent crime—that robbed them of the joy, satisfaction, and purpose in life they had previously known, leaving them feeling desolate and forsaken. For others, the condition has always been present because they have never felt a personal touch from the Creator in their lives.

The transformation of our environment in Genesis 1 gives answers to the problem of emptiness because God is the same God today that He was in the beginning. Through the power of His Word and the preparation by His Spirit, He changed planet Earth from its previous formless, empty, dark, and fluid condition into a place of life and beauty that brought Him pleasure and reflected His image. And He can do the same for you and me today!

12. Perhaps the sun, moon, and stars were actually created on the first day but because of the vapor canopy were not visible on earth until the fourth day.

13. Rev. 21:23.

14. It may be that the repetition of the phrase "and there was evening and there was morning—the first day" in verses 5, 8, 13, 19, 23, 31, suggests the earth was already rotating on its axis.
15. Ps. 119:130.
16. Ps. 119:105.
17. Phil. 3:5–6.
18. Acts 26:13.
19. 2 Cor. 4:6.
20. Saul of Tarsus became Paul, the apostle of Jesus Christ, who was inspired of the Holy Spirit to write most of the New Testament and who was the greatest evangelist, Bible teacher, and church planter the world has ever known.
21. 2 Tim. 4:8.
22. John 8:12.
23. John 1:4–5.
24. John 1:1–3, 14.
25. 1 John 1:5–7.
26. This increase in diameter is derived from the 1995 *Information Please Almanac* (Boston: Houghton Mifflin, 1995), page 332, which notes that the earth's atmospheric blend of 78 percent nitrogen, 21 percent oxygen, and 1 percent trace gases extends to a height of about sixty miles above sea level.
27. If it was a type of cloud cover, it was transparent by the fourth day when the sun, moon, and stars became visible from planet Earth.
28. Gen. 2:5.
29. We do know that Adam and Eve were perfectly comfortable without clothes (see Genesis 3:7).
30. *1995 Information Please Almanac*, 332.
31. Isa. 26:3; Ps. 4:8, 29:11, 37:11, 85:8, 119:165.
32. 1 Cor. 2:16; Rom. 5:5; Phil. 2:13.
33. Isa. 55:9.
34. Virtually all science now accepts the fact that the earth was one interconnected land mass. It may have been through the upheaval of the Flood that the ground broke apart into the continents as we know them today. Certainly when we look at a globe, the various continents look like pieces of a giant puzzle that at some point in time fit together.
35. 1 Cor. 3:11.
36. Heb. 13:8.
37. Heb. 13:5.
38. Rom. 8:35–39.
39. 2 Cor. 12:9.
40. Matt. 5:18; Ps. 119:89; 2 Cor. 1:20.
41. Matt. 7:24–25.
42. In Genesis 1:11 we have for the first time the phrase "after its kind" (KJV). This phrase recurs on the fifth day, when sea life was created, and on the sixth day, when animals and man were created. Everything reproduced after its kind. This means that within every living thing (plants, trees, animals, men) there is DNA containing the

genetic code that locks it in to reproducing exclusively "after its kind." A tremendous variety may exist within a species, but there is no crossover between the species. For example, there can be hundreds of different kinds of cats, but a cat will never become a horse. There can be hundreds of different kinds of roses, but a rosebush will never become a pine tree. Likewise, there may be hundreds of different kinds of monkeys, but a monkey will never become a man.

43.　It is interesting to note that on the third day of Creation the trees and plants came forth fully grown. I would assume if a newly made tree had been chopped down, rings of age could have been seen. The rings could have been counted, giving the appearance of years of age, when actually the tree was brand-new. Likewise, when Adam was created on the sixth day, he was created a full-grown man. He had the appearance of age when he was really brand-new.

　　This same astounding process was evident at the wedding at Cana of Galilee. The party ran out of wine. When Jesus, who was present, was informed of the problem by His mother, He instructed the servants to place water in the wine pitchers, then pour from the pitchers into the glasses of the guests. The master of the banquet tasted what had been poured into the glasses without knowing where it came from. "Then he called the bridegroom aside and said, 'Everyone brings out the choice wine first and then the cheaper wine after the guests have had too much to drink; but you have saved the best till now" (John 2:9–10). Jesus had turned the water not just into cheap wine but into the best wine. And best wine is aged wine, yet the wine at the wedding was created brand-new! It simply had the appearance—or taste—of age. (See John 2:1–11.)

　　In light of this fact, when scientists say the earth is billions of years old, should we think again? Maybe God created the entire earth with the appearance of age, just as He did the trees and plants and animals and people. The earth that seems to be very old may not be as old as it appears.

44.　See note 14, above.
45.　John 1:4.
46.　John 10:10.
47.　*Man* is used in a generic sense. The term describes the human species, which includes both male and female.
48.　Perhaps to be created in the image of God also meant that man, in his physical appearance, reflected something of what God is like. It is hard to conceive of a man created in the image of God stooping, crouching, ambling about on arms and legs, and grunting to communicate. Surely the first man was a perfect specimen, ideal in his height, weight, appearance, intellectual awareness, emotions, and communication skills—dignified, noble, intelligent—and upright on two legs.
49.　John 17:3.
50.　1 Peter 1:4.
51.　This alphabetized list of benefits is taken from Ephesians 1–2.
52.　Matt. 11:28–29.

Chapter 2: I Mend Your Brokenness
1.　Mark 6:3.

2. Acts 18:3.
3. Heb. 4:1–13.
4. Exod. 31:12–13.
5. Isa. 58:13–14.
6. God revealed His name to Moses as Jehovah, or Yahweh, at the burning bush. Its use in Genesis 2 helps to authenticate Mosaic authorship.
7. Five of the twenty-five verses in Genesis 2 are devoted to pinpointing the exact location of the garden of Eden. Although subsequent topographical changes make Eden difficult to locate, the two rivers described as flowing out of the garden can be located in the Middle East today, north of the Persian Gulf. Much archaeological evidence points to this area as being the "cradle of civilization" where the human race began. The careful, thorough, specific description of Eden's location emphasizes that it was a literal, historical place regardless of whether we can find it on a map today.
8. Gen. 2:19.
9. Gen. 3:8, italics added.
10. Gen. 18.
11. Gen. 32:22–32.
12. Josh. 5:13–6:5.
13. Heb. 1:3.
14. John 20:28.
15. John 2:1–11.
16. Matt. 21:17, 26:6; Mark 11:11–12, 14:3.
17. Prov. 6:20.
18. Robert Coles, "On Raising Moral Children," *Time* magazine, 20 January 1997, 50.
19. Deut. 4:9, 6:5–7, 7:9–10.
20. Gal. 5:22–23.
21. See Richards, *It Couldn't Just Happen,* 135–45.
22. Ps. 139:14.
23. Matt. 19:4; Mark 10:6, 13:19.
24. 2 Peter 3:5; Rev. 4:11, 10:6; Eph. 3:9; Col. 1:16, 3:10.
25. Rom. 12:1–2.
26. If the garden of Eden was Adam's home and God placed him there to work it, does that mean Adam—the man—did housework?!
27. Gen. 32:28.
28. Matt. 1:20–21.
29. John 1:42 and Matt. 16:18.
30. *Washington Post*, 15 February 1997, D-7.
31. Ps. 37:4–5.
32. Although the Hebrew word for man is "Adam," the genealogy of Jesus Christ in Luke 3:38 lists Adam as a very real, historical person. Jesus Himself referred to one man and one woman in Mark 10:6 when He explained, "At the beginning of creation, God 'made them male and female,'" and in Matt. 19:4–6 when He confirmed, "'The two will become one flesh.' . . . So they are no longer two, but one." This refers

240

to one man and one woman, because while two people can become one flesh, obviously three cannot.

33.  1 Peter 3:7 KJV.

34.  Gal. 3:28.

35.  Gen. 1:27. There is no possibility of a homosexual union in God's eyes. Homosexuality has never been and never will be an acceptable or alternate "lifestyle." Homosexuality is sin. Romans 1 describes the homosexual as far away from the Creator's design yet not beyond God's grace and redemptive power should the homosexual choose to repent and turn to God.

36.  Because of this intimate relationship, adultery is wrong in God's eyes. Three people cannot become one, as Adam and Eve were one.

37.  Dr. Ed Wheat, *Love Life* (Grand Rapids, MI Zondervan, 1980), 59.

38.  Matt. 19:6.

39.  Matt. 19:9. The apostle Paul seems to say in 1 Corinthians 7:15 that God also permits divorce on the basis of abandonment.

40.  Matt. 18:21–22.

41.  Matt. 19:9; Mark 10:10–12.

42.  1 Cor. 6:9.

43.  Eph. 5:25–33.

44.  Mal. 2:16.

45.  1 John 1:9.

46.  Jack and Susan's names have been changed.

47.  Nancy and Harold's names have been changed.

48.  Matt. 19:6.

49.  Jer. 18:1–6.

50.  2 Cor. 4:7–10, 17.

*Chapter 3: I Forgive Your Sinfulness*

1.  Rom. 3:23.

2.  2 Samuel 11.

3.  Rev. 12:9, 20:2.

4.  It is significant that the first principle of God's Word to be contradicted concerned judgment. People today perpetuate the contradiction with such statements as, "A loving God would never send anyone to hell."

5.  Gen. 39:12.

6.  Matt. 5:29–30.

7.  2 Tim. 2:22.

8.  Larry Crabb, *Finding God* (Grand Rapids, MI: Zondervan, 1993), 89.

9.  1 John 2:15–17 is a New Testament description of the intensifying steps of temptation.

10.  1 Tim. 2:14.

11.  John 8:44.

12.  Heb. 2:14.

13.  Rev. 20:10.

14.  John 18:12–13, 19.

15. John 18:20–21.

16. Today, in countries where Christianity has had little impact, such as those dominated by Islam, women don't have a much higher status than that of animals. They are treated as the property of the father or husband with no regard to their own feelings and desires. Yet in countries such as America, women enjoy an elevated status that is not due to legislation alone but to the permeation of Christianity. Because Jesus Christ, the Son of God, was born of a woman, He has elevated the position of all women. "Women's liberation" will occur not because we demonstrate for it or demand it but when we come into a right relationship with our Creator through faith in Jesus Christ—and society does the same. That's why the way a society treats women is directly related to society's attitude toward God and society's relationship with God. The further society drifts from God and His Word, the more society will experience a rise in pornography, wife abuse, sexual harassment, and a general degradation of women.

17. Rom. 6:23.

18. 1 Cor. 15:21–22.

19. Rom. 8:20–22.

20. Lev. 4:27, 32–35.

21. John 1:29.

22. Heb. 10:3–5.

23. The previous four paragraphs are taken from Anne Graham Lotz, *The Vision of His Glory* (Dallas: Word, 1996).

## Chapter Four: I Uproot Your Bitterness

1. James 2:10.

2. Thomas Merton, *The Seven Storey Mountain* (New York: Harcourt Brace, 1990, reprint), 75.

3. For Velma's autobiography, written while awaiting her execution, read Velma Barfield, *Woman on Death Row* (Nashville: Oliver Nelson, 1985).

4. Rom. 12:19.

5. Gen. 18:25.

6. Heb. 12:15. (The King James Version states this most clearly.)

7. Rev. 21:27 KJV.

8. A defiled life is like a life built out of wood, hay, and stubble, saved but as though by fire, with no eternal reward at the Judgment Seat of Christ. See 1 Cor. 3:12–15.

9. Heb. 11:4.

10. Gal. 2:16.

11. Heb. 9:22.

12. John 14:6; Acts 4:12.

13. Mal. 1:6–14.

14. Ps. 51:17.

15. See 1 John 3:12–13.

16. John 15:18–22.

17. Luke 11:47–51.

18. Although Genesis 4:8 implies Cain's murder of Abel was premeditated, perhaps it

was not. Perhaps Cain was acting on the impulse of the moment. The solemn lesson is that even the choices we make on impulse can be dictated by our sinful attitudes.

19.  Ps. 32:3–4.
20.  Heb. 12:5–6.
21.  1 Chron. 28:9; 2 Chron. 15:2.
22.  The Bible clearly states that Adam was the first man (1 Cor. 15:45) and that Eve was the mother of "all the living" (Gen. 3:20). Therefore, Cain's wife would have also been his sister or his niece (see Gen. 5:4). At this early stage of the human race, this would not have been genetically harmful. Later, such marriages were genetically damaging to such a degree that incest is forbidden in the Mosaic law (see Leviticus 18).
23.  1 John 4:16.
24.  Heb. 12:15.
25.  Luke 15:11–27.
26.  Ps. 32:5.
27.  Ps. 32:1 KJV.

## Chapter 5: I Redeem Your Wastedness

1.  *Wall Street Journal*, October 1983.
2.  Rom. 6:23.
3.  *USA Today*, 7 March 1997, 11A.
4.  The phrase "and he lived," or a phrase similar to it, is in every verse of Genesis 5 except verses 1, 2, 22, 24, 29, and 32.
5.  Eccles. 1:2–11, 3:11–14.
6.  Throughout history, genealogies have been very important, particularly to the Jews, who used them as actual proof they were the chosen people of God and therefore could lay claim to His promises. For example, Ezra, the great Jewish scribe and teacher who has been described as the Thomas Jefferson of his day, led the Jews out of captivity in Persia back to Jerusalem. As he prepared and organized the return, he required each Jew to produce his or her genealogy as proof that the person actually belonged to God. The only basis for claiming God's promises in regard to the land they were returning to was to have evidence of registration as an Israelite. In the time of Jesus Christ, the genealogies were kept in the temple in Jerusalem. Matthew and Luke probably got the information from the temple for the genealogies recorded in their gospels that validated the claim of Christ to the throne of David. In AD 70, the temple was destroyed and along with it, all the records kept there.

So there are no genealogies today that can be traced back to Adam. If someone today stands up and says he is the Messiah, he could not prove it, because he would have no genealogy to validate his claim. The genealogies had existed primarily for the purpose of recording the righteous remnant of God's people as well as proving the human lineage of Jesus of Nazareth. They revealed the fulfillment of prophecy in the life of Christ relating to the Messiah and the basis for His claim to the throne. When they had served their purpose, they ceased to exist.
7.  Rev. 20:11–12, 15.
8.  Rom. 7:1–4.

9. John 1:12, 3:16, 10:10; Rom. 3:23, 5:8, 6:23; Luke 13:1–5; John 14:6; Eph. 2:8–9; Rev. 3:20, 19:7–8.
10. 1 Kings 18:36–38.
11. Heb. 10:3–7.
12. Heb. 11:4.
13. Matt. 5:14.
14. Matt. 5:13.
15. Acts 1:8.
16. 1 Pet. 1:6–7.
17. God knows how to make up our losses.
18. Heb. 11:4.
19. John 4:19–24.
20. Some scholars see the statement in Genesis 4:26 ("At that time men began to call on the name of the LORD") as the first corporate worship in the Bible.
21. Jude 14–15.
22. Mark 12:30.
23. Heb. 11:5.
24. John 1:29
25. John 1:14; 1 John 1:1.

Chapter 6: I Share Your Loneliness
1. The name of the city when Mother and her family lived there was Tsing Kiang Pu in North Jiangsu Province.
2. 2 Cor. 6:14.
3. Amos 3:3.
4. However, we continue to pray for those three children, claiming God's promise in Joel 2:25: "I will repay you for the years the locusts have eaten."
5. Matt. 24:38–39.
6. Jude 6.
7. 2 Pet. 2:4.
8. Mark 12:25.
9. Rev. 12:7–12.
10. 1 John 4:4.
11. 2 Pet. 3:9.
12. Joel 1.
13. Heb. 9:27.
14. *Sports Illustrated*, 14 October 1996, 56.
15. Ps. 63:1–8.
16. Ps. 45:10–11; Zeph. 3:17.
17. The facts of this scene are accurately taken from Daniel 3, but many of the descriptive details are from my own imagination.
18. Dan. 3:15.
19. Dan. 3:16–18.
20. Dan. 3:24–25.

21. Rev. 12:11.
22. Mark 8:35.
23. James 1:22.
24. The word *ark* describes a floating barge designed for buoyancy rather than for speed or navigation. The Egyptians used arks to transport enormous quantities of grain and other cargo up and down the Nile River. An ark could turn on a ninety-degree angle without capsizing.
25. Gen. 2:5–6.
26. Compare Gen. 5:32 with 6:3 and 7:11.
27. Isa. 63:9.
28. Heb. 4:15 KJV.
29. 2 Cor. 5:21.
30. Matt. 27:46.
31. Heb. 13:5–18.
32. See Ezekiel 22:30 and 2 Chronicles 16:9.

Chapter 7: I Overcome Your Helplessness
1. Dan. 10:8.
2. Henry Morris, *The Genesis Record* (San Diego: Creation Life, 1976), 181–82.
3. Some scholars speculate that Noah was able to care for so many animals because many of them may have gone into hibernation. Every mammal has the latent capability to go into hibernation if the temperature drops in a certain way. It may be that when the temperature of the earth dropped during the Flood, it caused some of the animals to go into a type of hibernation, causing their bodily processes to slow down. See Morris, *The Genesis Record*, 186–87.
4. Gen. 6:14–16.
5. Ps. 118:7.
6. 2 Cor. 12:9–10.
7. See Elisabeth Elliot's biography of Amy Carmichael, *A Chance to Die* (Old Tappan, NJ: Revell, 1987).
8. Heb. 6:10–12.
9. Rom. 3:23, 6:23; John 3:16–18; Heb. 9:27; Luke 12:5; 2 Peter 2:4–9.
10. Matt. 13:49–50; Rev. 20:1, 20:10, 14–15; Jude 13; Matt. 5:22, 7:23.
11. See Romans 3:23.
12. See Ephesians 1:7 and Romans 3:25 KJV.
13. 2 Cor. 6:2.
14. Eph. 5:22.
15. One speculation for the delay comes from Genesis 5:27, where we read of Methuselah, who lived 969 years. His name means "when he dies, it will come," and he died the year the Flood came. Wouldn't it be interesting if Methuselah had just died? Just as the world held seven official days of mourning for Jacob when he died, perhaps the people of Noah's day, who would have known the meaning of Methuselah's name, mourned seven days for the oldest man who had ever lived. This could have been another way the gracious Creator sought to issue yet another warning of judgment to come.

16.  2 Peter 2:5.
17.  Rom. 5:9–10.
18.  Acts 27:13–44.
19.  Job 12:15 KJV.
20.  2 Peter 3:6 KJV.
21.  Three reasons for believing the Flood was universal are as follows: (1) Genesis clearly states that "every living thing on the face of the earth was wiped out." If the Flood had been a localized catastrophe, it could logically be assumed that at least a few living things could have escaped. (2) If, for some reason, all living things were localized in this vicinity and therefore a localized flood destroyed them all, then in the 120 years it took Noah to build the ark, he could have walked to safety. (3) Genesis reports that the waters "covered the mountains to a depth of more than twenty feet." The Bible records that the ark eventually landed on the Ararat range in Turkey, which today is seventeen thousand feet above sea level. It was able to land there only after the water level had been receding for nearly a year, which means the water must have been substantially higher than seventeen thousand feet at the peak of the Flood. Since water seeks its own level, how could a flood with a water depth of more than seventeen thousand feet be localized?
22. 2 Peter 3:5–7.
23. John 19:38–42.
24. Eph. 1:19–21.

*Chapter 8: I Calm Your Fearfulness*
1.  Columnist Ann Landers, quoted in Tan, *Encyclopedia of 7700 Illustrations*, 434.
2.  Charles Mayo, quoted in Greg Laurie, *Life: Any Questions?* (Dallas: Word, 1995), 38.
3.  2 Cor. 1:3.
4.  Isa. 49:16.
5.  Isa. 49:15.
6.  Josephus, a highly respected Jewish historian who lived in the first century AD, wrote that the ark was still visible in his lifetime. In World War II, a Russian airman flying over the Ararat range noticed a boatlike shape. He reported it to his commander, who sent an expedition that claimed to have found Noah's ark. About twenty years ago, *Life* magazine ran some interesting photographs with an accompanying article stating, "While routinely examining aerial photos of this country, a Turkish army captain suddenly gaped at the picture shown. There on a mountain twenty miles south of Mount Ararat, the biblical landfall of Noah's ark, was a boat–shaped form about five hundred feet long. The captain passed on the word, and an expedition including American scientists set out for the site. At seven thousand feet in the midst of crevices and landslide debris, the explorers found a clear grassy area shaped like a ship and rimmed with steep, pat earth sides. Its dimensions are close to those given in Genesis. A scientist in the group says, 'Nothing in nature could create such a symmetrical shape.'" The caption on one of the photographs notes, "They blasted the sides of this shape and wood came out." The area was above the tree line, with no trees growing at that height on the mountains. Although we may never be able to

definitely locate the site of Noah's ark and we may never be able to prove that the reported sightings are accurate, we do know the ark landed somewhere in the Ararat range of mountains.

7. Ps. 37:34.
8. Judg. 6:15.
9. Judg. 6:36–40.
10. John 5:6.
11. Matt. 7:7.
12. 1 Thess. 5:17 KJV.
13. Lam. 3:19–23.
14. Mark 14:1–9; John 12:1–8.
15. See Romans 3:23, 6:23.

*Chapter 9: I Understand Your Weakness*
1. The name and certain details of this true story have been changed to protect Wang's identity.
2. Gen. 1:29, 2:16, 3:17–18.
3. *USA Today*, 7–9 March 1997, 1.
4. Heb. 9:22.
5. Lev. 17:10, 11, 14; 1 Peter 1:18–19; 1 John 1:7; John 6:54.
6. Gal. 2:15–16.
7. Jer. 17:9 KJV.
8. Prov. 4:23 KJV.
9. Chance Conner, McVeigh trial reports, *Denver Post* online, 6 April 1997.
10. Rom. 6:23.
11. It is interesting to note that nowhere in the Bible is there a principle for imprisonment. God's principles deal with serious crime through either execution, retribution, or restitution. See Exodus 21:23–25 and Leviticus 24:17–22.
12. Deut. 6:7.
13. The other four covenants were given to Abraham in Genesis 15, to Moses in Exodus 19, to David in 2 Samuel 7, and the new covenant offered to you and me in Matthew 26.
14. 2 Peter 3:7.
15. Heb. 8:8–12.
16. Heb. 12:24.
17. Matt. 26:26–28.
18. John 15:5; Phil. 4:13.
19. Acts 2:1–4, 32–33, 37–39.
20. This is the first time wine is mentioned in the Bible. It has been suggested by some that before the atmospheric changes brought on by the Flood, grapes would not have decayed and fermented and therefore Noah drank the wine unsuspecting of its evil effect, but there is no evidence to support this theory.
21. 1 John 1:9.
22. Prov. 17:9.

23. 1 Cor. 13:6–7.
24. 1 Pet. 4:8.
25. 2 Pet. 1:21.

*Chapter 10: I Reject Your Religiousness*
1. 2 Peter 3:9.
2. 1 Thess. 5:18.
3. See John 1:12–13 and John 3:3.
4. 2 Cor. 8:5.
5. 1 Thess. 4:3.
6. Prov. 20:24.
7. See Matthew 12:30.
8. Archaeologists have excavated the area by the Euphrates River, which was the very beginning of the nation of Babylon and would have included the plain of Shinar where Babel was built. We are told that Babylon was a very advanced civilization for its day. The landscape was peppered with pyramid-shaped structures called "ziggurats." One of the ziggurats uncovered was more than 275 feet tall. On the flat plain of Shinar, it would have looked like a skyscraper reaching into heaven. It was an elaborate series of platforms, each twenty to sixty feet high. Each platform was a little smaller than the one below it so that it was tiered like a wedding cake. And each tier was decorated in brilliantly covered tile and mosaics. The very top platform was a shrine to a god that required prostitution as a form of worship. See Henry H. Halley, *Halley's Bible Handbook* (Grand Rapids, MI.: Zondervan, 1965), 83–84.
9. John 6:29.
10. Isa. 64:6.
11. Rom. 3:10 (see also Psalms 14:3, 53:3).
12. Heb. 12:14.
13. Matt. 7:21.
14. John 14:6.
15. Jim Trotter, "Cults Weren't Stupid and Didn't Start Out Crazy," *San Jose Mercury News*, 28 March 1997.
16. Dana Calvo, AP writer, "Ex–Cult Member Kills Self," *Washington Post*, 7 May 1997.
17. *Raleigh News and Observer*, 16 February 1997, 1A.
18. Rom. 1:18, 24, 26, 28.
19. Gen. 13:14–17.
20. 1 Chron. 11:4–9.
21. Ex. 1:1–15:21.
22. 1 Sam. 17:4–10, 34–37, 41–50.
23. Jonah 1:1, 3:10.
24. 2 Kings 25:1–21.
25. Josh. 3:9–10.
26. Ps. 106:34–43.
27. Job 1:1–22, 2:1–13, and 38:1–42:17.
28. Dr. William F. Albright, the world's leading authority on archaeology of the Near

East, quoted from "Recent Discoveries in Bible Lands," an article appended to *Robert Young's Analytical Concordance to the Bible* (New York: Funk and Wagnalls, 1936), 25.

29. Based on John 3:16.
30. John 14:6.
31. Rom. 1:19–20.

*Chapter 11: I Banish Your Hopelessness*
1. Prov. 13:12.
2. Ur was a seaport located at the mouth of the Euphrates River as it flowed into the Persian Gulf. It was a center for shipping by boats at sea as well as caravans by land to every corner of the known world. Archaeologists have excavated its ruins and discovered the homes in Ur were large, had central heating, indoor plumbing, running water, and were made of brick. They were located on wide, palm tree–lined boulevards that crisscrossed the city. The city itself was home to a university of science, a university of math, and a library of more than two hundred thousand tablets. The most prominent building in Ur was a square, solid-brick, multiterraced tower patterned after the Tower of Babel, with a shrine to the moon god Nannar, located at the pinnacle. See Halley, *Halley's Handbook*, 87–89.
3. Josh. 24:2.
4. Heb. 11:8–10, italics added.
5. Gen. 13:14–17.
6. Out of the sixty-six separate books included in the Bible, only two or three are not written by Jews—the gospel of Luke, Acts, and possibly Hebrews.
7. Deut. 18:18.
8. Acts 13:22.
9. Isa. 9:6–7.
10. Ezra 1:1–3.
11. Mal. 3:1.
12. Luke 2:10–12, italics added.
13. Luke 2:13–14.
14. Luke 2:20.
15. John 1:1, 14.
16. 2 Cor. 1:20.
17. John 3:16, italics added.

# A DEVOTIONAL GUIDE FOR

# GOD'S
# STORY

## DAILY STUDIES FOR
## PERSONAL OR GROUP USE

# A PERSONAL WORD FROM ANNE

My beloved friend, Jill Briscoe, once visited what had been an extremely poverty-stricken country in Africa. As she flew in, she looked down on miles and miles of African veldt that had previously been covered by a lush grasslike crop, but was now an unbroken, brown, dusty plain stretching all the way to the horizon. As Jill traveled to the mission station where she would be staying, mile after mile of barren, dry, poverty-stricken land passed by her window. Little dust devils danced in the hot afternoon sun, while shimmering heat waves made the emaciated, dust-covered people walking listlessly beside the road look more like ghostly apparitions than humans.

The relief workers told her the sad story: The veldt had once been a beautifully green, rolling expanse covered by a newly discovered crop that adapted easily to the climate and soil of the area. Within a few short years, this crop had promised to make the people in the area totally self-sufficient as it became the main, and plentiful, staple of their diet.

Sadly, the relief workers shook their heads as they explained what had happened: The crop had, indeed, become the main staple in the diet of the local people, but too late it had been found to have no nutritional value at all. The tragedy was that hundreds of people had starved to death—with their stomachs full!

Those pitiful African people seem to symbolize many church members in America today who are spiritually starving to death with their stomachs full! We have made the main staples of our "diet" those things that have no real nutritional value—political agendas, social issues, human rights, books about God's Word, musical videos, theological formulas for reaching the postmodern man, and marketing strategies for the local church, along with a myriad of conferences, seminars, retreats, dramas, and "special events." None of these things is harmful in itself, but when substituted for the nutrition of daily Bible reading and prayer, the result is increasing spiritual starvation.

For the past twenty years as I have crisscrossed America speaking in arenas, to conventions and churches, I have become convinced of one thing: the average church member is desperately hungry for God's Word. While we read books about it and hear sermons on it and live by principles from it, we are sadly devoid of it on a daily basis. When our lives begin to unravel due to pressure, problems, or pain, we don't seem to know how to access its power and truth in a personal, relevant way that makes a difference. As a result, thousands have spirits that are shriveling even while they are sobbing, "Please, just give me Jesus!"

What does your spiritual diet consist of? Although you may be an active church member and a committed Christian, could it be that you are actually starving for the Bread of Life? Are you starving for the Bread, which is Jesus Himself, offered to you and me through God's Word?

If so, then this workbook is for you! It has been designed to take you directly into God's Word. There is no middleman. There are no blanks to fill in. There is not even any cross-referencing required. The simple format for meditation has been developed from my own daily personal time in God's Word as a means of reading a passage in order to hear Him speaking to me personally through it. Day after day, as I use this method in my Bible reading, God has fed me and filled me to overflowing!

As you begin this Bible study, pray this simple prayer: "Dear God, *please, reveal yourself to me!*" Then open your Bible and enjoy the Food!

# GETTING STARTED

These worksheets are designed to be used as a companion to *God's Story*. Used together, they will provide a format for Bible study that is effective for group discussion (Sunday school classes, women's or men's church groups, home or neighborhood Bible classes, one-on-one discipleship) as well as for your private devotions. Believing that God speaks to us through His Word, we have designed these worksheets to lead you through a series of questions concerning the designated Scripture passage. The exercises enable you to not only discover for yourself the eternal truths revealed by God in the Bible, but also to hear God speaking personally to you through His Word and thus have a fresh encounter with Him.

*Getting Started on Your Own*

It is suggested that *Getting Started, Tips for Success, Take One Step at a Time,* and the Sample Chapter be used as an initial lesson in order to familiarize yourself with the format to be used. The worksheets are subsequently divided to correspond with the chapters of the book. If you make your way through this study using one set of worksheets each day, you will complete a chapter a week. The Scripture passage for each worksheet corresponds with the Scripture passage in the divisions of the book chapters. Each set of worksheets will provide a very rich, meaningful pathway for your daily walk with Jesus.

*Getting Started in a Group*

If you embark on this study through Genesis in a group, you may want to meet once a week to share the insights you've gained. It is suggested that *Getting Started,*

*Tips for Success, Take One Step at a Time,* and the Sample Chapter be used as an initial lesson in order to familiarize yourself with the format to be used. The worksheets are subsequently divided to correspond with the chapters of the book. If you make your way through this study using one set of worksheets each day, you will complete a chapter a week. Ideally, your group will gather each week under the leadership of a facilitator who will lead you through a meaningful discussion of what you've individually discovered. If the group is large (twelve or more), you may need to divide into smaller groups for discussion time, with moderators being chosen to lead each one.

The facilitator may offer a summation at the end of the group study, emphasizing specific applications from Genesis to meet the needs and characteristics of your particular group, depending on age, sex, and interests of the members.

Whether you choose to get started on your own or in a group, I pray that your time spent exploring Genesis will result in a fresh experience of God's love—from the beginning.

# TIPS FOR SUCCESS

I have taken countless trips in my lifetime—some long, some short, some far, some near. But every single trip involves a certain amount of preparation in order to be successful. And the preparation itself requires a measure of discipline. This Bible study is no exception.

Spiritual discipline is an essential part of an individual's ability to grow in his or her personal relationship with God through knowledge and understanding of His Word. It is my sincere prayer that whether you use these worksheets as a private daily devotion or in a weekly group Bible study, it will provide you with an easy, meaningful format for this growth to occur.

To stay on track and make this study most effective and meaningful to your life, I offer these specific suggestions:

- Set aside a regular *place* for your daily Bible study.
- Set aside a regular *time* for your daily Bible study.
- Pray before beginning each day's study, asking God to speak to you through His Word.
- Write out your answers for each step of the worksheets in sequence. Do not skip a step.
- Make the time to be still and listen, reflecting thoughtfully on your responses, especially in Step 5.

# TAKE ONE STEP AT A TIME

**Step 1. LOOK IN GOD'S WORD:** Begin by reading the designated passage of Scripture. This is printed for you on each day's devotional section. When you have finished reading the passage, move to Step 2.

**Step 2. LIST THE FACTS:** Make a verse-by-verse list of the outstanding facts. Don't get caught up in the details; just pinpoint the most obvious facts. As you make your list, do not paraphrase but use actual words from the passage itself. Take a moment to read the completed example of a worksheet on the following pages. When you have read the passage in Step 1, look over the facts listed in Step 2 so that you understand these instructions more clearly.

**Step 3. LEARN THE LESSONS:** After looking at the passage and listing the facts, you are ready for Step 3. Go back to the list of facts in Step 2 and look for a lesson to learn from each fact. Ask yourself who is speaking, what the subject is, where the action is taking place, when it happened, and so on. Ask, *What are the people in this passage doing that I should be doing? Is there a command I should obey? A promise I should claim? A warning I should heed? An example I should follow?* Look again at the completed example on the following pages. Note that you may have more than one lesson for each verse.

**Step 4. LISTEN TO HIS VOICE:** The fourth step is the most meaningful, but you cannot do it until Steps 1, 2, and 3 have been completed. In order to complete Step 4, rephrase the lessons you found in Step 3 and put them in the form of questions you could ask yourself, your spouse, your child, your friend, your neighbor, or your coworker. As you write out the questions, listen for God to communicate to you personally through His Word.

There are some challenging passages in Genesis. Don't get hung up on what you don't understand. Look for the general principles and lessons that can be learned. Remember, don't rush. It may take you several moments of prayerful meditation to discover meaningful lessons and hear God speak to you. The object of these devotional studies is not to get through the study, but to develop your personal relationship with God in order to satisfy your spiritual hunger and increase your spiritual health.

**Step 5. LIVE IT OUT:** Read the assigned Scripture passage prayerfully, objectively, thoughtfully, and attentively as you listen for God to speak. He may not speak to you through every verse, but He *will* speak. When He does, record in Step 5 the verse number, what it is He seems to be saying to you, and your response to Him. You might like to date it as a means not only of keeping a spiritual journal, but also of holding yourself accountable to following through in obedience.

God bless you as you seek to learn this simple yet effective method of reading His Word, that you might hear His voice speaking to you personally through it. My prayer is that as you walk daily in this study through Genesis, you will learn to love the Bread of Life.

# 1 LOOK IN GOD'S WORD:
Feel free to underline, circle, or otherwise mark text if it will aid your study.

# 2 LIST THE FACTS:
Make a verse-by-verse list of the most obvious facts. What does the passage say? Do not paraphrase.

## I SAMUEL 3:7–10

7 Now Samuel did not yet know the LORD; The word of the LORD had not yet been revealed to him.

3:7 Samuel did not know the Lord or His Word.

8 The LORD called Samuel a third time, and Samuel got up and went to Eli and said, "Here I am; you called me." Then Eli realized that the LORD was calling the boy.

3:8 For the third time God called Samuel, who went to Eli.

9 So Eli told Samuel, "Go and lie down, and if he calls you, say, 'Speak, Lord, for your servant is listening.'"

3:9 Eli told Samuel to lie down and, if He calls, say, "Speak, Lord, I'm listening."

10 The LORD came and stood there, calling as at the other times, "Samuel! Samuel!" Then Samuel said, "Speak, for your servant is listening."

3:10 The Lord called Samuel, who said, "Speak, your servant is listening."

## 3 LEARN THE LESSONS:
What lessons can be learned from these facts? What do the facts mean? Is there an example to follow? Warning to heed? Promise to claim? Command to obey?

## 4 LISTEN TO HIS VOICE:
What does this passage mean to you? Rewrite the lessons from Step 3 in the form of a question to ask yourself or another.

3:7 There are some people today in church who do not know the Lord or His Word.

3:7 How well do I really know the Lord and His Word?

3:8 Sometimes God speaks to us, but we don't recognize His voice.

3:8 Could God be speaking to me now, but I don't recognize His voice?

3:9 We need instructions on how to recognize and listen to God's voice.

3:9 Am I willing to follow these instructions on how to recognize and listen to God's voice?

3:10 God speaks to us personally, and we need to give Him our attention.

3:10 As I read my Bible, using this workbook, how expectant am I that God will speak to me?

## 5 LIVE IT OUT:
Pinpoint what God is saying to you from the passage. How will you respond? Write down today's date and what you will do now to live it out.

I confess I have neither listened for, nor recognized Your voice because I did not know You speak personally through Your Word. I now choose to approach Your Word as though listening for a voice. Speak, Lord, for I am willing to listen. Use this book to help me hear Your voice that I might get to know You better and love You more.

# CHAPTER 1

## *I am the God of Creation . . .*
## *I Fill Your Emptiness*

When have you observed the blazing glory of a tropical sunset
>or the soft, silvery shimmer of moonlight on the ocean waves,

or a baby's birth and first lusty cry,
>>or a bird weaving her nest, hatching and feeding her young,

>>>or an exquisite lady's slipper tucked into a rocky crevice in the forest,

>>>or a hummingbird suspended in air,

>>>>or a V-shaped flight of geese migrating north,

>>>or the blinding flash of a jagged bolt of lightning splitting

>>the darkness . . .

when have you observed these things and wondered, *Who made it?*

When we thoughtfully consider the world around us, we instinctively know our environment is not some haphazard cosmic accident but the handiwork of a Master Designer. The earth did not come about by the snap of some giant fingers but was deliberately planned and prepared in an orderly progression of events. Like planet Earth around us, our lives are not a haphazard cosmos, either. They were deliberately planned to be filled with the beauty of love and joy and peace and purpose—with God Himself.

# A DEVOTIONAL GUIDE

**1** LOOK IN GOD'S WORD:
Feel free to underline, circle, or otherwise mark text if it will aid your study.

**2** LIST THE FACTS:
Make a verse-by-verse list of the most obvious facts. What does the passage say? Do not paraphrase.

## GENESIS 1:1–8

1 In the beginning God created the heavens and the earth. 2 Now the earth was formless and empty, darkness was over the surface of the deep, and the Spirit of God was hovering over the waters. 3 And God said, "Let there be light," and there was light. 4 God saw that the light was good, and He separated the light from the darkness. 5 God called the light "day," and the darkness he called "night." And there was evening, and there was morning—the first day. 6 And God said, "Let there be an expanse between the waters to separate water from water." 7 So God made the expanse and separated the water under the expanse from the water above it. And it was so. 8 God called the expanse "sky." And there was evening, and there was morning—the second day.

264

**3** LEARN THE LESSONS:
What lessons can be learned from these facts? What do the facts mean? Is there an example to follow? Warning to heed? Promise to claim? Command to obey?

**4** LISTEN TO HIS VOICE:
What does this passage mean to you? Rewrite the lessons from Step 3 in the form of a question to ask yourself or another.

**5** LIVE IT OUT:
Pinpoint what God is saying to you from the passage. How will you respond? Write down today's date and what you will do now to live it out.

# 1 LOOK IN GOD'S WORD:

# 2 LIST THE FACTS:

**GENESIS 1:9–13**

9 And God said, "Let the water under the sky be gathered to one place, and let dry ground appear." And it was so. 10 God called the dry ground "land," and the gathered waters he called "seas." And God saw that it was good. 11 Then God said, "Let the land produce vegetation: seed-bearing plants and trees on the land that bear fruit with seed in it, according to their various kinds." And it was so. 12 The land produced vegetation: plants bearing seed according to their kinds and trees bearing fruit with seed in it according to their kinds. And God saw that it was good. 13 And there was evening, and there was morning—the third day.

**3** LEARN THE LESSONS:

**4** LISTEN TO HIS VOICE:

**5** LIVE IT OUT:

# 1 LOOK IN GOD'S WORD:

# 2 LIST THE FACTS:

## GENESIS 1:14–19

**14** And God said, "Let there be lights in the expanse of the sky to separate the day from the night, and let them serve as signs to mark seasons and days and years, **15** and let them be lights in the expanse of the sky to give light on the earth." And it was so. **16** God made two great lights—the greater light to govern the day and the lesser light to govern the night. He also made the stars. **17** God set them in the expanse of the sky to give light on the earth, **18** to govern the day and the night, and to separate light from darkness. And God saw that it was good. **19** And there was evening, and there was morning—the fourth day.

**3** LEARN THE LESSONS:

**4** LISTEN TO HIS VOICE:

**5** LIVE IT OUT:

# 1 LOOK IN GOD'S WORD:

# 2 LIST THE FACTS:

**GENESIS 1:20–25**

**20** And God said, "Let the water teem with living creatures, and let birds fly above the earth across the expanse of the sky." **21** So God created the great creatures of the sea and every living and moving thing with which the water teems, according to their kinds, and every winged bird according to its kind. And God saw that it was good. **22** God blessed them and said, "Be fruitful and increase in number and fill the water in the seas, and let the birds increase on the earth." **23** And there was evening, and there was morning—the fifth day. **24** And God said, "Let the land produce living creatures according to their kinds: livestock, creatures that move along the ground, and wild animals, each according to its kind." And it was so. **25** God made the wild animals according to their kinds, the livestock according to their kinds, and all the creatures that move along the ground according to their kinds. And God saw that it was good.

# 3 LEARN THE LESSONS:

# 4 LISTEN TO HIS VOICE:

# 5 LIVE IT OUT:

# 1 LOOK IN GOD'S WORD:

# 2 LIST THE FACTS:

## GENESIS 1:27–31

27 So God created man in his own image, in the image of God he created him; male and female he created them. 28 God blessed them and said to them, "Be fruitful and increase in number; fill the earth and subdue it. Rule over the fish and the sea and the birds and the air and over every living creature that moves on the ground." 29 Then God said, "I give you every seed-bearing plant on the face of the whole earth and every tree that has fruit with seed in it. They will be yours for food. 30 And to all the beasts of the earth and the birds in the air and all the creatures that move on the ground—everything that has the breath of life in it—I give every green plant for food." And it was so. 31 God saw all that he had made, and it was very good. And there was evening, and there was morning—the sixth day.

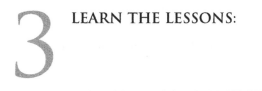

**3** LEARN THE LESSONS:

**4** LISTEN TO HIS VOICE:

**5** LIVE IT OUT:

## COMMITMENT:

What was the most meaningful lesson to you from each day's study this week?

*Study #1*

*Study #2*

*Study #3*

*Study #4*

*Study #5*

As you reflect on all the lessons, what one thing has God seemed to say to you from Genesis 1? Take a moment now to write out what He has said.

What has been your response?

Is there anything else you need to do in order to follow through completely?

Date your answer—then do it. Be committed!

# CHAPTER 2

## *I am the God of Creation . . . I Mend Your Brokenness*

Many people approach life as though it's so simple they can live it their own way. They sort of guess their way along. It's not until their lives don't work that it occurs to them to look around for directions.

God as our Creator has specific directions for our lives. If we live according to His directions, our lives work—we are blessed, and we experience life the way it was meant to be lived. If we ignore or reject His directions, we do so to our own detriment and experience much less than He intended.

But God did not just create you and me, plop us down on planet Earth, and say, "Happy birthday!  Now you can guess your way through life." Instead, He gave us directions, which form a pattern that—if we follow them—will prevent breakage of our lives and will help to mend the brokenness already present.

# 1 LOOK IN GOD'S WORD:

Feel free to underline, circle, or otherwise mark text if it will aid your study.

# 2 LIST THE FACTS:

Make a verse-by-verse list of the most obvious facts. What does the passage say? Do not paraphrase.

## GENESIS 2:1–3

1 Thus the heavens and the earth were completed in all their vast array. 2 By the seventh day God had finished the work he had been doing; so on the seventh day he rested from all his work. 3 And God blessed the seventh day and made it holy, because on it he rested from all the work of creating that he had done.

**3** **LEARN THE LESSONS:**
What lessons can be learned from these facts? What do the facts mean? Is there an example to follow? Warning to heed? Promise to claim? Command to obey?

**4** **LISTEN TO HIS VOICE:**
What does this passage mean to you? Rewrite the lessons from Step 3 in the form of a question to ask yourself or another.

**5** **LIVE IT OUT:**
Pinpoint what God is saying to you from the passage. How will you respond? Write down today's date and what you will do now to live it out.

# 1 LOOK IN GOD'S WORD:

# 2 LIST THE FACTS:

**GENESIS 2:4–7**

4 This is the account of the heavens and the earth when they were created. When the LORD God made the earth and the heavens— 5 and no shrub of the field had yet appeared on the earth and no plant of the field had yet sprung up, for the LORD God had not sent rain on the earth and there was no man to work the ground, 6 but streams came up from the earth and watered the whole surface of the ground— 7 the LORD God formed the man from the dust of the ground and breathed into his nostrils the breath of life, and the man became a living being.

**3** LEARN THE LESSONS:

**4** LISTEN TO HIS VOICE:

**5** LIVE IT OUT:

# 1 LOOK IN GOD'S WORD:

# 2 LIST THE FACTS:

## GENESIS 2:8–14

8 Now the LORD God had planted a garden in the east, in Eden; and there he put the man he had formed. 9 And the LORD God made all kinds of trees grow out of the ground—trees that were pleasing to the eye and good for food. In the middle of the garden were the tree of life and the tree of the knowledge of good and evil. 10 A river watering the garden flowed from Eden; from there it was separated into four headwaters. 11 The name of the first is the Pishon; it winds through the entire land of Havilah, where there is gold. 12 (The gold of that land is good; aromatic resin and onyx are also there.) 13 The name of the second river is the Gihon; it winds through the entire land of Cush. 14 The name of the third river is the Tigris; it runs along the east side of Asshur. And the fourth river is the Euphrates.

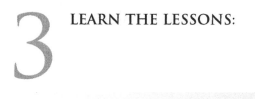

## 3 LEARN THE LESSONS:

## 4 LISTEN TO HIS VOICE:

## 5 LIVE IT OUT:

## 1  LOOK IN GOD'S WORD:

## 2  LIST THE FACTS:

**GENESIS 2:15–20**

**15** The LORD God took the man and put him in the Garden of Eden to work it and take care of it. **16** And the LORD God commanded the man, "You are free to eat from any tree in the garden; **17** but you must not eat from the tree of the knowledge of good and evil, for when you eat of it you will surely die." **18** The LORD God said, "It is not good for the man to be alone. I will make a helper suitable for him." **19** Now the LORD God had formed out of the ground all the beasts of the field and all the birds of the air. He brought them to the man to see what he would name them; and whatever the man called each living creature, that was its name. **20** So the man gave names to all the livestock, the birds of the air and all the beasts of the field. But for Adam no suitable helper was found.

**3** LEARN THE LESSONS:

**4** LISTEN TO HIS VOICE:

**5** LIVE IT OUT:

# 1 LOOK IN GOD'S WORD:

# 2 LIST THE FACTS:

### GENESIS 2:21–25

**21** So the LORD God caused the man to fall into a deep sleep; and while he was sleeping, he took one of the man's ribs and closed up the place with flesh. **22** Then the LORD God made a woman from the rib he had taken out of the man, and he brought her to the man. **23** The man said, "This is now bone of my bones and flesh of my flesh; she shall be called 'woman,' for she was taken out of man." **24** For this reason a man will leave his father and mother and be united to his wife, and they will become one flesh. **25** The man and his wife were both naked, and they felt no shame.

# 3 LEARN THE LESSONS:

# 4 LISTEN TO HIS VOICE:

# 5 LIVE IT OUT:

## COMMITMENT:

What was the most meaningful lesson to you from each day's study this week?

*Study #1*

*Study #2*

*Study #3*

*Study #4*

*Study #5*

As you reflect on all the lessons, what one thing has God seemed to say to you from Genesis 2? Take a moment now to write out what He has said.

What has been your response?

Is there anything else you need to do in order to follow through completely?

Date your answer—then do it. Be committed!

# CHAPTER 3

## *I am the God of Compassion . . .*
## *I Forgive Your Sinfulness*

What is sin? It has been defined as "not just that man is as bad as he could be but that he is not as good as he should be." The Greek definition of sin is of an archer who launches his arrow but "misses the mark." Sin is breaking God's moral law and therefore being unable to meet His standards of perfection.

Where does sin come from? Sin is a spiritual "disease" that has been transmitted to every single person in every single generation from the beginning of the human race. It infects the entire population of the world and is the cause of all the problems of war, greed, hate, prejudice, cruelty, corruption, and other ills that plague us.

While we all are born with a nature that has a strong tendency to sin, our lives bear the "fruit" of sin through the choices we make—which is where sin started in the beginning.

**1** LOOK IN GOD'S WORD:
Feel free to underline, circle,
or otherwise mark text if it
will aid your study.

**2** LIST THE FACTS:
Make a verse-by-verse list of
the most obvious facts. What
does the passage say? Do not
paraphrase.

### GENESIS 3:1–6

1 Now the serpent was more crafty
than any of the wild animals the
LORD God had made. He said to the
woman, "Did God really say, 'You
must not eat from any tree in the garden'?" 2 The woman said to the serpent, "We may eat fruit from the trees
in the garden, 3 but God did say, 'You
must not eat fruit from the tree that is
in the middle of the garden, and you
must not touch it, or you will die.'" 4
"You will not surely die," the serpent
said to the woman. 5 "For God knows
that when you eat of it your eyes will
be opened, and you will be like God,
knowing good and evil." 6 When the
woman saw that the fruit of the tree
was good for food and pleasing to the
eye, and also desirable for gaining wisdom, she took some and ate it. She
also gave some to her husband, who
was with her, and he ate it.

**3** LEARN THE LESSONS:
What lessons can be learned from these facts? What do the facts mean? Is there an example to follow? Warning to heed? Promise to claim? Command to obey?

**4** LISTEN TO HIS VOICE:
What does this passage mean to you? Rewrite the lessons from Step 3 in the form of a question to ask yourself or another.

**5** LIVE IT OUT:
Pinpoint what God is saying to you from the passage. How will you respond? Write down today's date and what you will do now to live it out.

# 1 LOOK IN GOD'S WORD:

# 2 LIST THE FACTS:

### GENESIS 3:7–13

**7** Then the eyes of both of them were opened, and they realized they were naked; so they sewed fig leaves together and made coverings for themselves. **8** Then the man and his wife heard the sound of the LORD God as he was walking in the garden in the cool of the day, and they hid from the LORD God among the trees of the garden. **9** But the LORD God called to the man, "Where are you?" **10** He answered, "I heard you in the garden, and I was afraid because I was naked; so I hid." **11** And he said, "Who told you that you were naked? Have you eaten from the tree that I commanded you not to eat from?" **12** The man said, "The woman you put here with me—she gave me some fruit from the tree, and I ate it." **13** Then the LORD God said to the woman, "What is this you have done?" The woman said, "The serpent deceived me, and I ate."

## 3 LEARN THE LESSONS:

## 4 LISTEN TO HIS VOICE:

## 5 LIVE IT OUT:

# 1 LOOK IN GOD'S WORD:

# 2 LIST THE FACTS:

### GENESIS 3:14–16

**14** So the LORD God said to the serpent, "Because you have done this, Cursed are you above all the livestock and all the wild animals! You will crawl on your belly and you will eat dust all the days of your life. **15** And I will put enmity between you and the woman, and between your offspring and hers; he will crush your head, and you will strike his heel." **16** To the woman he said, "I will greatly increase your pains in childbearing; with pain you will give birth to children. Your desire will be for your husband, and he will rule over you."

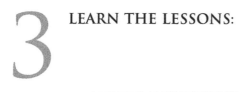

## 3 LEARN THE LESSONS:

## 4 LISTEN TO HIS VOICE:

## 5 LIVE IT OUT:

# 1 LOOK IN GOD'S WORD:

# 2 LIST THE FACTS:

### GENESIS 3:17–19

**17** To Adam he said, "Because you listened to your wife and ate from the tree about which I commanded you, 'You must not eat of it,' Cursed is the ground because of you; through painful toil you will eat of it all the days of your life. **18** It will produce thorns and thistles for you, and you will eat the plants of the field. **19** By the sweat of your brow you will eat your food until you return to the ground, since from it you were taken; for dust you are and to dust you will return."

3  **LEARN THE LESSONS:**

4  **LISTEN TO HIS VOICE:**

5  **LIVE IT OUT:**

# 1 LOOK IN GOD'S WORD:

# 2 LIST THE FACTS:

**GENESIS 3:20–24**

20 Adam named his wife Eve, because she would become the mother of all the living. 21 The LORD God made garments of skin for Adam and his wife and clothed them. 22 And the LORD God said, "The man has now become like one of us, knowing good and evil. He must not be allowed to reach out his hand and take also from the tree of life and eat, and live forever." 23 So the LORD God banished him from the Garden of Eden to work the ground from which he had been taken. 24 After he drove the man out, he placed on the east side of the Garden of Eden cherubim and a flaming sword flashing back and forth to guard the way to the tree of life.

# 3  LEARN THE LESSONS:

# 4  LISTEN TO HIS VOICE:

# 5  LIVE IT OUT:

## COMMITMENT:

What was the most meaningful lesson to you from each day's study this week?

*Study #1*

*Study #2*

*Study #3*

*Study #4*

*Study #5*

As you reflect on all the lessons, what one thing has God seemed to say to you from Genesis 3? Take a moment now to write out what He has said.

What has been your response?

Is there anything else you need to do in order to follow through completely?

Date your answer—then do it. Be committed!

# CHAPTER 4

*I am the God of Compassion . . .*
*I Uproot Your Bitterness*

Every descendant of Adam and Eve has been born with his or her "body" infected with the disease of sin, but until it breaks out all over in wrong habits and attitudes and actions and decisions, it can be difficult to diagnose. However, the New Testament tells us that the first spot of sin—

    the first worry

        or little white lie

           or selfish thought

               or flash of anger

                  or proud look

                     or angry word—

indicates our entire lives are riddled with it.

The disease of sin entered the human race through Adam and Eve's choice to disobey the Lord God. It was easily diagnosed in Cain, the very first child born to them, when he broke out in bitterness rooted in resentment.

# 1 LOOK IN GOD'S WORD:
Feel free to underline, circle, or otherwise mark text if it will aid your study.

# 2 LIST THE FACTS:
Make a verse-by-verse list of the most obvious facts. What does the passage say? Do not paraphrase.

## GENESIS 4:1–5

1 Adam lay with his wife Eve, and she became pregnant and gave birth to Cain. She said, "With the help of the LORD I have brought forth a man." 2 Later she gave birth to his brother Abel. Now Abel kept flocks, and Cain worked the soil. 3 In the course of time Cain brought some of the fruits of the soil as an offering to the LORD. 4 But Abel brought fat portions from some of the firstborn of his flock. The LORD looked with favor on Abel and his offering, 5 but on Cain and his offering he did not look with favor. So Cain was very angry, and his face was downcast.

## 3 LEARN THE LESSONS:
What lessons can be learned from these facts? What do the facts mean? Is there an example to follow? Warning to heed? Promise to claim? Command to obey?

## 4 LISTEN TO HIS VOICE:
What does this passage mean to you? Rewrite the lessons from Step 3 in the form of a question to ask yourself or another.

## 5 LIVE IT OUT:
Pinpoint what God is saying to you from the passage. How will you respond? Write down today's date and what you will do now to live it out.

1 **LOOK IN GOD'S WORD:**

2 **LIST THE FACTS:**

### GENESIS 4:6–8

6 Then the LORD said to Cain, "Why are you angry? Why is your face downcast? 7 If you do what is right, will you not be accepted? But if you do not do what is right, sin is crouching at your door; it desires to have you, but you must master it." 8 Now Cain said to his brother Abel, "Let's go out to the field." And while they were in the field, Cain attacked his brother Abel and killed him.

3 **LEARN THE LESSONS:**

4 **LISTEN TO HIS VOICE:**

5 **LIVE IT OUT:**

# 1 LOOK IN GOD'S WORD:

# 2 LIST THE FACTS:

**GENESIS 4:9–12**

9 Then the LORD said to Cain, "Where is your brother Abel?" "I don't know," he replied. "Am I my brother's keeper?" 10 The LORD said, "What have you done? Listen! Your brother's blood cries out to me from the ground. 11 Now you are under a curse and driven from the ground, which opened its mouth to receive your brother's blood from your hand. 12 When you work the ground, it will no longer yield its crops for you. You will be a restless wanderer on the earth."

## 3 LEARN THE LESSONS:

## 4 LISTEN TO HIS VOICE:

## 5 LIVE IT OUT:

# 1 LOOK IN GOD'S WORD:

## GENESIS 4:13–16

**13** Cain said to the LORD, "My punishment is more than I can bear. **14** Today you are driving me from the land, and I will be hidden from your presence; I will be a restless wanderer on the earth, and whoever finds me will kill me." **15** But the LORD said to him, "Not so; if anyone kills Cain, he will suffer vengeance seven times over." Then the LORD put a mark on Cain so that no one who found him would kill him. **16** So Cain went out from the LORD's presence and lived in the land of Nod, east of Eden.

# 2 LIST THE FACTS:

3 **LEARN THE LESSONS:**

4 **LISTEN TO HIS VOICE:**

5 **LIVE IT OUT:**

# 1 LOOK IN GOD'S WORD:

# 2 LIST THE FACTS:

## GENESIS 4:17–24

**17** Cain lay with his wife, and she became pregnant and gave birth to Enoch. Cain was then building a city, and he named it after his son Enoch. **18** To Enoch was born Irad, and Irad was the father of Mehujael, and Mehujael was the father of Methushael, and Methushael was the father of Lamech. **19** Lamech married two women, one named Adah and the other Zillah. **20** Adah gave birth to Jabal; he was the father of those who live in tents and raise livestock. **21** His brother's name was Jubal; he was the father of all who play the harp and flute. **22** Zillah also had a son, Tubal-Cain, who forged all kinds of tools out of bronze and iron. Tubal-Cain's sister was Naamah. **23** Lamech said to his wives, "Adah and Zillah, listen to me; wives of Lamech, hear my words. I have killed a man for wounding me, a young man for injuring me. **24** If Cain is avenged seven times, then Lamech seventy-seven times."

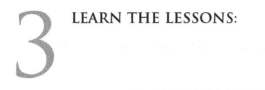

**3** LEARN THE LESSONS:

**4** LISTEN TO HIS VOICE:

**5** LIVE IT OUT:

## COMMITMENT:

What was the most meaningful lesson to you from each day's study this week?

*Study #1*

*Study #2*

*Study #3*

*Study #4*

*Study #5*

As you reflect on all the lessons, what one thing has God seemed to say to you from Genesis 4? Take a moment now to write out what He has said.

What has been your response?

Is there anything else you need to do in order to follow through completely?

Date your answer—then do it. Be committed!

# CHAPTER 5

## *I am the God of Compassion . . .*
## *I Redeem Your Wastedness*

Underneath all the progress and sophistication, our civilization is experiencing a bankruptcy of moral and spiritual values that threatens to erode our very existence. Our society is just as wicked and rebellious against God as Cain's civilization was.

The flashing red-light warning for you and me is to beware getting so caught up in the way everyone around us is living that we get swept away by the current of wickedness and waste our own lives in a meaningless existence. In the midst of spiritual dwarfs, we must strive to be giants by receiving, running with, and relaying the baton of truth that leads to personal faith in God that has been handed down to generation after generation since Creation.

# 1 LOOK IN GOD'S WORD:
Feel free to underline, circle, or otherwise mark text if it will aid your study.

# 2 LIST THE FACTS:
Make a verse-by-verse list of the most obvious facts. What does the passage say? Do not paraphrase.

## GENESIS 5:1–2

**1** This is the written account of Adam's line. When God created man, he made him in the likeness of God. **2** He created them male and female and blessed them. And when they were created, he called them "man."

**3** **LEARN THE LESSONS:**
What lessons can be learned from these facts? What do the facts mean? Is there an example to follow? Warning to heed? Promise to claim? Command to obey?

**4** **LISTEN TO HIS VOICE:**
What does this passage mean to you? Rewrite the lessons from Step 3 in the form of a question to ask yourself or another.

**5** **LIVE IT OUT:**
Pinpoint what God is saying to you from the passage. How will you respond? Write down today's date and what you will do now to live it out.

# 1 LOOK IN GOD'S WORD:

# 2 LIST THE FACTS:

**GENESIS 5:3–5**

3 When Adam had lived 130 years, he had a son in his own likeness, in his own image; and he named him Seth. 4 After Seth was born, Adam lived 800 years and had other sons and daughters. 5 Altogether, Adam lived 930 years, and then he died.

3 **LEARN THE LESSONS:**

4 **LISTEN TO HIS VOICE:**

5 **LIVE IT OUT:**

# 1 LOOK IN GOD'S WORD:

# 2 LIST THE FACTS:

### GENESIS 5:6–17

**6** When Seth had lived 105 years, he became the father of Enosh. **7** And after he became the father of Enosh, Seth lived 807 years and had other sons and daughters. **8** Altogether, Seth lived 912 years, and then he died. **9** When Enosh had lived 90 years, he became the father of Kenan. **10** And after he became the father of Kenan, Enosh lived 815 years and had other sons and daughters. **11** Altogether, Enosh lived 905 years, and then he died. **12** When Kenan had lived 70 years, he became the father of Mahalalel. **13** And after he became the father of Mahalalel, Kenan lived 840 years and had other sons and daughters. **14** Altogether, Kenan lived 910 years, and then he died. **15** When Mahalalel had lived 65 years, he became the father of Jared. **16** And after he became the father of Jared, Mahalalel lived 830 years and had other sons and daughters. **17** Altogether, Mahalalel lived 895 years, and then he died.

3 **LEARN THE LESSONS:**

4 **LISTEN TO HIS VOICE:**

5 **LIVE IT OUT:**

# 1 LOOK IN GOD'S WORD:

# 2 LIST THE FACTS:

### GENESIS 5:18–24

**18** When Jared had lived 162 years, he became the father of Enoch. **19** And after he became the father of Enoch, Jared lived 800 years and had other sons and daughters. **20** Altogether, Jared lived 962 years, and then he died. **21** When Enoch had lived 65 years, he became the father of Methuselah. **22** And after he became the father of Methuselah, Enoch walked with God 300 years and had other sons and daughters. **23** Altogether, Enoch lived 365 years. **24** Enoch walked with God; then he was no more, because God took him away.

# 3 LEARN THE LESSONS:

# 4 LISTEN TO HIS VOICE:

# 5 LIVE IT OUT:

# 1 LOOK IN GOD'S WORD:

# 2 LIST THE FACTS:

**GENESIS 5:25–32**

**25** When Methuselah had lived 187 years, he became the father of Lamech. **26** And after he became the father of Lamech, Methuselah lived 782 years and had other sons and daughters. **27** Altogether, Methuselah lived 969 years, and then he died. **28** When Lamech had lived 182 years, he had a son. **29** He named him Noah and said, "He will comfort us in the labor and painful toil of our hands caused by the ground the LORD has cursed." **30** After Noah was born, Lamech lived 595 years and had other sons and daughters. **31** Altogether, Lamech lived 777 years, and then he died. **32** After Noah was 500 years old, he became the father of Shem, Ham and Japheth.

3 **LEARN THE LESSONS:**

4 **LISTEN TO HIS VOICE:**

5 **LIVE IT OUT:**

## COMMITMENT:

What was the most meaningful lesson to you from each day's study this week?

*Study #1*

*Study #2*

*Study #3*

*Study #4*

*Study #5*

As you reflect on all the lessons, what one thing has God seemed to say to you from Genesis 5. Take a moment now to write out what He has said.

What has been your response?

Is there anything else you need to do in order to follow through completely?

Date your answer—then do it. Be committed!

# CHAPTER 6

## *I am the God of Salvation . . .*
## *I Share Your Loneliness*

What difference does your stand for righteousness and against wickedness make? When you stand alone against the tide of public opinion or the erosion of spiritual principles or the decay of personal morality, what difference can you make? You and I will never know the answer to that until we are willing to be one person, standing alone.

There was another man in history who took a lonely stand against the evil and wickedness of his day. His example emphasizes to you and me the power of one. Because if he had not stood against the wickedness of his day, the entire human race would have been totally eradicated by the Flood. His name was Noah, and he lived in the midst of Cain's godless world.

# 1

**LOOK IN GOD'S WORD:**
Feel free to underline, circle, or otherwise mark text if it will aid your study.

# 2

**LIST THE FACTS:**
Make a verse-by-verse list of the most obvious facts. What does the passage say? Do not paraphrase.

## GENESIS 6:1–6

1 When men began to increase in number on the earth and daughters were born to them, 2 the sons of God saw that the daughters of men were beautiful, and they married any of them they chose. 3 Then the LORD said, "My Spirit will not contend with man forever, for he is mortal; his days will be a hundred and twenty years." 4 The Nephilim were on the earth in those days—and also afterward— when the sons of God went to the daughters of men and had children by them. They were the heroes of old, men of renown. 5 The LORD saw how great man's wickedness on the earth had become, and that every inclination of the thoughts of his heart was only evil all the time. 6 The LORD was grieved that he had made man on the earth, and his heart was filled with pain.

## 3 LEARN THE LESSONS:
What lessons can be learned from these facts? What do the facts mean? Is there an example to follow? Warning to heed? Promise to claim? Command to obey?

## 4 LISTEN TO HIS VOICE:
What does this passage mean to you? Rewrite the lessons from Step 3 in the form of a question to ask yourself or another.

## 5 LIVE IT OUT:
Pinpoint what God is saying to you from the passage. How will you respond? Write down today's date and what you will do now to live it out.

A DEVOTIONAL GUIDE

# 1 LOOK IN GOD'S WORD:

# 2 LIST THE FACTS:

**GENESIS 6:7–8**

7 So the LORD said, "I will wipe mankind, whom I have created, from the face of the earth—men and animals, and creatures that move along the ground, and birds of the air—for I am grieved that I have made them." 8 But Noah found favor in the eyes of the LORD.

**3** LEARN THE LESSONS:

**4** LISTEN TO HIS VOICE:

**5** LIVE IT OUT:

# 1 LOOK IN GOD'S WORD:

# 2 LIST THE FACTS:

### GENESIS 6:9–12

**9** This is the account of Noah. Noah was a righteous man, blameless among the people of his time, and he walked with God. **10** Noah had three sons: Shem, Ham and Japheth. **11** Now the earth was corrupt in God's sight and was full of violence. **12** God saw how corrupt the earth had become, for all the people on earth had corrupted their ways.

**3**   **LEARN THE LESSONS:**

**4**   **LISTEN TO HIS VOICE:**

**5**   **LIVE IT OUT:**

# 1 LOOK IN GOD'S WORD:

# 2 LIST THE FACTS:

**GENESIS 6:13–17**

**13** So God said to Noah, "I am going to put an end to all people, for the earth is filled with violence because of them. I am surely going to destroy both them and the earth. **14** So make yourself an ark of cypress wood; make rooms in it and coat it with pitch inside and out. **15** This is how you are to build it: The ark is to be 450 feet long, 75 feet wide and 45 feet high. **16** Make a roof for it and finish the ark to within 18 inches of the top. Put a door in the side of the ark and make lower, middle and upper decks. **17** I am going to bring floodwaters on the earth to destroy all life under the heavens, every creature that has the breath of life in it. Everything on earth will perish.

**3** LEARN THE LESSONS:

**4** LISTEN TO HIS VOICE:

**5** LIVE IT OUT:

# 1 LOOK IN GOD'S WORD:

# 2 LIST THE FACTS:

## GENESIS 6:18–22

**18** But I will establish my covenant with you, and you will enter the ark— you and your sons and your wife and your sons' wives with you. **19** You are to bring into the ark two of all living creatures, male and female, to keep them alive with you. **20** Two of every kind of bird, of every kind of animal and of every kind of creature that moves along the ground will come to you to be kept alive. **21** You are to take every kind of food that is to be eaten and store it away as food for you and for them." **22** Noah did everything just as God commanded him.

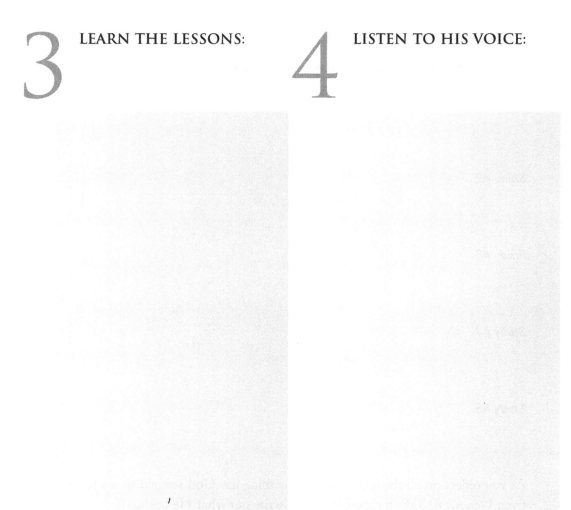

3 LEARN THE LESSONS:

4 LISTEN TO HIS VOICE:

5 LIVE IT OUT:

## COMMITMENT:

What was the most meaningful lesson to you from each day's study this week?

*Study #1*

*Study #2*

*Study #3*

*Study #4*

*Study #5*

As you reflect on all the lessons, what one thing has God seemed to say to you from Genesis 6? Take a moment now to write out what He has said.

What has been your response?

Is there anything else you need to do in order to follow through completely?

Date your answer—then do it. Be committed!

CHAPTER 7

*I am the God of Salvation . . .*
*I Overcome Your Helplessness*

When have you felt totally insecure and utterly helpless?

*When* your child ran away from home, leaving no trace?

*When* a spouse walked into the arms of another?

*When* the doctor diagnosed a fast-spreading, terminal disease?

*When* your income would not stretch to cover your expenses, and the creditors would not extend another loan?

*When* you stood watching as flames devoured your home?

*When* the river overflowed its banks, flooding your community?

*When* the sea rose up and claimed your property?

When our whole world falls apart, we can overcome our helplessness through God, our Savior.

Noah went through the equivalent of a nuclear holocaust when the entire world of his day was destroyed in a worldwide flood that was the judgment of God on Cain's civilization. Not only did Noah survive this devastation; he overcame triumphantly as he and his family were secure emotionally, mentally, spiritually, and physically throughout the living nightmare. His security and help rested in a moment-by-moment obedience and dependence upon God's Word.

**1** **LOOK IN GOD'S WORD:**
Feel free to underline, circle, or otherwise mark text if it will aid your study.

**2** **LIST THE FACTS:**
Make a verse-by-verse list of the most obvious facts. What does the passage say? Do not paraphrase.

### GENESIS 7:1–5

**1** The LORD then said to Noah, "Go into the ark, you and your whole family, because I have found you righteous in this generation. **2** Take with you seven of every kind of clean animal, a male and its mate, and two of every kind of unclean animal, a male and its mate, **3** and also seven of every kind of bird, male and female, to keep their various kinds alive throughout the earth. **4** Seven days from now I will send rain on the earth for forty days and forty nights, and I will wipe from the face of the earth every living creature I have made." **5** And Noah did all that the LORD commanded him.

**3** LEARN THE LESSONS:
What lessons can be learned from these facts? What do the facts mean? Is there an example to follow? Warning to heed? Promise to claim? Command to obey?

**4** LISTEN TO HIS VOICE:
What does this passage mean to you? Rewrite the lessons from Step 3 in the form of a question to ask yourself or another.

**5** LIVE IT OUT:
Pinpoint what God is saying to you from the passage. How will you respond? Write down today's date and what you will do now to live it out.

# 1 LOOK IN GOD'S WORD:

# 2 LIST THE FACTS:

### GENESIS 7:6–10

**6** Noah was six hundred years old when the floodwaters came on the earth. **7** And Noah and his sons and his wife and his sons' wives entered the ark to escape the waters of the flood. **8** Pairs of clean and unclean animals, of birds and of all creatures that move along the ground, **9** male and female, came to Noah and entered the ark, as God had commanded Noah. **10** And after the seven days the floodwaters came on the earth.

## 3 LEARN THE LESSONS:

## 4 LISTEN TO HIS VOICE:

## 5 LIVE IT OUT:

## 1 LOOK IN GOD'S WORD:

## 2 LIST THE FACTS:

### GENESIS 7:11–16

**11** In the six hundredth year of Noah's life, on the seventeenth day of the second month—on that day all the springs of the great deep burst forth, and the floodgates of the heavens were opened. **12** And rain fell on the earth forty days and forty nights. **13** On that very day Noah and his sons, Shem, Ham and Japheth, together with his wife and the wives of his three sons, entered the ark. **14** They had with them every wild animal according to its kind, all livestock according to their kinds, every creature that moves along the ground according to its kind and every bird according to its kind, everything with wings. **15** Pairs of all creatures that have the breath of life in them came to Noah and entered the ark. **16** The animals going in were male and female of every living thing, as God had commanded Noah. Then the LORD shut him in.

## 3 LEARN THE LESSONS:

## 4 LISTEN TO HIS VOICE:

## 5 LIVE IT OUT:

# 1 LOOK IN GOD'S WORD:

# 2 LIST THE FACTS:

**GENESIS 7:17–19**

**17** For forty days the flood kept coming on the earth, and as the waters increased they lifted the ark high above the earth. **18** The waters rose and increased greatly on the earth, and the ark floated on the surface of the water. **19** They rose greatly on the earth, and all the high mountains under the entire heavens were covered.

**3** LEARN THE LESSONS:

**4** LISTEN TO HIS VOICE:

**5** LIVE IT OUT:

# 1 LOOK IN GOD'S WORD:

# 2 LIST THE FACTS:

## GENESIS 7:20–21

20 The waters rose and covered the mountains to a depth of more than twenty feet. 21 Every living thing that moved on the earth perished—birds, livestock, wild animals, all the creatures that swarm over the earth, and all mankind.

**3** LEARN THE LESSONS:

**4** LISTEN TO HIS VOICE:

**5** LIVE IT OUT:

## COMMITMENT:

What was the most meaningful lesson to you from each day's study this week?

*Study #1*

*Study #2*

*Study #3*

*Study #4*

*Study #5*

As you reflect on all the lessons, what one thing has God seemed to say to you from Genesis 7? Take a moment now to write out what He has said.

What has been your response?

Is there anything else you need to do in order to follow through completely?

Date your answer—then do it. Be committed!

# CHAPTER 8

## *I am the God of Salvation . . .*
## *I Calm Your Fearfulness*

Have you ever been a victim of crime? If statistics are accurate, more than half of the American population will be victimized at some time during their lives. Ann Landers once said that out of the ten thousand letters she got each month, one problem surfaced more than any other, and it was fear.

Fear of the future,
fear of the unknown,
fear of consequences,
fear of violence,
fear of exposure,
fear of poverty,
fear of old age,
fear of loneliness,
fear of rejection,
fear of death,
fear of God . . .

And right on the heels of fear is worry. What are you afraid of that has you literally sick with worry? Medical studies have proven that worry attacks the central nervous system, the circulatory system, and the digestive system of our bodies. Charles Mayo, of the Mayo Clinic, said, "You can worry yourself to death, but you cannot worry yourself to a longer life." The word *worry* comes from a root word in Old English that means to "choke or to strangle," and it can strangle our good health as well as choke our emotions until we are not able to adequately function.

Surely Noah knew the paralysis of fear and the total paranoia of worry. But he also knew by experience that the God of the storm is also the God of all comfort, able to calm his fears as he kept his faith in God and his focus on God.

**1** LOOK IN GOD'S WORD:
Feel free to underline, circle, or otherwise mark text if it will aid your study.

**2** LIST THE FACTS:
Make a verse-by-verse list of the most obvious facts. What does the passage say? Do not paraphrase.

### GENESIS 8:1–5

**1** But God remembered Noah and all the wild animals and the livestock that were with him in the ark, and he sent a wind over the earth, and the waters receded. **2** Now the springs of the deep and the floodgates of the heavens had been closed, and the rain had stopped falling from the sky. **3** The water receded steadily from the earth. At the end of the hundred and fifty days the water had gone down, **4** and on the seventeenth day of the seventh month the ark came to rest on the mountains of Ararat. **5** The waters continued to recede until the tenth month, and on the first day of the tenth month the tops of the mountains became visible.

# 3 LEARN THE LESSONS:
What lessons can be learned from these facts? What do the facts mean? Is there an example to follow? Warning to heed? Promise to claim? Command to obey?

# 4 LISTEN TO HIS VOICE:
What does this passage mean to you? Rewrite the lessons from Step 3 in the form of a question to ask yourself or another.

# 5 LIVE IT OUT:
Pinpoint what God is saying to you from the passage. How will you respond? Write down today's date and what you will do now to live it out.

## 1  LOOK IN GOD'S WORD:

## 2  LIST THE FACTS:

### GENESIS 8:6–12

6 After forty days Noah opened the window he had made in the ark 7 and sent out a raven, and it kept flying back and forth until the water had dried up from the earth. 8 Then he sent out a dove to see if the water had receded from the surface of the ground. 9 But the dove could find no place to set its feet because there was water over all the surface of the earth; so it returned to Noah in the ark. He reached out his hand and took the dove and brought it back to himself in the ark. 10 He waited seven more days and again sent out the dove from the ark. 11 When the dove returned to him in the evening, there in its beak was a freshly plucked olive leaf! Then Noah knew that the water had receded from the earth. 12 He waited seven more days and sent the dove out again, but this time it did not return to him.

3 **LEARN THE LESSONS:**

4 **LISTEN TO HIS VOICE:**

5 **LIVE IT OUT:**

# 1 LOOK IN GOD'S WORD:

# 2 LIST THE FACTS:

**GENESIS 8:13–14**

13 By the first day of the first month of Noah's six hundred and first year, the water had dried up from the earth. Noah then removed the covering from the ark and saw that the surface of the ground was dry. 14 By the twenty-seventh day of the second month the earth was completely dry.

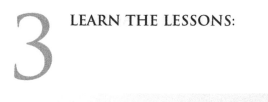

3 LEARN THE LESSONS:

4 LISTEN TO HIS VOICE:

5 LIVE IT OUT:

# 1 LOOK IN GOD'S WORD:

# 2 LIST THE FACTS:

**Genesis 8:15–19**

**15** Then God said to Noah, **16** "Come out of the ark, you and your wife and your sons and their wives. **17** Bring out every kind of living creature that is with you—the birds, the animals, and all the creatures that move along the ground—so they can multiply on the earth and be fruitful and increase in number upon it." **18** So Noah came out, together with his sons and his wife and his sons' wives. **19** All the animals and all the creatures that move along the ground and all the birds—everything that moves on the earth—came out of the ark, one kind after another.

# 3 LEARN THE LESSONS:

# 4 LISTEN TO HIS VOICE:

# 5 LIVE IT OUT:

# 1 LOOK IN GOD'S WORD:

# 2 LIST THE FACTS:

### GENESIS 8:20–22

**20** Then Noah built an altar to the LORD and, taking some of all the clean animals and clean birds, he sacrificed burnt offerings on it. **21** The LORD smelled the pleasing aroma and said in his heart: "Never again will I curse the ground because of man, even though every inclination of his heart is evil from childhood. And never again will I destroy all living creatures, as I have done. **22** As long as the earth endures, seedtime and harvest, cold and heat, summer and winter, day and night will never cease."

## 3 LEARN THE LESSONS:

## 4 LISTEN TO HIS VOICE:

## 5 LIVE IT OUT:

## COMMITMENT:

What was the most meaningful lesson to you from each day's study this week?

*Study #1*

*Study #2*

*Study #3*

*Study #4*

*Study #5*

As you reflect on all the lessons, what one thing has God seemed to say to you from Genesis 8? Take a moment now to write out what He has said.

What has been your response?

Is there anything else you need to do in order to follow through completely?

Date your answer—then do it. Be committed!

# CHAPTER 9

*I am the God of Salvation . . .*
*I Understand Your Weakness*

There is not a more outstanding man of God in all of the Old Testament Scriptures than Noah. Because he was righteous before God and blameless before men, he had found such favor in God's eyes that God had used him to save the entire world of his day. As he stepped off the ark, he stepped into a brand-new life. And the human race, represented by Noah and his family, could begin all over again.

How thrilling to experience a brand-new beginning! But the Flood that had washed away the wickedness of Cain's civilization had not washed away the sinfulness in the human heart. It lurked like a dark shadow in the brilliant sunshine of the new day.

But God understands our weakness and has made provision for it. We experience His provision first when we heed His principles.

1 **LOOK IN GOD'S WORD:**
Feel free to underline, circle, or otherwise mark text if it will aid your study.

2 **LIST THE FACTS:**
Make a verse-by-verse list of the most obvious facts. What does the passage say? Do not paraphrase.

**GENESIS 9:1–4**

1 Then God blessed Noah and his sons, saying to them, "Be fruitful and increase in number and fill the earth. 2 The fear and dread of you will fall upon all the beasts of the earth and all the birds of the air, upon every creature that moves along the ground, and upon all the fish of the sea; they are given into your hands. 3 Everything that lives and moves will be food for you. Just as I gave you the green plants, I now give you everything. 4 But you must not eat meat that has its lifeblood still in it."

## 3  LEARN THE LESSONS:
What lessons can be learned from these facts? What do the facts mean? Is there an example to follow? Warning to heed? Promise to claim? Command to obey?

## 4  LISTEN TO HIS VOICE:
What does this passage mean to you? Rewrite the lessons from Step 3 in the form of a question to ask yourself or another.

## 5  LIVE IT OUT:
Pinpoint what God is saying to you from the passage. How will you respond? Write down today's date and what you will do now to live it out.

# 1 LOOK IN GOD'S WORD:

# 2 LIST THE FACTS:

## GENESIS 9:5–7

5 "And for your lifeblood I will surely demand an accounting. I will demand an accounting from every animal. And from each man, too, I will demand an accounting for the life of his fellow man. 6 Whoever sheds the blood of man, by man shall his blood be shed; for in the image of God has God made man. 7 As for you, be fruitful and increase in number; multiply on the earth and increase upon it."

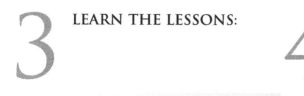

3 LEARN THE LESSONS:

4 LISTEN TO HIS VOICE:

5 LIVE IT OUT:

# 1 LOOK IN GOD'S WORD:

# 2 LIST THE FACTS:

**GENESIS 9:8–11**

8 Then God said to Noah and to his sons with him: 9 "I now establish my covenant with you and with your descendants after you 10 and with every living creature that was with you—the birds, the livestock and all the wild animals, all those that came out of the ark with you—every living creature on earth. 11 I establish my covenant with you: Never again will all life be cut off by the waters of a flood; never again will there be a flood to destroy the earth."

## 3 LEARN THE LESSONS:

## 4 LISTEN TO HIS VOICE:

## 5 LIVE IT OUT:

# 1 LOOK IN GOD'S WORD:

# 2 LIST THE FACTS:

**GENESIS 9:12–13**

**12** And God said, "This is the sign of the covenant I am making between me and you and every living creature with you, a covenant for all generations to come: **13** I have set my rainbow in the clouds, and it will be the sign of the covenant between me and the earth."

## 3  LEARN THE LESSONS:

## 4  LISTEN TO HIS VOICE:

## 5  LIVE IT OUT:

# 1 LOOK IN GOD'S WORD:

# 2 LIST THE FACTS:

### GENESIS 9:14–17

**14** "Whenever I bring clouds over the earth and the rainbow appears in the clouds, **15** I will remember my covenant between me and you and all living creatures of every kind. Never again will the waters become a flood to destroy all life. **16** Whenever the rainbow appears in the clouds, I will see it and remember the everlasting covenant between God and all living creatures of every kind on the earth." **17** So God said to Noah, "This is the sign of the covenant I have established between me and all life on the earth."

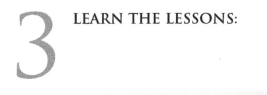

3 **LEARN THE LESSONS:**

4 **LISTEN TO HIS VOICE:**

5 **LIVE IT OUT:**

## COMMITMENT:

What was the most meaningful lesson to you from each day's study this week?

*Study #1*

*Study #2*

*Study #3*

*Study #4*

*Study #5*

As you reflect on all the lessons, what one thing has God seemed to say to you from Genesis 9? Take a moment now to write out what He has said.

What has been your response?

Is there anything else you need to do in order to follow through completely?

Date your answer—then do it. Be committed!

# CHAPTER 10

## *I am the God of Redemption . . .*
## *I Reject Your Religiousness*

A professor of religion at one of the most prestigious and intellectual universities in our country told me that although she considered herself to be a Christian, she was confused by all the other religions in the world. She had recently written an article for the university newspaper, describing a trip she had taken to India. She related that when she arrived in Calcutta, she was deeply impressed with how good the Hindu people seemed to be. And she remembered that her godly grandmother had prayed for their salvation for years—prayers that to this professor seemed to be totally unnecessary. Why did the Hindus need to be "saved" when they were so "nice"?

Why do we pray for the salvation of people in other countries, cultures, and religions? Why does the Christian church send out missionaries? Why can't you believe what you want and I believe what I want and everyone in the world believe whatever they want as long as we don't hurt each other?

The answers are to be found in Genesis, where we see that the root of every religion in our world today outside of Judaism and Christianity can be traced back to the Tower of Babel.

**1** LOOK IN GOD'S WORD:
Feel free to underline, circle, or otherwise mark text if it will aid your study.

**2** LIST THE FACTS:
Make a verse-by-verse list of the most obvious facts. What does the passage say? Do not paraphrase.

**GENESIS 10:8–12**

8 Cush was the father of Nimrod, who grew to be a mighty warrior on the earth. 9 He was a mighty hunter before the LORD; that is why it is said, "Like Nimrod, a mighty hunter before the LORD." 10 The first centers of his kingdom were Babylon, Erech, Akkad and Calneh, in Shinar. 11 From that land he went to Assyria, where he built Nineveh, Rehoboth Ir, Calah 12 and Resen, which is between Nineveh and Calah; that is the great city.

**3** LEARN THE LESSONS:
What lessons can be learned from these facts? What do the facts mean? Is there an example to follow? Warning to heed? Promise to claim? Command to obey?

**4** LISTEN TO HIS VOICE:
What does this passage mean to you? Rewrite the lessons from Step 3 in the form of a question to ask yourself or another.

**5** LIVE IT OUT:
Pinpoint what God is saying to you from the passage. How will you respond? Write down today's date and what you will do now to live it out.

# 1 LOOK IN GOD'S WORD:

## GENESIS 11:1–2

1 Now the whole world had one language and a common speech. 2 As men moved eastward, they found a plain in Shinar and settled there.

# 2 LIST THE FACTS:

3 **LEARN THE LESSONS:**

4 **LISTEN TO HIS VOICE:**

5 **LIVE IT OUT:**

# 1 LOOK IN GOD'S WORD:

# 2 LIST THE FACTS:

**GENESIS 11:3–4**

3 They said to each other, "Come, let's make bricks and bake them thoroughly." They used brick instead of stone, and tar for mortar. 4 Then they said, "Come, let us build ourselves a city, with a tower that reaches to the heavens, so that we may make a name for ourselves and not be scattered over the face of the whole earth."

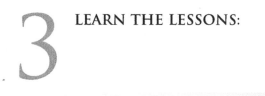

## 3   LEARN THE LESSONS:

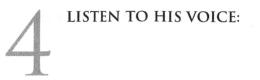

## 4   LISTEN TO HIS VOICE:

## 5   LIVE IT OUT:

# 1 LOOK IN GOD'S WORD:

# 2 LIST THE FACTS:

**GENESIS 11:5–7**

5 But the LORD came down to see the city and the tower that the men were building. 6 The LORD said, "If as one people speaking the same language they have begun to do this, then nothing they plan to do will be impossible for them. 7 Come, let us go down and confuse their language so they will not understand each other."

3 **LEARN THE LESSONS:**

4 **LISTEN TO HIS VOICE:**

5 **LIVE IT OUT:**

# 1 LOOK IN GOD'S WORD:

# 2 LIST THE FACTS:

**GENESIS 11:8–9**

8 So the LORD scattered them from there over all the earth, and they stopped building the city. 9 That is why it was called Babel—because there the LORD confused the language of the whole world. From there the LORD scattered them over the face of the whole earth.

**3** LEARN THE LESSONS:

**4** LISTEN TO HIS VOICE:

As you reflect on all the lessons
from Genesis 1–37, the . . .

What has been your greatest . . .

**5** LIVE IT OUT:

## COMMITMENT:

What was the most meaningful lesson to you from each day's study this week?

*Study #1*

*Study #2*

*Study #3*

*Study #4*

*Study #5*

As you reflect on all the lessons, what one thing has God seemed to say to you from Genesis 10? Take a moment now to write out what He has said.

What has been your response?

Is there anything else you need to do in order to follow through completely?

Date your answer—then do it. Be committed!

# CHAPTER 11

## *I am the God of Redemption . . .*
## *I Banish Your Hopelessness*

Following the rebellion at the Tower of Babel, the human race, which was separated from God, was scattered all over the world in absolute, utter, total, complete, endless, eternal hopelessness.

There was no chance in a lifetime that the people could ever . . .

fulfill their potential

or experience lasting satisfaction

or enjoy deep peace

or find real joy

or be unconditionally loved

or live forever!

They would never know the Creator for whom they were created. They would never know the very reason for their existence. They were utterly hopeless in themselves. And their descendants who fill our world today are still utterly, absolutely, completely, finally hopeless! Yet there is hope in God!

# A Devotional Guide

**1 LOOK IN GOD'S WORD:** Feel free to underline, circle, or otherwise mark text if it will aid your study.

**2 LIST THE FACTS:** Make a verse-by-verse list of the most obvious facts. What does the passage say? Do not paraphrase.

## Genesis 11:10–18

**10** This is the account of Shem. Two years after the flood, when Shem was 100 years old, he became the father of Arphaxad. **11** And after he became the father of Arphaxad, Shem lived 500 years and had other sons and daughters. **12** When Arphaxad had lived 35 years, he became the father of Shelah. **13** And after he became the father of Shelah, Arphaxad lived 403 years and had other sons and daughters. **14** When Shelah had lived 30 years, he became the father of Eber. **15** And after he became the father of Eber, Shelah lived 403 years and had other sons and daughters. **16** When Eber had lived 34 years, he became the father of Peleg. **17** And after he became the father of Peleg, Eber lived 430 years and had other sons and daughters. **18** When Peleg had lived 30 years, he became the father of Reu.

## 3 LEARN THE LESSONS:
What lessons can be learned from these facts? What do the facts mean? Is there an example to follow? Warning to heed? Promise to claim? Command to obey?

## 4 LISTEN TO HIS VOICE:
What does this passage mean to you? Rewrite the lessons from Step 3 in the form of a question to ask yourself or another.

## 5 LIVE IT OUT:
Pinpoint what God is saying to you from the passage. How will you respond? Write down today's date and what you will do now to live it out.

# 1 LOOK IN GOD'S WORD:

# 2 LIST THE FACTS:

**GENESIS 11:29–32**

**29** Abram and Nahor both married. The name of Abram's wife was Sarai, and the name of Nahor's wife was Milcah; she was the daughter of Haran, the father of both Milcah and Iscah. **30** Now Sarai was barren; she had no children. **31** Terah took his son Abram, his grandson Lot son of Haran, and his daughter-in-law Sarai, the wife of his son Abram, and together they set out from Ur of the Chaldeans to go to Canaan. But when they came to Haran, they settled there. **32** Terah lived 205 years, and he died in Haran.

**3** LEARN THE LESSONS:

**4** LISTEN TO HIS VOICE:

**5** LIVE IT OUT:

# 1 LOOK IN GOD'S WORD:

# 2 LIST THE FACTS:

### GENESIS 12:1–4

**1** The LORD had said to Abram, "Leave your country, your people and your father's household and go to the land I will show you. **2** I will make you into a great nation and I will bless you; I will make your name great, and you will be a blessing. **3** I will bless those who bless you, and whoever curses you I will curse; and all peoples on earth will be blessed through you." **4** So Abram left, as the LORD had told him; and Lot went with him. Abram was seventy-five years old when he set out from Haran.

3 **LEARN THE LESSONS:**

4 **LISTEN TO HIS VOICE:**

5 **LIVE IT OUT:**

# 1 LOOK IN GOD'S WORD:

# 2 LIST THE FACTS:

**MATTHEW 1:1–2; 15–17**

1 A record of the genealogy of Jesus Christ the son of David, the son of Abraham: 2 Abraham was the father of Isaac, Isaac the father of Jacob, Jacob the father of Judah and his brothers . . .

15 Eliud the father of Eleazar, Eleazar the father of Matthan, Matthan the father of Jacob, 16 and Jacob the father of Joseph, the husband of Mary, of whom was born Jesus, who is called Christ. 17 Thus there were fourteen generations in all from Abraham to David, fourteen from David to the exile to Babylon, and fourteen from the exile to the Christ.

**3** LEARN THE LESSONS:

**4** LISTEN TO HIS VOICE:

**5** LIVE IT OUT:

# 1 LOOK IN GOD'S WORD:

# 2 LIST THE FACTS:

### MATTHEW 1:18–25

**18** This is how the birth of Jesus Christ came about: His mother Mary was pledged to be married to Joseph, but before they came together, she was found to be with child through the Holy Spirit. **19** Because Joseph her husband was a righteous man and did not want to expose her to public disgrace, he had in mind to divorce her quietly. **20** But after he had considered this, an angel of the Lord appeared to him in a dream and said, "Joseph son of David, do not be afraid to take Mary home as your wife, because what is conceived in her is from the Holy Spirit. **21** She will give birth to a son, and you are to give him the name Jesus, because he will save his people from their sins." **22** All this took place to fulfill what the Lord had said through the prophet: **23** "The virgin will be with child and will give birth to a son, and they will call him Immanuel"—which means, "God with us." **24** When Joseph woke up, he did what the angel of the Lord had commanded him and took Mary home as his wife. **25** But he had no union with her until she gave birth to a son. And he gave him the name Jesus.

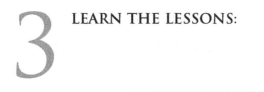

**3** LEARN THE LESSONS:

**4** LISTEN TO HIS VOICE:

**5** LIVE IT OUT:

## COMMITMENT:

What was the most meaningful lesson to you from each day's study this week?

*Study #1*

*Study #2*

*Study #3*

*Study #4*

*Study #5*

As you reflect on all the lessons, what one thing has God seemed to say to you from Genesis 11:10–12:4; Matthew 1? Take a moment now to write out what He has said.

What has been your response?

Is there anything else you need to do in order to follow through completely?

Date your answer—then do it. Be committed!

Additional resources from Anne Graham Lotz
are available at:

AnGeL Ministries
5115 Hollyridge Drive
Raleigh, NC 27612
Phone: 919-787-6606
www.AnneGrahamLotz.com

CPSIA information can be obtained at www.ICGtesting.com
Printed in the USA
LVOW03s0644241213

366403LV00005B/7/P